You and Your Tween

By Netmums and available from Headline

Baby Sleep Solutions
Baby's First Year
Feeding Kids
Getting Ready to Start School
How to Be a Happy Mum
Toddling to Ten
You and Your Tween
Your Pregnancy

You and Your Tween

Managing the years from 9 to 13

 netmums

Parents and experts share advice and experience

with Hollie Smith

headline

First published in 2011
by HEADLINE PUBLISHING GROUP

1

Cataloguing in Publication Data is available from the British Library

ISBN 978 0 7553 6109 0

Typeset in 11/15pt Clearface by Palimpsest Book Production Limited, Falkirk, Stirlingshire

Printed and bound in the UK by
Clays Ltd, St Ives plc

Headline's policy is to use papers that are natural, renewable and recyclable products and made from wood grown in sustainable forests. The logging and manufacturing processes are expected to conform to the environmental regulations of the country of origin.

HEADLINE PUBLISHING GROUP
An Hachette UK Company
338 Euston Road
London NW1 3BH

www.headline.co.uk
www.hachette.co.uk

Contents

Author's note

To avoid the awkward use of 'he/she' or 'his/her' throughout the book, we have used male and female children as the main examples in alternate chapters. Obviously the same advice applies whether you have a boy or a girl!

Some of the Netmums contributors' names have been changed.

Introduction

You've survived the sleepless nights, battled through the terrible twos, cried at the gates on their first day at big school and worked out what they will and won't eat . . . finally you feel you've got a handle on this parenting business.

And then, something starts to happen. Your baby starts to behave differently. At first we think perhaps they are tired, or worried about something, or just being naughty. But little by little we realise that there is something new emerging here. And along with this something-new comes huffing, stomping, tutting, arguing and door slamming. Let me introduce you to . . . your tween.

The years between nine and thirteen can be complicated, confusing and overwhelming both for parent and child. Your child is feeling their way through new social pressures as they start to wonder how they appear to others, whether they are 'normal' and how they can fit in. But while you want to give them security, reassurance and normality, they are pushing you away and demanding more privacy and independence.

Our job is to walk the fine line in between – letting them go just enough to start finding their own way, whilst allowing them to feel safe and secure.

This book has been researched and written by regular Netmums author Hollie Smith, herself a mum of a tween-age daughter. Hollie has worked with the guidance and advice of our expert panel: psychotherapeutic counsellor and Netmums parent supporter Crissy Duff, and parenting coach Elaine Halligan. And as always, we have drawn on the invaluable real-life experiences of hundreds of Netmums who have safely navigated their children through this phase of their journey.

You'll find out here just how far to allow them to push their new independence; where, when and how to set boundaries; how to listen – and how to encourage them to talk to you; and how to respect their privacy, whilst keeping them safe.

Most of all, you'll learn how to help your child to be a happy, confident, responsible Tween – who still feels able to come to Mum and Dad for advice, guidance . . . or just a hug on a bad day.

Siobhan Freegard
Founder, Netmums

Meet the team

Hollie Smith is a freelance journalist and author of eight books about parenting, five of them written for Netmums. She's married and has two daughters, aged nine and six.

Crissy Duff is a qualified psychotherapeutic counsellor and a member of the British Association for Counselling and Psychotherapy. She works with clients in her private practice as well as for her local council, and is a volunteer therapist at a GP surgery. Having been a popular member of the team at Netmums since 2004, she now works as one of the site's parent supporters, counselling members with a wide range of problems. Crissy is married and has daughters aged twelve and ten, and a son aged seven.

Elaine Halligan has a law degree and a background in accountancy and finance, but decided on a career change after seeking help for her own family on a parenting course run by London's New Learning Centre. In 2002 she began training as a parenting coach with the New Learning Centre South, now The Parent Practice. She's been a member of the team ever since, helping hundreds of parents to learn skills and strategies such as raising self-esteem, developing better communication, and managing challenging behaviour. She also has a particular interest in Special Educational Needs. Elaine is married and has a son of fifteen and a daughter of twelve.

1 Conflict and communication

Welcome to the tween years, what sometimes feels like the most challenging phase of parenting you've encountered so far. You've made it through the blur of babyhood, tackled the terrible twos, and negotiated the ups and downs of the primary school period. It's got to get easier now, right? But of course nothing's ever easy with kids. Your cuddly and compliant child seems to have been kidnapped by aliens and replaced with a different young person altogether: one who regularly unleashes her surly moods, bad attitudes, cheeky backchat, and downright defiance in your direction. No longer is she willing to do what you ask of her, even when you've asked her repeatedly. And worse, you face a barrage of grumbling or rude remarks if you insist on her cooperation, or attempt to pull her up when she's done something of which you don't approve. Working out how to respond to all this is beyond you. You're losing your rag on a regular basis. And, since she's almost up to your shoulders in height and the naughty step is now defunct, you're no longer sure what to issue in the way of consequences. Suddenly, you've got serious doubts about who's the boss any more – and you're wondering what on earth you did to deserve it. Still, there is some good news: if you're getting bad attitude and unacceptable behaviour from your tween, and it's causing conflict, it's *absolutely normal*.

Whatever happened to your 'baby'?

So why does it take place, this transformation from child to alien? What is it that makes her unable to respond to your repeated requests, so quick to answer back, or just so infuriatingly indifferent? Well, there's more than one good reason for this less-than-desirable behaviour. Part of it is biological: the approach of puberty, followed by adolescence, means that from as early as eight years old, there's a massive release of hormones that can have a very real effect on your child's mood. There are also dramatic changes afoot in the structure of the brain, which can be very significant. But of course, much of it is emotional, too, as her mind develops and she starts forming her own independent thoughts and opinions – very often the opposite of yours! The influence of her peers and the media will probably be relevant, as well. And it's quite likely that a child in this age group has a lot on her mind right now – worries about school, perhaps, or about friendships, her image, or how she herself is going to cope with this business of growing up, and how she fits within her own family. Chances are these worries will manifest themselves in a succession of bad moods: moods that are likely to end up being dumped on you – and quite rightly, as you're the one who she feels secure enough to dump them on.

Your feelings are normal, too

It's natural to feel totally infuriated when your tween shows attitude or misbehaves – probably because you feel you've lost control, and that's always a horrible feeling. It may also leave you feeling rejected and hurt, if things get personal – after all, this is your baby calling you a rotten cow. And then there's the fact that when our kids behave badly, we can't help but feel it's somehow our fault, and that we must have gone wrong somewhere. Going deeper still, it's possible our tweens' terrible behaviour reminds of us of our own awkward transition from childhood to adult-hood, and makes us painfully aware of what old fogeys we are, whilst they have their whole lives ahead of them. With all that in mind, it's not really surprising that rude or rebellious behaviour – as natural and under-standable as it is – can trigger some pretty strong reactions in us. So maybe, as parents, we need to beat ourselves up a bit less when we find this period difficult to cope with.

What's certain is that, in spite of the apparent push for independence and the claims that she couldn't care less, a tween needs her parents' love and support as much as she always did. More so, in fact. After all, she's undergoing huge upheaval – biologically, physically, emotionally, and socially – in the space of a few years. The one thing she could really do *without* right now is a parent who can't empathise with her. So, as hard as it can seem sometimes, that's what we should always be aiming for.

What the experts say

Crissy says: As she enters the tween years, your child becomes more self-aware, more capable of greater emotional and spiritual depth, and has a need for greater autonomy that inevitably leads her to reject parental values in favour of her own, and those of her peers. The child who once hung on your every word is now eager to work things out for herself, and as her sense of self develops she'll be placing herself firmly under the microscope. She may not yet know who she wants to be, she's just damned sure she doesn't want to be you! She needs to learn how to handle complicated emotions and make relationship choices for herself, and so she'll find herself spending a whole lot of time thinking about herself and her own needs, hopes and fears – which goes some way towards explaining why we often find our own advice and instructions being 'tuned out'. This process is further complicated by the mass of hormonal and brain changes, and the many social pressures she faces during these few brief but chaotic years. So when she behaves badly it's often more about her need to push boundaries than to push your buttons, and what looks like defiance may simply be frustration and a desire to experiment.

This pre-teen rebellion can come as a huge shock to parents, and sometimes it can seem more like a violent rupture than a gradual process of growing apart. But, painful as these changes can be, they represent a vital stage in your child's journey towards becoming an autonomous adult. Of course as parents we will always get things wrong or wish we had handled things better, and it's important that we do take responsibility for our role in the unfolding drama that is the tween years. At the same time, beating ourselves up over behaviour that is essentially a natural and inevitable part of growing up just turns that drama into a crisis.

Elaine says: As our children go through these years, we parents are becoming middle-aged, and that makes us sensitive to their developing powers of criticism and judgement. So when they tell us to get stuffed, or call us names, it can really hurt. We also have a lot of anxiety about them, often worrying about their safety, their studies, and their values. That means we tend to react more negatively and can end up nagging and criticising a lot.

Whilst many tween behavioural issues occur because of all the difficult changes they are going through, it's up to us as parents to share the responsibility for them. And sometimes, these issues are actually down to a lack of 'connective parenting', which is all about communicating respectfully and with empathy. That means really listening to your child's point of view (even if you can't allow the outcome she wants) and giving her lots of messages of support through praise.

Our job is to understand her changing temperament and characteristics, as well as the physical changes that are happening in her body. It's a difficult task: most of us, if we're honest, find it takes years to understand our children. And then, just as we're starting to understand them, they start going through yet more changes again.

What the netmums say

Living with an alien!

I seem to be living with someone else's daughter at the moment

– my ten-year-old has acquired the mouth and attitude of a sixteen-year-old! Just lately, anything I ask her to do is of the highest inconvenience: laying the table; putting up her hair for school; taking a shower; going to bed. We've tried a range of sanctions, but it doesn't seem to change the behaviour for long. To be honest, I'm close to tears some days.

Amanda, mum to three girls aged ten, seven and six, and a one-year-old boy

My daughter is a tween in teen training. We get a lot of huffing and stomping. I have to make sure I don't get drawn into an argument with her and just ignore these tantrums. She reminds me of myself at her age. I was a drama queen, too. Her dad jokes she should be auditioning for *EastEnders*.

Katie, mum to two girls aged nine and six

I started getting attitude from Carys when she was eight, and by the time she was thirteen, I thought I had a monster in my house. I kept looking for the sweet little girl I once knew but finding this whirlwind of emotions in her place! There were times when she was so sweet and nice and I thought we'd turned the corner. Then it would be tears, tantrums, attitude, and pushing the boundaries again. Thankfully, at seventeen, she's now almost returned to that lovely girl, and I couldn't be more proud of her.

Mandy, mum to a son, twenty-four, and two girls, seventeen and three

Every day, I find myself being wound up by our daughter. Everything's an issue, from getting dressed in the morning to getting undressed at night, and I am so fed up with having to ask ten times for everything to happen. This week she is not going dancing, nor is she watching TV, nor playing with her DS or on the computer, because of her one-hour tantrum last night. Yet she's so well-behaved when at school or at friends' houses, you wouldn't believe that it's the same child. I find it hard staying philosophical, because I don't see the difficulty in doing as you're

told the first or at least the second time you are asked. She's apologetic afterwards, but it never lasts.
Gemma, mum to a girl, twelve, and a boy, nine

Recently my husband told our eldest off for annoying her younger sister, despite being asked repeatedly to stop what she was doing, and for being just generally argumentative. She stormed off, shouting, stomped up the stairs, and slammed her bedroom door. When I went up to check up on her a little later I found a sign on her door saying, 'Go away, leave me alone'! She then sent my husband a text message: 'I am moving out because I don't like you and never will.' Fortunately he's seen the funny side, and hasn't taken it to heart. (She seemed to have forgiven him the next morning.) Nothing is ever her fault, and getting an apology from her is like extracting teeth. The best we can hope for is a begrudging, muttered 'sorry'. Oh, and when she's being told off she puts her fingers in her ears and sings 'la-la-la-la' so she can't hear us. The joys of parenting a tween.
Esther, mum to two girls aged eleven and eight

It's not so bad now, but the years between nine and twelve were terrible. There were tantrums and tears and strops, and sometimes full-blown screaming matches between us. Although he's better now there's still the odd day where it all blows up and then I'm the biggest cow in the world again (well, in his world, anyway). I have been known to send him to bed at 6 p.m. for the rest of the day, normally because the arguments have escalated. I've allowed myself to get dragged in and I worry about saying something I regret in the heat of the moment. He's exactly like me at that age, and I'm really hoping that because he's a boy he will actually start to settle down over the next couple of years rather than turn into the full-blown tearaway that I did!
Kelly, mum to two boys aged twelve and four

My son has a very 'up-and-down' personality anyway, but over the last year or so he's become really difficult to communicate

with. Everything is my fault: I'm mean, he hates me, I always 'ruin everything' and 'spoil his fun'. That's all for things like asking him to tidy his room or taking him to the local shop for five minutes to buy something, when he wasn't expecting me to! His moods are so unpredictable, and I've spoken to the headmistress at his school about it, because he has me in tears on a regular basis and I worry about telling him things that are likely to anger him. She thinks that he's well-developed for his age and that it's just puberty kicking in. In some ways he's still really naïve and childlike, and it's hard to believe. Guess I'll have to get used to it, though.
Phillippa, mum to two boys aged nine and seven

My daughter had such a big strop last night. She wanted to go out with her friends instead of doing her homework and as soon as I said 'no', she started throwing things and telling me to shut my mouth; that I was fat, and a horrible mum, and that I don't care about her. Today when she comes home from school she's grounded – but to be honest I'm dreading her coming home in case I get the same performance.
Jane, mum to a girl, ten

Laying down the laws

You'll have fewer problems with bad behaviour and conflict if everyone understands what's expected and accepted in the first place. Deciding on what your values are and establishing whatever rules you need to keep them in place is vital. And doing all this as early as possible will really reap rewards later: although, of course, you'll need to make regular revisions to the rules as she grows older and more independent, and as her needs change over time.

What one family has in its 'golden rules' book may well be different to another's, but whatever's on yours, try to stick with it. It's confusing for kids if some things are allowed on some days, but not on others. Don't have too many rules, or make them too strident, otherwise they simply won't be stuck to. And make sure your other half, or co-parent, is on board: if you have different ideas about the guidelines that govern your kids, it will cause conflict between the two of you, and that's the last thing you need. Negotiate and find a middle ground, if need be.

What the experts say

Elaine says: It makes it so much easier for you and your child to have firm rules and boundaries in place, because you both know what's expected. In fact, it's key. And as long as the rules are clear you don't need to keep on explaining what they are and why they're in place. All families have different values – it's down to you what your values will be. For instance, it's a really important value to me personally that my kids don't smoke, and I don't want to hear them swearing. Of course, if those are your values, you can't really smoke or swear yourself – it would be sending very mixed messages.

We need to be very clear on where we stand on things. It's not about laying down laws in a draconian way, but more about gently but clearly making sure she knows how you feel and why, and consistently following through on our rules. All you can hope for then is that as she gets older and gains more independence, she will make the right decisions herself, having absorbed some of your values over the years.

Crissy says: As our tween begins to withdraw and separate from us, it can be difficult as parents not to feel rejected and unvalued. It's crucial, however, that we don't react by also distancing ourselves from the relationship. Just as a young child needs firm boundaries in order to feel safe and loved, older kids needs a sense of consistency and security as well as something substantial to push or rebel against.

Any family rules or boundaries need as far as possible to be mutually agreed and also realistic and achievable. Try to let your child have her say and make sure she is listening, too. Boundaries should be age-appropriate, which means you need to be prepared to adapt them when the time comes. Take time to decide what's acceptable and what isn't. We all have different limits. Most of us would agree though that whilst it's OK to feel angry and to show it – after all, anger is a natural response and repressing it can cause real emotional damage – expressing your anger through aggression or physical violence is not.

Talking and listening

Good communication is more important than ever before when you've got a tween, and that means listening, as well as talking to her. If you've got good communication going, it will help you pre-empt conflict – and deal with it if it does arrive. And it will also help you to get results when you need your tween to do as you ask her.

Tell me about it: Tips for talking and listening

- Always acknowledge your tween's feelings, even if you don't necessarily agree with her. Allow her to have her say, and don't override it with what you think on the matter.
- When she's talking, give her your full attention, and listen reflectively – let her know you're taking it in by making eye contact, and adding comments that confirm hers.
- Try to empathise – even if you're furious. Aim to see everything from her point of view. You might not remember being her age – but you should try!
- If she's reluctant to talk to you, try chatting whilst you're both busy doing something else. It can make a conversation less intense, which will help her open up.
- Explain yourself if you're laying down laws she doesn't like, or outlining values and expectations that she doesn't agree with: don't just say 'because I said so'.
- Try to avoid shouting, nagging and repeating yourself whenever possible. It's simply counterproductive!

What the experts say

Elaine says: When it comes to communication, the onus lies with us as parents to lead the way. Good communication is really important between parent and child, and even more so once your child reaches the tween years. But it can only happen if you've got a relationship based on mutual respect – we need to be clear that we're talking to our kids in a respectful way. Sometimes it's hard to listen without judgement or criticism. And often, it's us not listening that leads to conflict. For example, perhaps you don't want her to go to a certain party and when she says she wants to go, you refuse. If you say no straight away, without listening to why she wants to go, you've cut out all communication, and that's not respectful. She needs to believe that you have heard her, and understand how she feels, even if you still don't want her to go. Explain why you don't want her to go, and accept that she may not see the validity of your reasons – she doesn't have the same ability to reason or the same level of experience that you do. That makes you the adult! And if she's talking to you, then listen . . . and really listen, by imagining what she's feeling, and reflecting it back to her – for example, 'It sounds to me as if you're feeling really frustrated that you're not able to go to this party tonight. I know how much you want to go and it must be disappointing for you.'

Crissy says: If you find yourself saying the same thing over and over again and being accused of nagging, it's time to brush up your communication skills, because eventually she will stop listening and just 'tune out'. Say what you need to say once, but make absolutely sure she hears you. Sit down with her and encourage her to stop what she's doing, and make eye contact. Be firm but also quiet, calm and respectful. If you're shouting from the kitchen while she's engrossed in a computer game, you're unlikely to get your point across and may end up saying the same thing twenty times. Better to take the time to go up to your child, get down to her level and say quite simply, 'I would like you to go and do your homework now please.'

Stay positive

You probably read all about positive parenting when your child was younger. But it continues to be a useful policy as she gets older – just like small children, tweens will usually respond well to praise (even though she might not let you see it!). So remember to 'big up' your tween whenever the going is good. Bouts of bad behaviour and unacceptable attitudes tend to come and go – in between, she'll no doubt behave perfectly well, so don't take it for granted when she does: give loads of praise and encouragement every time she acts in a way that pleases you, and it will help motivate her to behave better in future.

As well as praise, it's a good idea to keep your tween well rewarded for good behaviour. You might wonder if she's a bit past the sticker-chart phase now, but she'll still get a kick out of receiving a tangible token of merit from you, sometimes, when one is well deserved. Not everyone agrees that good behaviour should be conditional on reward, seeing it as something to expect as par for the course. But many parents do feel it's a fair system: the trick is not to dangle rewards as 'carrots', in exchange for cooperation, but to make sure they're offered as an unexpected bonus, and every so often rather than every single time. (Although if your tween needs extra incentive because you're trying to overturn an entrenched habit or tackle a long-running behavioural issue, it can work well to set up a temporary, routine system of rewards to be offered at each positive step along the way.)

Once she hits the tweens, if you haven't already, you might want to start giving your tween an appropriate amount of pocket money, and – although again, views vary – this is something that can be tied in with positive behaviour. However, rewards for tweens certainly don't have to involve cold, hard cash. That sticker chart can still have its uses, certainly for younger tweens, or you might give a small gift like a favourite comic or a pack of trading cards, or suggest a trip to the cinema. Avoid rewarding with sweets or other sorts of food, as it's not considered wise by health experts (see Chapter 6). And do be wary of using a reward system in reverse as a way to apply sanctions: it's not really fair to take away something you've previously bestowed for good behaviour, as it negates the efforts she made in order to earn it. Better to withdraw a privilege that she has yet to earn. In theory, giving praise and reward when things are going well should have a motivating effect on your tween which makes it less necessary to sanction her when they aren't!

As well as praising and rewarding good behaviour, positive parenting allows you scope to simply ignore some of the bad – and that may be just as well, as for most parents it would be impossible to keep on top of every little misdemeanour. As a general rule, though, don't let anything go that's in your golden rules book, otherwise you can't reasonably expect it to be adhered to in the future.

What the experts say

Elaine says: If we're positive, our kids are more likely to do the right thing because they know that we value them. Being in charge in a positive way is not about being authoritarian. So, instead of just saying, 'You need to turn the TV off now,' be sure to praise her when she does so: 'I appreciate you doing that. I know how much you enjoy watching the television and that took some self-control.' Consistently doing this when she gets the little things right will help keep her motivated and make her more likely to comply next time round. Try to use 'descriptive praise', in other words be very clear about specifically what you're praising her for.

Being positive means that when pulling up your child for something, you don't come down on her like a ton of bricks, but you quietly and calmly let her know it's not acceptable to you. For instance, if your child swears – assuming not swearing is high on your list of expectations – you might simply say, without making a huge deal out of it, 'I can hear you're upset. Would you please rephrase that?' The less constructive alternative would be to say, 'Don't you dare use that word!' but that's not positive parenting, and it's not respectful. It's also ineffective – in other words it won't get you the results you want and may even encourage more of the same poor behaviour, or language.

Rewarding our tweens in order to motivate and incentivise, especially in areas where they're reluctant, such as homework or household chores, is part of positive parenting. A good way to reward is by granting privileges, such as television time, which should be earned rather than seen as an absolute right.

What the netmums say

Being positive parents

I make sure I keep talking to my son, and hug him after we've argued. It can be hard, though, as it hurts when he answers back. I've noticed it gets worse when I'm stressed: he seems to bounce off me and we end up arguing. Generally when it gets to this point we need to spend time together. It's difficult, but this always seems to get us back on track. I think a lot of this behaviour is because he needs something but doesn't know how to get it across. It's easy to forget that they're still children sometimes, because they want so much independence and it seems like a constant battle. I just keep hold of the thought that one day it'll be over (then my other two will start!).
Andrea, mum to two boys aged thirteen and nine, and a girl, two

Trying to get my eldest daughter to keep her room tidy was becoming a constant battle and, unlike some parents, I could never quite let it go because I think tidy rooms are important – otherwise she can never find anything when she needs it! Then I realised that all the nagging was just a pointless waste of energy – in fact, it was almost certainly counterproductive, because I think she gets a kick out of being a little bit rebellious. So now I bite my lip and don't say anything – but if she ever does make an effort to tidy up (or rather, to keep it tidy for a while after I've been in and blitzed), I make sure I buy her a little 'room improvement' present like a new desk tidy or lampshade. I get them from charity shops or boot sales, so it's not much of an outlay, but I think the message is sinking in.
Julia, mum to two girls aged nine and six

I always found that grounding and confiscating things was not the way to go with my two when they were tweens. If play times or going-out times were an issue we would discuss it together and come to a compromise with them or explain why we thought it was best for them to stick to a certain hour at that time. Our kids were far from perfect and sometimes we had to be firm, usually by keeping them in. However, we made sure we spent that time with them doing something. I think the more parents get heavy with punishments, the more the children resent it and rebel more. Mine are grown up now and we haven't had any trouble from either of them so we must have done something right!

Angela, mum to a boy aged twenty-one and a girl, nineteen

We had difficulties when our son was a bit younger – I even mentioned his behaviour to my GP. She talked about positive parenting and from then on, things improved a lot. I don't get embroiled in arguments. If things start to get tricky, I try my best to respond positively rather than getting angry. He loves it when I take some time to talk to him, and let him know what a special child he is.

Sandra, mum to a boy, thirteen, and a girl, ten

In my opinion, positive parenting is definitely the way to go. If you shout and argue back, things only escalate and it's showing your children that this is the correct way to deal with things, when really it isn't. Kids of this age can be horrible at times and say really hurtful things, so you need to always remember it's only a phase. Of course you need to show them who's in charge but I've always tried to do that in a calm, friendly manner, and always be there for them ready to talk things through when they've calmed down. You need to develop a tough skin. Easier said than done, sometimes, but if you can stay positive you'll come out the other side better people, with a better relationship.

Hayley, mum to a girl, sixteen, and a boy, thirteen

Ignoring the bad and praising the good is the policy I try to use. If what they've done is unacceptable I will normally have a quiet word so they know I am aware of the way they are behaving and will not tolerate it. I'm generous with rewards, too: they get extra pocket money or treats like trips to the cinema or a take-away for good school reports, or doing their chores.
Caroline, mum to two boys aged twelve and eleven

We have a reward chart on which they collect stars for behaving well and, depending on how many stars they've got, they will get rewarded. It's not allowed to be the same thing week after week: it might be a couple of quid, or it might be a magazine.
Emma, mum to a girl, eleven, and a boy, nine

I find a mixture of positive parenting and appropriate conse-quences work best. For example, my daughter tore up a drawing my son had done. Rather than telling her off, I explained why that was wrong, and we talked about how she could have handled her frustration differently. I also made her take my son's turn in the washing-up rota for two days, as a way of making it up to him. I find it's important to choose my battles carefully. Some things are just not worth arguing about whereas others can't be ignored – I suppose which things fall into which categor-ies will be personal to each family. I can overlook the odd swear word *about* something, as I know they are just showing off. However I will not tolerate them swearing at each other and will deal with that more strongly. I think it's important to have clear boundaries but also I feel that you can compromise on some things if they meet you halfway.
Lucy, mum to a girl, eleven, and a boy, eight

When you need to take action

Of course, if your tween's behaviour has been truly unacceptable, there should usually be a consequence. The point of consequences is that they help a child reflect on where she's gone wrong and, hopefully, make her think twice before doing it again – as opposed to dishing out punishment, which is more about making her pay for her mistakes, and is likely to leave her thinking nothing apart from how much she resents you.

It's impossible to say what's acceptable and what isn't when it comes to bad behaviour – different parents are bound to have different ideas about that! And it's hard to say what will be an appropriate consequence. How old your child is; what she's done wrong; and what's most likely to actually be useful will all need to be taken into account. Most parents of tweens find that some kind of withdrawal of privilege – whether that be her allowance for the week; sessions on her computer; a valued possession; or the chance to spend time out of the house, with her friends – is the best way to make their point.

Do carry out a consequence if you've threatened it – your tween will very soon start to exploit it if she knows your threats are empty. And with that in mind, don't threaten a consequence you can't possibly hope to carry out!

What the experts say

Elaine says: Whenever you do issue a consequence, it needs to be as relevant as possible, so that it means something, and it needs to be delivered without criticism or shouting. If you can't do that in the heat of the moment, wait until you're calmer. As parents, we often come up with consequences that don't particularly fit the misdemeanour. Let's say she's failed to do her homework before using her computer – the consequence could be withdrawal of her computer for a period. You know when a consequence is working if the behaviour goes away. If it's repeated, maybe the consequence isn't hitting the mark.

Consequences have to have an educative function – if the child doesn't learn something from them, they're just an abuse of parental power. And if we issue punishments in an authoritarian way it becomes more about making her feel bad, and rarely is this effective. We need her to feel that she is OK even if her behaviour is unacceptable.

Crissy says: Parents will have differing views on what is and isn't appropriate, realistic and effective when it comes to consequences. For example, if your son's idea of heaven is sitting in front of the computer all day, grounding him may be pretty pointless, just as telling your daughter she has to miss her best friend's party because her room is untidy is out of proportion. For me, when important rules and boundaries are broken there does need to be a consequence. But that's not the same as punishing your child. Consequences are a form of positive discipline, which encourage your child to reflect and to reason upon her behaviour and ultimately to develop her own ability to practise self-control. When we become overly punitive, however, we're effectively controlling our children by exerting power over them.

Learning which types of behaviour are acceptable and which are unacceptable in our families and wider society is an important life lesson for us all, particularly where inappropriate behaviour can also be dangerous to ourselves or to others. Imposing your will upon your child, getting wound up and barking orders will ultimately be counterproductive because you're effectively stopping her from thinking for herself and developing self-control, and chances are you'll both end up feeling resentful and unheard. Being too prohibitive can make the very behaviour you're trying to avoid seem illicit and exciting, so it's important not to be too rigid, and to aim to strike a balance in the tween years. That way, you're more likely to avoid a major rebellion in the – even more testing – teenage years to come.

What the netmums say

What works when it comes to consequences?

My eldest started [playing up] at about eight, becoming worse by twelve. Whilst we're definitely seeing light at the end of the tunnel there are still some explosive moments. A friend recommended that I did not engage in shouting matches and instead should just take away something that was precious to her, then refuse to discuss it until she had calmed down – this really worked for us. When her sister started down the same route I tried the same tactic, but she is quite happy to carry on and on regardless, so we now just put her in her room until she's calm enough to talk (ear plugs help!). I guess what I'm saying is that each child is different and what might work for one sibling will not always work for another. But you do need stick to any consequences issued, or it won't stop them next time.

Melanie, mum to two girls aged thirteen and eleven

'Whatever' has been my twelve-year-old's favourite word for the past two years. Everything is an effort for her, and she can be very mean to her younger sister. I've tried taking her mobile phone away, grounding her, stopping her pocket money. But what really seems to work is making her go to bed ten minutes earlier every time she's disrespectful. She ended up going to bed an hour and a half earlier than usual the other Saturday night, which meant she was in bed before her sister. We've had two good days, since.

Laura, mum to two girls aged twelve and nine

If we've had a really bad day or week, my daughter doesn't get to go to her much-loved gymnastics class. She'll give Oscar-winning temper tantrums but I cover my ears or turn the television up. Some days are better than others – remembering them helps to get you through the rough patches!

Anna, mum to a girl, eleven, and a boy, three

One thing I've learned is that it's not worth shouting: it does no good, as they don't listen if you're roaring like a madwoman. I've found taking their 'third limb' – their mobile phone – works a treat. They act like they're dying, which amuses me, but it gets the message across.

Jackie, mum to two girls aged seventeen and twelve

I find grounding my daughter and/or removal of her laptop works wonders. On the whole she is a good kid, but she does like to answer back. She is normally given several warnings to stop and then she is just grounded. She will moan and complain but I point out that I had told her to stop arguing, and now I've had enough. I only really needed to do it a few times – now she always stops when she is given a warning!

Natalie, mum to two girls aged twelve and five

I definitely agree with the sentiment of picking your battles wisely. It isn't worth causing upset over every little thing, as tweens like to have some control over their lives. What definitely works with both of mine is withdrawal or reduction in pocket money – the amount would be dependent on what they had done and whether they had had any warning. In addition for my son, I threaten him with missing his football training or some other activity he is keen to do. I think I've only had to actually do it once in recent months as the threat usually works.

Angela, mum to a girl, fourteen, and a boy, eleven

Since they were tiny, I've found that to get your children to behave and understand there are consequences to bad behaviour, you must carry through with any stated punishment. You hear some parents making empty threats and promises of punishments that just cannot be met: for example, 'If you carry on, you won't come on holiday and I will leave you at home on your own!' I knock time off my son's and daughter's bedtime. They get a warning and then, if the behaviour continues, it is bed five minutes earlier. I have never got beyond knocking more than ten minutes off. They know we mean it!

Louise, mum to a boy, eleven, and a girl, ten

I still haven't yet found a suitable way to deal with my thirteen-year-old when he gives me backchat – I'm open to suggestions! He doesn't go out, so I can't ground him, and he doesn't play computer games, so I can't confiscate those. As for my daughter, just the threat of being sent to her room and missing out on what we're doing seems enough at the moment. I'm sure that will change.

Jill, mum to a boy, thirteen, and a girl, eleven

Losing your cool

So you thought your toddler knew how to 'press your buttons'? Actually, your toddler didn't – kids of that age are not mature enough to truly know what rattles your cage. Your tween, on the other hand, has probably got you pretty well sussed by now. But just because she's lost it, doesn't mean you have to, too. Do your best not to let personal remarks about you and dramatic statements hurt: it's highly unlikely that's her genuine intention, and it might help if you can tell yourself that. Stop to listen before rushing to contradict, or to shout back. It may even be that she's got a fair point.

Trying to stay cool when conflict rears its head is easier said than done. But if you can, you should! Blowing your top may be an instinctive reaction, and one that in the very short term can feel satisfying, but it's likely to be counterproductive if you're trying to make a point, reprimand your child, or get something done.

Coping with conflict: How to avoid blowing your top with your tween

- It's a cliché, but counting to ten really can help when you feel your temperature start to rise. Breathing slowly and deeply can also slow you down before you say or do something you wish you hadn't. Try leaving the room for a few moments to calm down.
- Don't beat yourself up when you do lose it with your tween – and you're bound to, sometimes. Try to smooth things over as soon as possible after things have gone pear-shaped, though allow sufficient cooling-off time for both of you, first. Then move in with some reassuring words, and perhaps a hug, or some other physical acknowledgment of your love, like a rub on the back (if she'll allow it).

- Try to talk about what went wrong, if you can. If you can talk about minor conflicts when they arise, you'll be better equipped to cope when the big ones rear their head. Allow her to vent any thoughts of her own on the matter (without allowing it to disintegrate into another shouting match), and be sure to listen.
- Don't be tempted to give in when an important value's at stake just because you feel guilty about a loss of temper. If you need to carry through that consequence, then carry it through!
- If conflict with your tween is really getting you down, you're not alone. Try to talk about it with someone you know will be sympathetic, perhaps because they're going through it too, or have done in the past. If no one's around locally, there's support and friendship aplenty available at www.netmums.com.

What the experts say

Elaine says: When you do have a disagreement with your tween, make sure you listen and talk to her, and find a resolution that she can accept (even if she doesn't particularly like it). Try to avoid reprimanding and scolding in the heat of the moment, instead stopping to listen to what she's said to you. Take a moment to compose yourself if you need to – 'time out' for a parent is a really good strategy, to ensure we don't do or say something we will regret in the next moment.

State your feelings, but stay calm and in charge. If she disappears for an hour without giving you any idea where she was, for example, and you were worried, tell her so. Then state your expectations – so you might say, 'I expect you to let me know when you're going somewhere, so that I don't worry.' Then ask her to make amends – perhaps she could take on an extra chore or responsibility that week. Finally, if you need to, take action, not by way of retribution for what's happened, but rather as a way of working out how can you stop it happening again. That may mean putting an appropriate consequence into place – maybe she's grounded for a few days; or perhaps it means adding a new rule to your list, so maybe she must always phone or text you to let you know where she is when she's out. If you're consistent in upholding your values, by modelling the desired behaviour yourself as well as requiring it of your child, she will eventually absorb that value even if she rebels in the moment. It pays to take the long-term view here.

Crissy says: In times of conflict, try to remember who's the adult and who's the child. Aim to respond rather than overreact – if you lose the plot you may end up saying or doing something you'll regret. Learn to identify the signs that you're losing control and when that happens be prepared to take some time out and deal with it later. After all, if you can't manage your own anger, how can you expect your child to manage hers?

It's true that kids of this age really do know how to get under your skin. If she's upset you, I think it's OK to let her see that and to let her know that her behaviour has crossed the line. But no matter how wounded you may be, no matter how fiercely she may battle with you, don't withdraw emotionally. She may seem like she's not hearing you and she doesn't need or want you in her life, but it's important that you maintain a constant presence. She needs to know she has your permission to make her own choices (within reason, of course) and that if it all blows up in her face she can always come back to you. It's particularly crucial to let your child know that you're still there for her even after a blazing row, so if you don't feel ready to hug and make up it's fine to say that aloud: 'I love you, but right now I'm still upset and I want to take a little time out.' Most kids will respond in a positive way to this message.

When your tween rebels and rejects you and your values, try not to take it to heart. It's all part of a necessary process of growing up and she needs your support to learn how to control this complex mix of emotions. She might say she hates you, and in that moment she probably does – but it's absolutely possible to feel you hate someone whilst still really loving them, and that's another lesson she needs to learn. Equally it's OK for us as parents to have mixed feelings about our children in the heat of the moment. The difference is that as adults we need to have enough self-control not to say it out loud!

Big trouble

You may well find yourself facing one or more quite serious behavioural problems at some point in this period, with the likelihood increasing as your tween gets older. Perhaps you discover your child has been persistently lying; maybe she's been a bully; perhaps she's truanted from school; or tried smoking.

If you had no inkling something like this was going on in your child's life, chances are you'll be deeply shocked. Try not to panic. Don't rush to voice your anger, or issue a punishment, however serious the deed. Talking about it – and listening to her side of the story – is the first thing you need to do: it's very likely there's a good reason for the behaviour and sympathy may be called for. Don't be tempted just to 'wash your hands' of a major problem, though, and leave it untackled in the hope it will go away by itself. She'll need your help in getting out of trouble, and staying out.

What the experts say

Crissy says: If you are faced with more serious issues, try to take a deep breath and avoid a kneejerk reaction at all costs. If you come down on her like a ton of bricks at the first sign of major trouble you run the risk of alienating her and it may discourage her from coming to you for help in the future.

When a tween is behaving badly it's easy to focus on the act itself rather than the reasons behind it. Take nothing for granted and take time to explore how it has happened. It's not enough just to listen to your child's side of the story: she needs to know she is really being heard. It may be that she's deeply unhappy about something in her life and the behaviour is a coping mechanism or a cry for help; she may be desperate for your attention – even at this age, for some children, negative attention is better than no attention at all. It may be that she's struggling to contend with peer pressure or even bullying. If you don't listen, then you won't know.

Let's put this in perspective. Although comparatively rare, really serious behavioural problems can nevertheless happen to any child and within any family at any time. Plenty of kids will find themselves in stormy waters at some time during this tricky phase of life. A few will sink, but most will swim. As parents, it's our job to provide as many flotation aids as possible!

2 Education

School is a big deal for tweens. Let's face it, a vast chunk of any child's time is spent there, and that's before you count all the extra time on school-based extra-curricular activities, homework and socialising with fellow pupils beyond the school gates. For most, it's the second most significant place after home.

Thankfully, school has loads of great things to offer. Chief among them is the chance to meet and mix with a wide range of different peers, and a host of learning and leisure opportunities that will stand them in good stead through to adulthood.

However, school life can also bring big pressures for many tweens, and for their parents too. This is particularly so once the leap up from primary school comes, which for the majority comes at the end of Year Six, at the age of eleven (whilst for the minority living in an area where there's a three-tier system, there are two leaps to make, typically after Years Four and Eight). There'll be masses of change to adapt to, a huge increase in responsibilities, and the daunting business of being a small fish plunged into a big pond. So any child approaching this all-important transition will need tons of love and support, as well as plenty of practical help in preparing for the move and in coping when he actually gets there.

The build-up begins early

Your child's teachers will be helping him to prepare for secondary education well before he's left primary school, and as parents, you can help with the process too, by building up self-confidence and self-esteem in your child. If he's got these qualities in abundance it will help him settle into the upper tier of his education when the time comes, and to deal with any difficulties that arise. The best way to do this for your child is to be liberal with praise at his every achievement, small and large.

You can also start to give him his first steps of freedom and independence well in advance of his eleventh birthday, increasing the amount of this you give him gradually during his final few years at primary school. Of course, how much freedom to give comes down to how you feel as parents – and will also take into account the sort of tween you've got. (There's more exploration of this issue in Chapter 8.) Teaching him to take responsibility for organising himself is another vital bit of preparation you can set in motion early on, if you haven't already. Getting his act together, without any help from you, is a skill he'll certainly need to call on once at secondary school.

A whole new system

Secondary-school is certain to be very different to primary school: for starters, there'll be a bigger pupil population and a larger, more complex site, which is unlikely to have the same colourful and cosy feel of the average primary. The workload will be greater, with many assignments expected to be completed at home, and there'll be lots of new subjects, with a teacher for each, and different methods of teaching, learning and assessment. There'll be timetables to juggle, numerous classrooms to find, and lots more books and other sorts of kit and equipment to remember – and to carry!

A different or longer journey to and from school is also something that may take a while to get to grips with – especially if it now involves your child getting there under his own steam, whether that's walking, cycling or by public transport.

There will very likely be huge changes to his usual social set-up, too. He may have left some or even all of his old friends behind, but in any case there'll be the challenge of forming many new friendships and acquaintances ahead – and the likelihood of running into peers he won't get on with so well. (There's more on the subject of friends and peers in the next chapter.)

But it's not just your child who'll need to adapt. You too must get to grips with the timetable; be on hand to help with homework; and offer your sympathy when the going gets tough. The cosy school-gate culture you may have experienced at primary school will no longer exist – so you'll need to find other ways of keeping in touch with fellow parents, if you want to. And you probably won't be encouraged to pop in and out as you might have done before (which, from your child's point of view, is probably just as well), so chatting to teachers will be a more formal affair.

Don't be surprised if you get some snappy attitudes or bad behaviour at around this time: it's very likely to be anxiety manifesting itself in a negative way. Try to find some extra reserves of empathy – and make sure all lines of communication are kept fully open.

Moving on up: Tips for a smooth transition to secondary

- Find out as much as possible about the school, by reading its website or chatting to existing pupils and their parents. Look for the things you know will particularly appeal – exciting extra-curricular opportunities, for example, or great facilities for music or sport – and use it to build a positive view of this new horizon. You could also look to see what strategies the school has in place to welcome 'newbies' – many offer special orientation sessions, or operate a 'buddy' or mentoring system, where first years are allocated an older pupil to show them the ropes.
- Have at least one practice run of the route to school, there and back. Get a timetable for any buses and trains he'll be taking, highlighting the relevant information. Bear in mind he

should always leave plenty of time to get to school, so he's never late for registration.

- Make sure he's got everything he needs in the way of uniform and equipment – your shopping list will probably include items he hasn't needed until now, such as a calculator or a French dictionary.

- Arrange for your tween to spend time with friends going to the same school, or get to know other peers he's on less-familiar terms with. It will be a boon if he's got at least one friend to make the journey to and from school with, even if only at the outset. Perhaps they could do the practice runs together?

- Make sure you both attend any open days or induction meetings, or take any other opportunities to get a look round the school. Secondary schools can seem enormous and layouts horribly confusing if you've never been in one before.

- Listen carefully to any concerns he has about the move, whether he's deeply worried about major issues like bullying or academic pressure, or simply sweating the small stuff, like having the right PE kit. Offer whatever help you can, practically and emotionally, in resolving them.

- Try to show loads of interest in the move up, generally, and be positive about it yourself, even if you do feel a bit wobbly at the thought. Help him see it as an exciting move forward, and the chance for a fresh start.

- Ease him into the business of taking responsibility for himself, if you haven't already, by getting him to make decisions whenever possible (offering a shortlist of choices you're happy with). For instance, how can he help you when it comes to getting breakfast on the table in the mornings? If a daily bath or shower is likely to be a good idea now, would he prefer to take it at the beginning or the end of the day? What sort of bag will he best fit all his new folders in?

- Help him sustain links with old friends he's leaving behind. In time, he'll make plenty of new pals, but for a while, hooking up with familiar faces outside of school is sure to be a big comfort.

What the experts say

Crissy says: By the age of nine, like it or not your child is officially a 'tween', and it's definitely time to stop babying him and to begin preparing him for what lies ahead. I'd advise that you begin experimenting with 'letting go' of your tween in the two years before he starts secondary school. Mutually negotiated new freedoms such as walking to school with his mates, popping to the local shops and staying in the house alone for short periods are all good preparation. Give him his own tasks and chores around the house, and leave it up to him to tidy his room, put the washing in the basket and pack his school bag. In this way you're preparing him for the increased personal responsibility that going to secondary school will bring. As he begins to pursue a greater sense of autonomy, it's vital that you neither let him go nor hold him on too tight a rein. Loosen the apron strings little by little, so he'll have something to hold on to should he stumble, but still giving him the freedom to move away from you and explore freely. It's worth remembering that this process of separation and increasing self-awareness will really pick up speed once he gets to secondary school.

By this age, tweens are becoming increasingly conscious of how others see them, so it's not surprising that the move to secondary school can be a worrying time. He'll have heard rumours from older siblings or classmates and may be afraid he won't fit in, and will be acutely aware of an imminent demotion to the bottom of the pecking order, which may make him feel insecure, even afraid. He won't know the 'big-school' rules and may be fearful of being considered a geek for having the wrong hairstyle, or the wrong bag. There's a whole lot of uncertainty swirling around and he'll have a lot to learn outside as well as inside the classroom. This is where other people's kids can come in very handy – cousins, neighbours or friends' children who attend the same school can be a mine of information, as can the previous year's primary graduates. And the more familiar your child is with the school itself, the less intimidating it will be when term begins, so as well as going to any open days or evenings, perhaps you could also go along to events held there such as car-boot sales or plays in the run-up to the start of term.

Another good idea is to make sure you involve your child in all the shopping and planning that leads up to starting secondary school, and to try to make this a positive experience, and a chance for the two of you to spend time together. Don't just present him with a pile of stuff – show him the uniform and equipment lists, and discuss what he'll need it all for, and when. Don't forget to make a fuss of him when he tries his uniform on for the first time. He may complain, but he will be secretly really pleased if you take photos for Grandma and tell him how proud you are of him.

If he hasn't been out and about on his own before, the thought of your child travelling to and from school on his own by public transport or on foot can be worrying for both of you. But remember this is one step towards 'letting go' that we all have to take at some point. Try to encourage him to hook up with other tweens who live nearby, and don't insist on taking him to school every day, unless of course he asks you to. He needs to explore his new-found independence and you need to learn to trust him to stay safe and behave sensibly.

If at all possible, try to ensure you're around either before or after school at least for the first few days, and build in some special one-on-one time for him to tell you about his day. Familiarity and routine will be important now, so if he goes to a breakfast club or spends time with a childminder, try to make sure it's not a brand-new arrangement. You may also need to raise your tolerance levels for a while: he may well be stressed or anxious or tired, which may leave him grouchy or difficult at home. It's very much a time to choose your battles.

All children develop and mature at different rates, so take nothing for granted and be aware that although your child may say everything's hunky dory and appear to be coping really well with the myriad of fresh challenges, deep down he may be a mass of fears and insecurities. You may feel like you're being pushed away and ignored and that your tween needs you less and less, but in most cases the opposite is true. So stick close and be available.

Elaine says: All children are different. Most cope with change while some find it very difficult. But however able your child is, rather than leaving things to chance, you should aim to do as much as you can to ensure he's successful from day one, and that it's as easy an experience as possible. Coping with change is often difficult because of fear of the unknown, but when we're well prepared we're much better able to deal with whatever's thrown at us. So, do your research, get to know the school, find out about the curriculum, go to the open days and purchase what he needs well ahead of time. Thankfully, schools these days are very good at preparing children and will offer induction days and parents' evenings in advance of term starting. Often we as parents can also get stressed in this run-up period, but it's important to ensure we give our children that 'can do' feeling. Children are more likely to do their best when they are well prepared.

We can do an enormous amount to build up confidence – for school, and for life in general – and the best way to do this is to give lots of descriptive praise. He's going to be faced with many new changes and will need lots of messages about how much you value him, and he'll need plenty of new qualities such as bravery, adaptability, self-reliance, independent thinking, good organisation and strong self-esteem to survive in his new environment. So if he shows any of those qualities in other areas of life – perhaps he walked to the local shop to get you a pint of milk, or tried out a new hobby for the first time – he should be praised for it. What you're doing is carefully building up his image of himself as a child who can cope with new and challenging things. As your children get older, it's so easy to overlook the opportunities to praise and he'll need it now more than ever with all the challenges he's about to face.

When the time comes to start at school, he'll be feeling a range of emotions. Fear and anxiety is very likely, but a lot of that is based on the unknown, so just talking things through and offering your understanding can really help. Be careful not to give too much advice too quickly – the key is to listen without judgement. Once a tween feels heard and understood, problem-solving together is far more effective. Talk through all the situations and scenes he's likely to find himself in, and explore with him what will happen if things go wrong, for instance if he forgets his bus pass, or can't find his way to the science lab.

It may be that he shows feelings of fear or anxiety with a change in behaviour – perhaps rudeness, disrespect, defiance or unkindness to a sibling – or he may be unusually quiet and with-drawn. So just be aware that any change in behaviour is almost always down to a feeling, and many tweens may not be able to identify how they feel or may be unable to express what they are feeling in an effective way. The way to respond is to validate what he's trying to tell you, and show how much his feelings matter. Reflective listening is really key at times like this. The first step is to stop what you are doing and pay attention to his words or actions. If he's talking to you, then listen . . . and really listen, by imagining what he's feeling, and reflecting it back to him in words. For example, 'It sounds to me as if you're feeling really frustrated that you weren't picked for the football team this term. I know how hard you've worked at your dribbling skills and to end up not in the squad must be disappointing for you.' Don't deny his feelings – or try and fix it! There's a huge temptation to go and speak to the football coach and fix the problem, but by doing that we send the message to our child that he can't sort out his own issues. Once his feelings are listened to, he will often feel ready to look for his own solutions – a perfect result.

Being organised

Life can become a lot more complicated when you've got a child at secondary school – although the good news is he should now be mature enough to take much of the strain on his own shoulders.

You no doubt had an established weekday routine carved out whilst he was still at primary school, so perhaps you won't have to do too much tweaking to create a new one. If you need him to be up earlier than before because his school now starts at a different time, or the journey takes longer, set alarm clocks with plenty of time to spare – if he hasn't got his own by now, it could be the time to get him one. Schedule in time for breakfast – the first meal of the day is even more important now, as his growing body and brain will require plenty of fuel to get him through a demanding school day. (There's more on food and fitness in Chapter 7.)

There'll almost certainly be a more complex to-do list to tackle now, so you'll need to crank up some kind of admin system that's going to help you both to stay on top of it all. Your ultimate aim is for your tween to be entirely responsible for leaving for school with absolutely everything he needs for that day on his person, but in the early months you'll no doubt have to do a bit of hand-holding – and some kids will continue to need 'nudging' well beyond that! So it's essential to have a copy of his timetable pinned up in a prominent place, and a list of what's required and when. (And – although it may sound obvious – don't forget to actually look at it, or rather, make sure that *he* has looked it, before leaving for school.)

Although a very well-worn piece of advice, it's true that getting ready the evening before is the best way to avoid stressful mornings. Encourage him to unpack his school bag as soon as he gets in so you don't have to deal with soggy sandwich leftovers, dirty PE kit and forgotten homework when the heat's on the following morning. Whether or not you encourage homework to be done immediately after school, or later, is up to you: there's more ideas for helping with homework a bit further on in this chapter. But a quiet, screen-free lead-up to a reasonable bedtime is a good idea – even for this age group – as tweens need plenty of sleep to function well. The first term, in particular, is likely to be pretty exhausting as he adapts to his new schedule. There's more on bedtimes and sleep in Chapter 6.

Chances are you'll have many more extra-curricular and social activities to fit in now, too: most parents find that demands on them as a taxi service increase once secondary school starts. It's great for kids to have opportunities to do other things and meet other kids outside school, so do – as far as possible – help to facilitate that. Of course, too much structured activity can come at the expense of rest and relaxation, so don't let him overdo it.

What the experts say

Elaine says: Many parents do find that all the organisation required for successful secondary-school life a big challenge – particularly those with boys. (It's a generalisation, but girls *tend* to be better at taking responsibility for staying organised.)

The main thing you need is a checklist in a really prominent place, which details everything he needs on which day. Then, without nagging, you need to ask him daily if he's checked the list, and encourage him to do it for himself. Try not to rescue your child but let him learn over time the natural consequences of his actions if he doesn't keep on top of things. You don't want to be running to the school gates with his rugby kit every time he's forgotten it: you need him to be in good habits so that eventually he will remember it without you having to nag, repeat and remind.

Alongside this system you'll probably have some rules and consequences – so the rule is that he has to read the list and make sure he's got exactly what he needs for the day, and the natural consequence if he doesn't is probably a telling-off from his teacher or the embarrassment of having to wear ill-fitting spares. Of course for the first few weeks you may need to give him a helping hand, but that doesn't mean doing it for him: it means having all the information he needs there, and gently prompting him to check it, every day. Your aim is to get him to do his own thinking, with your support and encouragement.

What the netmums say

Coping with the move up to secondary

I think I was more worried than my daughter about the start of secondary school, as she's quite shy and usually takes a while to adjust to new situations. However, she's taken it all in her stride. I have to say that the school must take much of the credit. She had three induction days towards the end of the summer term so she got a taster of some of the lessons and the opportunity to have a good look round. She was also introduced to her teacher and fellow classmates, so there would be some familiar faces when she started for real. And her first day in September was what they called a 'bonding day'; the school was only open to the Year Sevens and Year Twelves and they spent the day doing fun activities and team-building exercises – a brilliant idea. They were also allowed separate break times and no homework for the first two weeks to ease them in gently, which she really appreciated.
Esther, mum to two girls aged eleven and eight

They say every child is different and that saying is so true. My first daughter adjusted fine to secondary school, but my youngest is not doing so well. It's actually quite painful watching her go, knowing she's not happy. Her dad and I are giving all the support we can, trying to give good advice, and speaking to her teachers. It's a similar pattern to when she started at primary school, so I know it will probably take a while for her to be OK, and a few years for her to be happy. Meanwhile, we are giving her all the love and support we can.
Jayne, mum to two girls aged fourteen and eleven

My son absolutely loves secondary school and I'm extremely proud of the way he's adapted to the change. He'd outgrown his primary school and was probably getting a bit too big for his boots there, but this move has grounded him again – he's grown up overnight. He now gets himself up, fed, washed, dressed, and sorts his bag, and is out of the door at 7.55 a.m. Then he walks to school with his friends, which takes them about twenty minutes. He loves his uniform, especially wearing the shirt and tie, and takes great pride in his appearance. The amount of homework is a shock – he's got on with it, though. At the moment it's all good. Long may it continue!

Ali, mum to a girl, eighteen, and a boy, eleven

Francesca has just started secondary and so far it's going well, although she does seem to have morphed into a sullen teenager almost overnight! I was really worried as we've only just moved to the area so, although she did manage to go to a local primary school for a couple of weeks, she didn't really have an established peer group and didn't get to go to the induction days. But she seems to have made a nice group of friends. She's dyslexic and I'm worried she won't get the help she needs. So far she's had no support at all but I feel it only fair to give the school a couple of weeks for the new term to settle until I go in with all guns blazing! She's coping pretty well with the amount of homework; it's still a novelty so she quite enjoys it, although I'm not sure how long that will last. But the organisation is a problem – I am trying to make sure she has what she needs without taking over. I'm a teacher myself and have always dreaded having to steer my own kids through the pitfalls of starting secondary school, but in my experience it's far harder for parents than the kids, and most children settle in pretty well. So I'm trying very hard to take a step back and let her enjoy all the good – as well as the bad – that secondary has to offer.

Abbie, mum to two girls aged eleven and four

James was really lucky to be going to my old school so I was able give him loads of advice and information before he started, which I hope helped put him at ease. He was given a three-day induction in the summer, to get to know the school, meet his form group and build a relationship with his tutors before the big move in September. He has to get the bus there himself on a morning and get it back home again, which I thought he might struggle with, but he's managed fantastically.

Claire, mum to five boys aged eleven, nine, six, five and one, and a girl, three

As the only girl going from her primary school, Natalie was quite anxious about starting secondary school. So she took down telephone numbers for seven girls during her induction day, and we arranged a barbecue at home in August, which she invited them to. It was a great way of breaking the ice and it meant there were some familiar faces on her first day.

Hayley, mum to a girl, sixteen, and a boy, thirteen

My eldest coped fine with homework, getting himself up for the bus and remembering everything, but he is quiet and bright, and has suffered from bullying. His younger brother Sam started this September. I struggle to get him up; he's forgotten his PE kit and his planner; lost his bus pass and needs to be prompted to do his homework. On the other hand, he sticks up for himself in the face of bullies, and seems to be making plenty of new friends. It just shows that different children cope in different ways. I don't think Sam was mature enough to cope with high school, but you don't get a choice so he's had to get on with it. I just hope he doesn't lose too many bus passes though, because they're expensive!

Shauna, mum to two boys aged thirteen and eleven

Morgan started senior school this September and he's enjoying it but he's always struggled with learning – we're still waiting for him to have an assessment for this – and he's been having great difficulty with the homework. Within the first two weeks, he'd got three detentions because of homework not done or not handed in. It turned out that because he was concentrating so much on writing down the classwork from the board to his book, he was missing anything the teacher was telling them to do for homework. To combat this we notified his form teacher of his learning problems and we've told Morgan to approach his

teachers after the class and ask them if there was anything he has missed. It's worked to an extent, but we're having problems getting him to remember all he has to do.
Sam, mum to a boy, eleven

My daughter has a coordination problem, which means she was awful at listening and doing what she needed to do for school in the morning. I made sure that everything she needed was put out the night before – and tried my best not to get frustrated and shout when she wouldn't move her bum. I also did her a list, to begin with, of what she had to do in the morning, so that when she had done it she could tick it off. Now the routine's set firm and she does what she needs to do on her own – although I still need to shoo her out the door sometimes! I always find that if I'm up half an hour before the girls it gives me time to have a cuppa and prepare for the morning madness.
Jackie, mum to two girls aged seventeen and twelve

I found life was actually easier once my girls started at secondary school. The school run stopped as they walked themselves there and back, and although they're involved in after-school clubs, they're independent enough to juggle those themselves. And really that's what high school is all about: getting them to become more independent and take responsibility for themselves. I suppose the tricky part is making yourself aware as a parent as to what's going on – the *children* are put in charge of knowing what their homework is, so it's their responsibility, not yours – and without the school run you suddenly haven't got the same school-gates grapevine to rely on for those times when letters are left at the bottom of the school bag. Sadly a crystal ball doesn't come as standard issue to parents, so if you want to keep track of what's going on you have to ask: check homework diaries, actively ask if there have been any letters, keep a check on the school website, etc. A family calendar of important dates can be handy for keeping track of everything.
Natalie, mum to two girls aged fifteen

Your role in his education

Just as at primary school – but perhaps even more so now – your role in how happy and successful your child is at school is vital. Research shows that kids whose parents take an active interest and give oodles of support in all aspects of school life and learning do better. The way to do this is by asking questions and listening; helping with homework (see overleaf); and regularly attending events like parents' evenings, fundraisers, sports fixtures or shows. Make a point of knowing the names and subjects of teachers, and finding out which of these he likes, and which he doesn't.

Of course, helping with learning goes far beyond taking an interest in what's written in his homework book, and is probably something you do every day without realising, anyway: for example, talking through ideas, and answering his questions – or helping him to research the answers to them himself. It's a great idea to chat about news and current affairs, and encourage him to have his own opinions: as well as boosting his knowledge and understanding of the world, it will help give him confidence to pipe up in class if he's required to. Dinnertime's the perfect chance for this kind of forum – in fact, eating together as a family is a healthy habit generally, so aim to do it whenever busy timetables allow. It's also a great time to discuss the school day and gently ask questions about, or ease, any anxieties that have cropped up.

Try to encourage reading, too. Even if he's not that keen on literature, you can help boost his enthusiasm by sourcing reading material that will inspire his interest – there's loads of good tween fiction out there right now, and if he prefers comics or specialist magazines that relate to his hobby, that's all good reading practice.

Help to keep him motivated by offering tons of praise when he's done well – or has simply made impressive efforts to do so – and the odd reward, perhaps. And don't forget that praise isn't just for academic achievements: music, sport and other extra-curricular stuff is important, as is his social life – so if he's made an effort to make friends with someone new, or shown some kindness to a fellow pupil, then make sure you let him know you're pleased about that, too.

Of course, some days, school life won't go well for him, and you'll have to help him overcome disappointment or failure. As ever, listening carefully is your first move. Remind him that failing some stuff is inevitable, for everyone – and let him know you are proud of other recent achievements.

Be wary of having *too much* input in your child's education. The line between giving lots of support and pushing a bit too hard is a fine one.

What the experts say

Crissy says: We all want what's best for our children and to give them a good start in life, but we need to tread carefully and make sure we're not pushing them too hard to achieve. Be interested in your child's homework, make suggestions, share ideas by all means, but his work is very much his work, not yours. We're talking parental input here, not a takeover bid by an overly ambitious adult. Show him you take school and schoolwork seriously and it will almost certainly rub off on him. Let him know you're always available, interested, willing and able to help. But if he feels you're taking over or telling him how he 'should' be doing his work, it could dent his self-confidence and leave him frustrated and resentful – and after all, you can't sit next to him in class or take exams for him when the time comes.

Always celebrate, never denigrate your child's efforts. Help him learn how to stretch rather than overstretch himself. Check he's meeting targets and deadlines, and support him to do so, but make sure you also schedule in downtime – kids need fresh air and exercise, plenty of sleep and fun with their family and friends just as much as a good education. Your aim is to help him develop into a happy, healthy rounded human being, not a frazzled academic. If your child is forever telling you to butt out, be prepared to have a long, hard look at yourself. Where is your motivation coming from? Do you want what's actually best for your child, or what *you* have decided is best for your child?

Show him when you're impressed but don't go over the top. If your child achieves a high mark, concentrate on praising his hard work and effort, rather than the grade, and don't be tempted to take the credit! Know and acknowledge what he's capable of, and make goals and expectations achievable and realistic. Make it clear from the outset that it's OK to get things wrong, to not understand and to fail, and that you will love him no matter what.

Elaine says: Children will feel pressured if they get messages from us that they are never good enough, and it can very quickly happen. We don't mean to – we mean to bring out the best in our child – but negative comments or nagging can so easily be interpreted as criticism, which will be a disaster in terms of getting the best out of him. What's called for is descriptive praise, whenever you get the opportunity. So maybe he remembered to take in his guitar last week, having forgotten the week before – let him know you're pleased he did so. You might say, 'I'm pleased to see you remembered to take your guitar today – you are getting good at organising yourself with no prompting or nagging from me! That's really self-reliant.' Perhaps he's got his biology book out of his bag and put it on the table ready to make a start on his homework – and you know it's his least favourite subject. You might say, 'It's hard for you to get started on your biology homework, isn't it? It takes self-discipline to be able to do something you have to do when you don't want to, like yesterday when you put all your books away in your bag before playing with the PlayStation. I was really pleased about that.' This kind of appreciative comment is much more effective than just 'good boy' or 'well done' in relation to achievements. It's much better to praise specifically regarding the effort, attitude and the strategies he's using.

Helping with homework

Homework is a fact of life for tweens. Government guidelines are that children in Years Five and Six (in other words, in the final two years of primary school) should be doing around thirty minutes of homework a day; and that children in Years Seven and Eight (the first two years of secondary) should be getting forty-five minutes to an hour and a half of homework a day. It's up to schools and teachers to decide exactly how much homework they dole out, but it can amount to a pretty hefty after-school study schedule for this age group.

It can be miserable trying to make tired children do the homework that's expected of them, and a definite challenge, sometimes, providing help. But however you feel about homework, it's regarded as a very necessary part of a pupil's education by schools, so it's something you need to stay positive about. If it helps, remind yourself that as well as filling in the gaps in the day's learning, regularly completing homework can boost self-discipline and the ability to make a deadline – and they will be useful skills for later in life.

It's good if you can be around as much as possible when it comes to homework. If you work until late in the day, and someone else keeps an eye on your tween for you, ask them to show an interest on your behalf.

Encourage your tween to take responsibility for completing his own homework – whether or not you need to check that he's done so will probably depend on him, and as he matures, hopefully he will get to a point where you never need to. Offer appropriate choices where possible when it comes to homework so he feels he's got some control over the situation – for instance, you might let him decide which part of the day he prefers to do it, or whether it might be possible to take one or more days off homework altogether, assuming it can be fitted in elsewhere in the week.

After-school studies: Hints on helping with homework

- Show him you're really interested in his homework – ask if you can see what's in his homework diary, and whether or not you can help with it. Give plenty of praise where it's due – and perhaps a reward every now and then if he's consistently made an effort to do what's required.
- Set aside a regular time for homework and stick to it. You might find that straight after school isn't a great slot, as he'll probably want to unwind and de-stress first, and re-energise with a snack and a drink. Equally, last thing at night isn't

ideal, because he'll be tired. Encourage him to spread homework out over the week, doing a little every day, rather than a lot on some days (although it's good to have at least one non-homework day, if possible). Allot a quiet part of the weekend, too, to help with longer projects and to avoid squeezing in too much in the short space between tea and bedtime. Ideally, homework sessions should be relaxed rather than rushed, so allow all the time you're likely to need.

- Help him to be organised so he can keep track of exactly what needs doing and when. Most schools provide a homework book or diary to keep notes in, but some kind of 'in-tray' or filing basket kept in a prominent place for storing the latest assignments could be useful.

- Set up conditions that will help him do his homework without distractions. Make sure tellies and games consoles are turned off, and that he's sitting at a comfortable desk or table, in a well-lit room. It's common for teachers to set homework that involves internet research, printing out, or even typed presentation, so access to a computer is a must these days.

- Offer help when needed, but remember it's up to him to get his homework done on his own. If in doubt about the level of support it's OK to give, ask his teacher. Don't feel bad if he needs some help but you don't understand – you're definitely not alone! His teacher can also tell you the best resources to turn to for the answers you need. Think of it as a useful learning curve for yourself.

- Don't hover over him, but be close by when he does his homework if possible (or make sure someone else is). Depending on how old he is (or rather, how much you can trust him), ask to see it when it's done. Don't lose your temper or be critical if you suspect he hasn't done a good job. Just ask gentle questions about how he might change or improve it.

- Encourage siblings to do homework together, or ask a friend over for tea with the promise that they can let rip on the

Xbox or in the garden once they've both got homework done. If you've got younger kids too, it's only fair that they take noisy distractions elsewhere. You might suggest they do some 'homework' of their own and set them up with some colouring, reading or quiet games.

- There are loads of useful learning and homework resources on the internet, and this kind of research is usually encouraged by schools. Help your child explore what extra resources are available.

What the experts say

Elaine says: If homework is a 'hotspot' area, there's usually a rule missing. One simple rule that might work for your family – it's one that works for mine – is that there's no screen-time, in other words television, consoles, computers or online social networking, at all before homework is done. Certainly there should be some sort of relaxation before starting out on homework, whether that's walking the dog or playing footie in the park. But my personal view is that allowing screen-time as a form of relaxation will usually make it harder to persuade your child it's time for home-work, and can often be a recipe for disaster.

There is always a reason if tweens don't want to do home-work, and it's usually generated by emotion: maybe he would simply prefer to be doing something else! Many times, avoidance of homework is due to a feeling that he can't do it or can't do it well enough, either for his own expectations, or the adults in his life. The question to ask is, is he feeling his efforts go unappre-ciated, and therefore that he is never going to be good enough? If this is the case, the main problem is a lack of motivation, and that's where we parents have the biggest part to play. For a tween to have checked out of homework, you'll normally find there are issues with self-esteem that may have been building up over a period of time. How we as parents react to this is key to what happens next. If indeed there has been a lot of nagging

and reprimanding, or even labelling as 'lazy', don't be surprised
if he hears criticism and in turn gives up on homework. Why?
Because he feels he just isn't good enough to get it done.

Getting on well with teachers

On the whole, it's harder to build relationships with teachers at secondary school. You're unlikely to be welcome to pop in and out of school
for a chat as you may have been at primary school, and as it's usual to
have one teacher for each subject at secondary school, there'll be far
more to get to know.

All the same, it's a good idea to keep communication lines open and
build goodwill with your child's teachers wherever possible. The most
important member of staff at school is likely to be his form tutor – in
most schools, this is the member of staff who takes registration at either
end of the day and will usually have some responsibility for pupils'
personal and social wellbeing – so it's worth getting to know them. As
a general rule, he or she will be the first port of call if you need to discuss
a problem or worry (unless it involves a specific subject, in which case
you could go direct to the subject teacher). Your child's head of year or
head of house will also have a significant role, usually taking overall
responsibility for monitoring your child's academic progress, behaviour
and general wellbeing within school.

Reports and parents' evenings will provide you with useful feedback
about how your tween is doing, but you should also be free to make
contact with a teacher if necessary in between. Find out how and
when they would prefer you to do this: they may be happy to take a
telephone call outside teaching hours, or they may prefer to be reached
by email. (Be wary of sending a written note in with your child, in
case it gets lost in the depths of his school bag.) If you want to see a
teacher in person, you'll almost certainly need to make an appointment first.

If your child's school has some kind of system for written communication between home and school, such as homework books, this will
be a very useful and important record, so make sure it's always kept in
a safe place. Check it daily and – if necessary – write in it yourself.

Coping with SATs

At present, Key Stage 2 national curriculum tests – more commonly known as SATs – continue to loom large for all Year Six children. It means they undergo formal assessment throughout their final year at primary school and, at the end of it, must sit a series of short exams in maths and English (although teacher boycotts of SATs have taken place recently in some schools, and it's possible the system will be changing some time soon, as the Government has pledged a review).

Although SATs shouldn't be a cause for alarm – since in theory they are supposed to be about judging schools' performances, not pupils' – they can nevertheless cause a fair amount of stress and worry and, whilst some teachers work hard to minimise pressure, others take them pretty seriously. It's likely that quite a bit of classroom time will be taken up in preparing for the tests, and your tween's teacher may set homework with this in mind, too, for example practising past questions. You may also be urged to buy revision books, although you certainly shouldn't come under pressure to fork out for these – there are plenty of free resources online if you feel the need to tap into them.

Try to be upbeat about SATs, if possible, whatever your personal view about them, and offer all the help and encouragement you usually would for homework, without increasing the pressure. You certainly shouldn't press upon your tween that he must do well in them. Explain that SATs are simply a way of showing what he knows and measuring the whole school's standards – and emphasise that SATs cannot be failed.

During SATs week itself, aim to keep the pressure down by sticking to your usual routines and encouraging your child to play and relax as he would normally. Try to make sure he gets enough sleep, and eats a good breakfast on the day of the test.

When there's a problem

It's a rare tween who won't run into difficulty of one sort or another at school, whether social, behavioural or academic. Perhaps he'll go through a phase of refusing to do his homework, or encounter problems keeping up in the classroom. Maybe he'll come up against a teacher he simply can't get on with, or develop a disproportionate dislike for a particular subject. Ruined friendships and bullying are also, sadly, fairly common stories (there's more about both in the following chapter). Thankfully, most schools these days have a good standard of pastoral care, with zero-tolerance policies for bullies, mentoring and support systems commonly in place, and help available for those with special educational needs. Even so, loving parents will clearly want to be involved if the course of their child's school life doesn't run smooth for one reason or another.

If and when you experience a problem, rest assured you won't be the first parent who's been there – or the last. Try not to panic, but equally don't dismiss any problem, even if it seems trivial at first: it's probably better tackled earlier rather than later, before it escalates into something worse. And even if it doesn't seem a big deal to you, it could be to your child.

Before attempting to fix any school-based problem, make sure you've got the full story. If your child seems worried, or has complained that something's making him unhappy, your first task is to gently encourage him to open up on the matter, so you know exactly what you're dealing with. Bear in mind that sometimes a problem at school actually has its roots at home (as well as vice versa), so be careful not to jump to any conclusions.

Talking to a teacher will be a necessary step if the problem can't be thrashed out at home. If you do need to approach a member of staff, or they have come to you, try not to be defensive and try to stay calm, positive and friendly – even if you suspect they've handled things badly so far, or even if you blame them for causing the problem – because it will be counterproductive if you're confrontational about it. Don't be critical of school rules or any member of staff in front of your child.

If a problem seems to be linked to a specific teacher, hear your child out on the subject, but stay neutral and keep calm. Don't be tempted to dash immediately into school to hunt the teacher in question down: there are always two sides to a story. Continue to keep talking and listening to your child's concerns, and give extra support with any homework set by the teacher in question. If things don't seem to get better, you'll have to arrange to chat to the teacher (as horrendous as this may seem to your child). And if that still doesn't seem to resolve things, you may want to discuss it with an appropriate and sympathetic alternative member of staff, such as a head of year or a form tutor. However, it may be that you need to be philosophical and put it down to a personality clash: your child probably won't get on with every one of his teachers, just as in adult life he won't get on with all the people he meets. If this is the case, you'll just have to urge him to keep his head down and live with it as best he can.

Getting in trouble

Your tween may well find himself on the receiving end of some form of disciplinary action at secondary school. Detention is probably the most common sanction against bad behaviour used in secondary schools, and involves a kid being kept in either during lunchtime or after school. Teachers don't need to get your permission to give a detention, but for those that take place outside normal school hours, they must give you at least twenty-four hours' advance warning in case you need to make alternative travel arrangements – usually in the shape of a detention form which you'll need to sign and return. For more serious offences, schools may issue fixed-period exclusions – what used to be known as suspensions – which means a child is not allowed in school at all, usually for five days or fewer.

As a general rule, you should always back the school on disciplinary action. However, if being punished seems to have become a regular thing for your child, make an appointment with an appropriate member of staff to find out why, and how you can help to change things. In the case of an exclusion which you feel is unfair, you can get all the advice and information you need to take things further from the website of ACE, the Advisory Centre for Education.

What the experts say

Crissy says: If a problem arises at secondary school your child may feel vulnerable, unsure of himself and isolated. All his hard-won self-confidence can quickly vanish, and so it's vital that difficulties are addressed as soon as possible. Open lines of communication between parent and child, and between parent and the school will always be helpful. If a child feels able to speak to his teachers and/or his parents about what he's experiencing that will help enormously. If in turn those adults are able to listen without judgement or criticism and to support that child, so much the better.

Your child needs to understand that it's OK to tell his teachers if someone is bullying him, and he needs to know that you will listen, understand and support him if he feels uncomfortable taking a shower after PE, or is struggling with his maths homework. He needs to feel confident that, although generally the school will be on his side if he feels a particular teacher is picking on him, or pushing him too hard, or behaving in an inappropriate way, *you* will always listen and will work with him to put a plan in place to deal with the situation.

If you have to go into school to tackle a problem, be sensitive to your tween's feelings. Let him know when and why you will be there and if you bump into him in the corridor or playground, be guided by him. If he wants to talk that's fine, if not keep your distance and, above all, steer clear of a motherly kiss and hug in front of his mates. He may feel deeply uncomfortable with you even setting foot inside his school, seeing it as his territory to be defended at all costs. Painful as it is to consider the possibility he feels embarrassed by you, remember that he's been busy building an image and identity for himself at school and may not want you coming along and contradicting that. Remember your boundaries, and don't share intimate secrets about your child with his teacher that may leave him feeling exposed or self-conscious, unless it's explicitly for the good of his welfare or wellbeing.

Elaine says: It's really important that as a parent you support the school rules, even if you don't agree with them, or something seems trivial, or you don't think it's a good way of administering positive discipline. So if your daughter's school says 'no dyed hair please', but you allow your daughter to go in one Monday morning with streaks in, that's sending a very mixed message. Occasionally, if you feel strongly, you might want to address a school rule you don't think is sensible – but if you do, keep calm. Don't go in with the certainty that you are right and they are wrong. If there *is* a big issue there and you really are at logger-heads, maybe your tween is attending the wrong school with the wrong values for you.

I'd add that if your child is struggling with workload and content, it's worth remembering that some specific special educational needs can often go unchecked throughout the primary years, but come to the fore in secondary school. Issues such as mild dyslexia, dyspraxia, dyscalculia or language process-ing problems can impact enormously on a tween's self-esteem and ability to access the curriculum. If you have any concerns, don't hesitate to talk to the school's Special Educational Needs Coordinator (SENCO) about them.

I don't want to go to school

Your tween will very likely try to wangle the odd 'duvet day' by feigning illness in an attempt to get the day off school. And for many parents of older children, it can be a struggle to simply turf them out of bed in the mornings. But beyond general apathy and extreme tiredness, or just the odd longing for a cosy day at home, a prolonged habit of 'school refusal' amounts to a pretty serious problem, not least because you have a legal responsibility to make sure your child attends school from ages five to sixteen, and, in theory, you could be prosecuted if he does not. When school refusal strikes during the tween years it may well be as a result of difficult transitions to secondary school. It's not necessarily the same thing as truancy (which is defined as 'wilful avoidance' of school, and is most likely to be done without parents' knowledge), and usually has a root cause that's based on anxiety or fear. But it's by no means always the case that school refusal problems are to do with school – sometimes a need to stay away can reflect a need for security, comfort or attention that for some reason has been lacking at home.

Do get your child checked by a doctor before passing off recurrent complaints of illness with no obvious symptoms as 'faking'. And bear in mind that, even if a doctor can't find anything wrong, or there are no overt symptoms such as a temperature, it's still possible that genuine problems like tummy pains, nausea, headaches or difficulty breathing can arise as a result of stress or worry.

We don't need no education: Tips for tackling school refusal

- Listening and communicating will be all-important if you're trying to get to the bottom of a school refusal problem, so encourage him – when he seems to be in the mood for chatting, or perhaps whilst you're both engaged in another activity – to talk through any concerns. Promise that whatever the problem, you can help him get to the bottom of it. Give plenty of space, too, though. Wait until he's ready to talk.

- Look out for a pattern – if your child is refusing to go to school on certain days, it may be a specific subject, or teacher, that's worrying him. Talking and reassuring him through the problem may be all that's needed: or you may need to address the issue with someone at school and go from there.

- Cooperation, support and sympathy from the school will be vital in getting your child through the phase and back to normal attendance, so be sure to talk to his teachers about what's happening. It's likely the school's Education Welfare Officer – whose main job is ensuring pupils' attendance – will become involved. She should be sympathetic, and offer help to find ways round the problem, or suggest special measures that will enable him to make a return: for instance, pairing him up with a mentor or offering counselling, inviting you to take him in to school and sticking around for a while (if he'll go for that), or allowing him to make a return in stages, perhaps attending just one lesson a day for a while, or spending time quietly studying alone in the library.

- If the problem seems to be rooted in academic difficulties, make your concerns clear and ask for an assessment from the school's Special Educational Needs Coordinator (SENCO) or an educational psychologist.

- Try not to panic if you've got a school refusal issue on your hands. In most cases, it's a phase that needs to be ridden out, so aim to stay calm and firm, but continue to give plenty of love and support. Shouting, criticising or being heavy-handed in an effort to get him to school is unlikely to be productive, however frustrated you feel about the situation. Give lots of praise for any positive moves forward.

- A school refusal problem which you and the school combined cannot seem to resolve may be a sign that your child has an underlying depressive or anxiety disorder which needs tackling. If this is the case, the school (or your GP) may suggest referral to your local Child and Adolescent Mental Health Service (CAMHS). In some areas of the country, you may be able to access a service called School Home Support, a charity that links up trained practitioners with families in need – details for the service's website are included in the back of the book, and your local education authority will be able to tell you if they work in your area.

- There's more information on this subject at the websites of Young Minds; the Advisory Centre for Education (ACE); and Family Lives (formerly Parentline Plus). Details for all of these are also in the back of the book.

What the netmums say

Kids who don't want to go to school

My daughter has had a lot of sick time since starting secondary school, with abdominal pains, but the doctor can't find anything physically wrong with her, and I do wonder if she's faking it. I now tell her when she complains of pain that she must take a painkiller and go in – if she had a fever or vomiting it would be different and I would keep her at home.

Lucy, mum to a girl, thirteen, and two boys aged nine and seven

I'm at my wits' end with my twelve-year-old son. He leaves for school in the morning and some days he actually gets there, but he simply refuses to go to his lessons – and the school says they cannot make him. We've tried talking but I can't see a reason for it. We had a meeting at school yesterday and it was agreed he would go in for just one lesson a day, but even that seems to be too much. I really don't know what to do next.

Carla, mum to a boy, twelve, and two girls aged ten and seven

My daughter went through a stage of not wanting to go to school and has never really enjoyed school, unlike my son who loves it. You need to get the school involved as soon as you realise there is a problem, and keep pestering them for help and advice – in my opinion, they don't offer unless you ask. Keep the lines of communication open. There's a lot schools can do, such as providing extra help from learning support staff, coun-selling and access to outside organisations for more specific problems. But you might only get it if you ask for it.

Hayley, mum to a girl, sixteen, and a boy, thirteen

There have been times when I know that illness has been faked by my kids. I find that making life very dull when they are at home helps – so no computer or television, on the grounds that they must stay in bed and rest if they are poorly. They usually

seem pretty keen to get back to school the following day!
Nina, mum to two boys aged fifteen and eleven

At ten, my son started school refusing after going through a tough time at school with bullying and self-esteem issues, as well as several changes at home, too. I was honest with the school and kept them informed, but I don't feel they were sympathetic. I also went to the GP for help and got us into a family therapy group, which was useful. I even rang the Education Welfare Officer before they called me, but they didn't have much to offer in the way of strategies and just threatened me with prosecution. In the end, I persevered, giving him lots of praise on the days when he did go to school. Thankfully, the problem sorted itself out with time and commitment, and he's back full-time now.
Julie, mum to a boy, thirteen, and a girl, nine

I have a thirteen-year-old girl who often refuses to go to school. She cries and gets very distressed when I try to make her go, and I find it really hard. At first I used to give her the benefit of the doubt and if she said she was ill I would let her miss school. But I'm more forceful in making her go now, and often end up driving her there myself. However, I can't do this on the days that I work. I contacted the school's welfare officer and she keeps a special eye on my daughter for me. They also have a counselling service which my daughter accesses. I know that the problem does not relate solely to school but is also influenced by my daughter's perception of her home life, and I work hard to keep talking and be approachable to her. I also reassure her that she is in a difficult stage of life and that I can remember feeling the same, and that these feelings will pass.
Jan, mum to a girl, thirteen

Removing your child from school

As a very last resort in the case of a major problem, you may look at taking your child out of school. If you want to change schools, you should speak to your local education authority and ask for a school transfer request form, but you'll need first to get the agreement of the authority and any new school you or your child has got hopes set on.

If it's feasible, you might consider some private tuition or home schooling (and if your child is spending a significant amount of time away from his school, you might *have* to, unless you want him to fall very behind with his learning). Home education isn't something to be lightly considered, but parents who've made the move often say it was a positive one. There are some links to further sources of information about home education in the back of the book. There's also information and support for bullied children who have been forced out of school at the website of the charity Red Balloon. Details are given in the back of the book.

3 Friends and peers

Friends really matter to your tween: they become an increasingly important source of comfort and companionship as your child naturally grows
less dependent on her family to provide these things. She needs to have
people around who are going through all the same ups and downs (unlike
Mum and Dad, who are old, and don't understand!), and who can accompany her through this tricky phase of life. And having a wide variety of
friends and peers is helpful in getting to grips with the huge mix of
characters, cultures, and lifestyles that she will encounter in later life.
Choosing and losing friends are developmental processes that will help
her work out who she is and what she's about, and provide valuable
lessons in essential skills such as sharing, listening, tolerating, empathising, compromising and assertiveness. And even if she selects friends of
whom you don't approve; or her friendships go pear-shaped; or peers
turn nasty; it may not be all bad news, since these experiences can also
be useful preparation for adult life.

Nevertheless, friends and peers *can* cause heartache, and it can seem
impossible not to jump in to make things better. Truth is, though, we
really need to let our kids make their own choices in friendships, and
encourage them to find their own way through conflict. Our aim should
be to offer support whenever it's needed – and to understand when we
need to butt out and leave them to get on with it!

Helping her to make (and keep) friends

Kids aged nine or above are usually quite able to make and keep their own friends, and as a general rule, won't need us to do so for them. But sometimes, a nudge in the right direction can be useful – especially if she's looking to make friends from scratch, having started at a new school, perhaps, or after moving to a different area.

One thing that's worth doing is to make sure her friends – or potential friends – are welcome in your home. So encourage her to invite her mates regularly round for tea; shared homework sessions; movie nights; the occasional sleepover (there's some tips for these in the box overleaf); or simply to hang around sometimes at the weekends. Keep a low profile on these occasions. Help her to get the date in the diary, offer food and drink (or suggest they help themselves), and then leave them to it. At some point your tween may want to play host to one or more of her friends when you're not at home and, when the time does come, you can reasonably ask that together they stick to any rules you have for being in the house alone. When it comes to her going to her friends' houses, you'll no doubt want to know who she's with, and where they live.

Whilst school is likely to be the main backdrop to friendships forming, it's a great idea if she can have friends outside school, too. In fact, these can often be the best friendships as they're not affected by pressures like academic rivalry or playground squabbling, and also because there's less chance for familiarity to breed contempt. So you might want to do all you can to encourage these friendships in particular – perhaps neighbours or children of your own friends are likely candidates, or maybe there were old pals left behind during the jump to secondary school that you can help her to maintain links with. Out-of-school groups, clubs or activities are another great way to boost social opportunities.

Your tween is very likely to have a 'best' friend at some point. Girls in particular tend to form special bonds. These very close relationships can be a great thing when the going's good, but are likely to cause all the more hurt when things go bad. Loyalty's a positive thing, and there's certainly no need to discourage special relationships like these. But always support other friendships too, so there'll be someone else to fall back on if necessary.

If you want your child to have good friends, then you'll need to teach her to be a good friend, herself. You don't want to intrude on the friendships she has, but it's important to pass on your thoughts about what makes a good friend: let her know that values such as respect, loyalty, kindness and empathy are essential. Help her understand that everyone is equal in life: she'll pick up messages by seeing the way you behave, so be conscious of how you treat other people, your own friends in particular, in front of her.

You may find it tough to accept once your child starts preferring her peers' company to yours. Try not to feel hurt when it happens: it's not so much a rejection of you as an exploration of other, important relationships. She still needs you very much – which you're likely to find out if and when those wonderful buddies turn out to be less wonderful than she thought. Meanwhile, don't push it, but try to keep *some* family time on the agenda: whether regular meals together, or the odd outing or activity. Even if she claims not to enjoy these occasions, she probably does!

Popcorn and pyjamas: Steps to successful sleepovers

- Keep the numbers small. Anything more than three guests is probably too much!
- Make sure all the invited guests get on well. An even number's sensible, so one individual doesn't end up 'left out'.
- Only ever have a sleepover during school holidays, or at the weekend. Friday's a better bet than Saturday, as it gives an extra day's recovery time.
- Provide comfortable sleeping arrangements: if they're sleeping on the floor, make sure they have plenty of cushions and covers.
- Gently but firmly lay down some ground rules in advance. You might say, for example, that lights must go out at 10 p.m. and, after that, no one's to get out of bed and only quiet chatting is allowed.
- Keep sugar consumption down. Try to make sure they eat any sweet treats a couple of hours before bedtime, and

that any snacks consumed later than that are sugar-free. In particular, steer clear of fizzy drinks that contain caffeine, as well as sugar.

- Be philosophical. Accept in advance that it's going to be a late night, there'll be a lot of noise, and everyone's going to be exhausted the next day. Be prepared for an early start, too: you might want to request that they tiptoe downstairs for some quiet television time in the morning, rather than waking you.

If she doesn't have friends

Don't jump to assume it's a major problem if she doesn't make friends easily, or appears to have few friends, or maybe even none at all. Some tweens are happiest sticking with a small number of reliable peers. Others prefer to cling on to home life and their parents' company for longer than others in lieu of friends, and for them, friendships will almost always come later.

However, if a lack of friends seems to be a long-term issue and is genuinely worrying, you may need to explore the potential reasons for it. It may be down to poor self-confidence and if that's the case, you'll need to boost the way she feels about herself. Or it may be that you have to face the fact that she's got a character trait that's making her unpopular (for example, maybe she's a bossy-boots) and, if so, you might have to sit down with her and talk about what makes a good friend, and why.

What the experts say

Crissy says: We all want our kids to be happy and, if we're honest, many of us would also like them to be popular. But it's the quality rather than the quantity of friendships that is really important. And friendship patterns vary from child to child. Some prefer to be part of the crowd whilst others are more comfortable with their own company; some need the intimacy that comes with having close friends, whilst others prefer more casual attachments.

If your tween complains that she has no friends, don't get upset as you imagine her cutting a lonely figure in the playground. Sit down and talk things through. It could be that she's exaggerating and what she really means is she wishes she could get close to the 'cool' girl or get picked first for netball. Children, just like adults, often see the grass as being greener elsewhere and may actually be turning their noses up at the friendships on offer in favour of membership of the in-crowd.

If you suspect the problem goes deeper and your child really does struggle to make or maintain friendships then you should find out precisely what the issue is and make it clear you are firmly in her corner. Letting your child know how much you enjoy and value her company and encouraging her to acknowledge and reflect upon her personal qualities and strengths can help to mend that wounded ego. Ask her what she looks for in a friend and support her to approach her own relationships in that way. Encourage your child to go to after-school clubs and activities and when appropriate be prepared to invite other children into your home. But keep it casual, and always tread carefully when it comes to inviting other children into your home: nothing puts kids of this age off quicker than the sour smell of desperation.

When your child does have friends round, keep your distance, and don't try to be one of the gang or you'll leave her cringing with embarrassment. Be respectful and give them some space and privacy, within reason. Never monopolise the conversation, ask a friend what their dad does for a living or barge into the room they're in without knocking.

For tweens, and especially female tweens, friendships may be fragile or short-lived. If she places all her emotional eggs into one basket, any subsequent breakdown of that friendship can feel devastating. So it may be wise to downplay the importance of forming really intense one-to-one attachments to a best friend, by emphasising the benefits of having a wider group of friends.

Elaine says: We definitely need to let our tweens find their own way in friendships and the fact is, you can't choose her friends – one of the worst things you can do is tell her not to be a friend with someone. In fact, when we tell our children we don't like their friends we can be seen as rejecting their choices and they may take it personally. Most of the time, she will choose appropriate friends because she'll automatically be drawn to people who like her for who she is. And sometimes, she won't. It helps to be positive and to notice and mention the good qualities about her friends. She'll be more likely to see for herself what's not so good then. It doesn't matter how many friends your child has and it may be important to stress that there is no popularity contest, measured by the number of contacts she has on MSN, but that the kind of friend you are is what counts.

It's important that we as parents let our children see us treating our own friends well. We need to model healthy, supportive friendships so they can learn from our behaviour. It's also very important that our kids get lots of approval from us, so that they don't depend entirely on peer approval. If they don't get appreciation at home they might seek it elsewhere and that's when they might get involved with groups or peers that we would prefer they avoided – kids who are attracted to gangs, for example, will often have low self-esteem. If their self-esteem is not good they may also do unhealthy or ineffective things to attract attention or be accepted, such as bragging, showing off, joining in with bullying someone else or taking part in other undesirable activities, such as smoking or playing truant.

Coping with peer pressure

Pressure to conform to whatever her friends do and say is very likely to be an issue in the life of your average tween. Around now, the desire to 'fit in' can be strong – probably because she's not quite sure of her own identity, yet – so the other kids she mixes with could well have a powerful influence on her. As the tween years progress, we increasingly need to allow our children to make their own choices, even if we don't like them much. Keeping up with a group isn't necessarily a bad thing, as it shows she has enough social awareness to be able to adapt to the norm. And let's face it, showing strong disapproval for something is a sure way to make it more attractive! So your best bet is to acknowledge that peer pressure is inevitable, and give in graciously as far as your values will allow: whether it's an outfit she wants to wear, a party she wants to go to, or a television programme she wants to watch. Do encourage any attempts she makes to find her own identity and strike out from the crowd – even if this too causes you some pain!

Of course, if you can't accept something because you really don't think it's suitable – or if you fear it could be damaging or dangerous – then you should stand firm in saying 'no'. Often, standing firm is exactly what she needs you to do: if she always gets your approval in following the crowd, she won't feel secure enough or brave enough to fight against the tide when what's being suggested is a *really* bad idea. In fact, it may even be that she *wants* you to provide her with an excuse. If she can tell her friends her mum will go mental if she succumbs to their influence, then perhaps that will let her off the hook.

Wherever possible, peer pressure is best tackled pre-emptively. And that means you should aim to boost her confidence and self-esteem at every opportunity, to arm her with the strength she needs to know her own mind, and to resist the lure of someone else's. You can do this by giving praise whenever the chance arises, and also by allowing her to make as many of her own choices as you can bear. Always listen to her feelings, ideas and opinions. Let her know how good she looks if she's put together a nice outfit, or how proud you are if she's stuck her neck out to support another friend, or a sibling.

It's also a good idea to keep on encouraging that wide range of friends, so that it's less likely one specific individual or group comes to wield disproportionate power over her. And don't overlook the positive flipside of peer pressure: if she has friends whose influence helps her to enjoy school, take an interest in a worthwhile hobby or to simply be a kind person, then those friendships are worth celebrating. So, wherever possible, allow her to host social gatherings, and try to include those 'good' friends sometimes during family events and outings. That way, you'll get to know them a little yourself and, as she spreads her wings and starts to explore the world without you, it will give you peace of mind knowing that she's got one or more reliable companions by her side as she does so.

Friends you don't like

Much as you may dislike the thought, it's probably a good idea if friends you aren't so keen on are also welcome in your house. There's no point trying to be heavy-handed in keeping less desirable pals at bay – it will probably just make her want to see them more. And in your own home, at least, you can keep a subtle eye on things (make it subtle though, or your child will know exactly what you're up to and is likely to object). It will also help reinforce the message that your tween has got your support, come what may, and that if she does get to a point where she wants to distance herself from the friendship, she'll feel free to do that without losing face.

She may at some point hook up with peers whose influence is a serious worry for you. If this happens, and you need to step in, then do so with as much sensitivity as you can muster, and try to think of ways you can make your actions less drastic. For instance, rather than a blanket ban on time spent with them, perhaps you could suggest a 'home-only' rule for meeting times? If the friendship seems to be affecting her behaviour or outlook at school, it's worth sharing your concerns with a sympathetic teacher, who may agree to monitor the situation, and even consider tactics for keeping them apart. And, again, it's a good idea to encourage her pursuit of other friendships, and to suggest outings and activities that don't involve the offending parties. Your own time and attention will be invaluable, too: don't let her preferences right now alienate you from her. She needs your approval and love more than ever (even if she doesn't show it).

Meanwhile, try to bear in mind that friendships, good and bad, tend to come and go during the tween years. She'll almost certainly shake any undesirable connections eventually, with or without your input.

What the experts say

Crissy says: Many tweens really feel a need to fit in and be one of the crowd. At this age it's often not about standing out but about blending in – at all costs! In short, they have to fit in before they can break out. So they will probably find comfort in the notion that they are not alone. Unique as their experience may feel, there will be a couple of hundred other tweens with precisely the same fears, hopes and dreams. It's important to make sure they understand that and to encourage them to confide in a trusted friend who they feel sure won't laugh or ridicule them for feeling afraid.

Chances are, your tween will strike up friendships that you feel are far from ideal. It's quite possible you may regard some of her attachments with complete horror and will be tempted to start plotting to separate your child from them, but resist the urge to interfere at all costs: try to hang back and allow the friendship to run its course. Your child is all about rebellion at this age and so in the long run, pulling friends apart may simply serve to push them more firmly together. It might last for life, but the more likely result is that it will last until your child moves on and forms new relationships with peers you do feel happy about. So bide your time, bite your lip and in the meantime, leave her be, but don't take yourself out of the picture entirely. She needs to know she can still lean on you from time to time.

If you genuinely believe a friendship is risky or even toxic for your child, you may have no choice but to step in. However, as a general rule of thumb, aim to respect your child's own friendship choices. These may not be the friends you would have chosen for her, but don't forget you're not the one who has to hang out with them every day. Friends can seem the be-all and end-all to tweens, and having or not having friends can impact upon their self-esteem, self-value and social status, which makes it even more crucial that they are left to choose and be chosen by their own friends.

Remember too that not all peer pressure is bad peer pressure. Sometimes the desire to fit in and the need for approval can motivate your child to challenge herself in positive new ways and help develop her sense of self. The difficulties arise when your child experiences pressure to do things either she and/or you are not comfortable with, or when activities move beyond mischief to mayhem. Kids will be kids and most are not angels, but when peer pressure turns bad, it's vital she knows where you stand. Get to know your child's friends better so any judgement you may make is an informed one. Offer your child boundaries. Of course she wants her friends to like her, but that friendship should not be conditional on her bending to the will of others. The more self-esteem you can foster in your child the more likely she is to be able to draw the line for herself, but when she needs a bit of extra help, be prepared to be the bad guy. An outright ban seldom works, though, and can often make things worse – so aim to steer, rather than drive, your tween away from trouble.

Elaine says: When you know she's mixing with someone who is a bad influence on her, and it's causing upset, there's a temptation to want to go in and tell her they're not good for her, and to leap in with solutions because we think we're wiser. But what you don't want to do is take away her opportunity to learn to manage on her own, which is what she will eventually need. If we try to control our kids it will give them the impression that they're not responsible enough to make their own decisions and find solutions for themselves.

Our job is to listen. There's a huge temptation to give advice but if you give it too quickly, it will give the message that she's not capable of sorting it out on her own. You don't want her to feel abandoned either, though. The main thing is taking time to listen to how she's feeling, and reflect it back to her in words. If she has friendship issues, or let's say there's some bullying going on, it can be very difficult for her to admit to it, and if the communication channels aren't there she could be going through it alone. It's natural to want to question her if you're trying to get to the bottom of a problem, but you have to do it in a very subtle way if you don't want her to just say 'I'm fine'. So you might phrase it like this: 'I can see from the way that you're talking and behaving that something's troubling you. I'm wondering if something is upsetting you in your friendship group just now, that's making you feel lonely?' You may not get an answer straight away but you've opened the doors for a conversation.

Work on establishing trust with your tween by giving her lots of messages of approval and non-judgemental listening – then she'll be more likely to listen if you have to say there's something you don't like about a friend's behaviour or manner. If you're passing on your values right, she'll probably be aware when friends fall foul of them.

What the netmums say

Forging friendships . . . and coping with peer pressure

My eldest is very shy and during her formative years she only had a couple of friends. I wasn't overly worried about it – sometimes it's better to have a few close friends than a lot of loose friendships. I encouraged her to go to Brownies and craft classes, and to go and call on other children. Some of this she managed fine, and enjoyed (like the Brownies, which was in a different area and therefore different girls from those at school), but sometimes she would be very low and wanted to stay home and not go out. However, at seventeen she's really starting to blossom, and now has a good network of friends of both sexes.
Ruth, mum to two girls aged seventeen and eleven

We enrolled our daughter into a drama club when she was nine, as she sometimes found it difficult to make friends, and she loved it. It really helped her confidence generally, and she soon started to find socialising easier. Now that she's older she has a few really good, close friends.

As for my son, at the moment, Luke really wants a newly released computer game that all his friends have, but it's a Certificate '18', so I refuse to get it for him. He constantly asks me for it and gets quite upset when I say no, as he thinks he's the only one that hasn't got it. I think you have to stick to your guns as a parent and do what you feel best no matter how much pressure they're under from their peers! I've explained to him why I won't let him have it, and that he's almost certainly *not* the only one not to have it. It's because I love him and worry about his wellbeing that I put down these boundaries.
Hayley, mum to a girl, sixteen, and a boy, thirteen

I try really hard to encourage my daughter to have lots of different friendships. She has a 'best' friend who I suspect is a bit manipulative and it worries me a little. So, although I would never mention this fact to her, and I don't discourage her from spending time with her outside school, I do urge her to knock around with other girls, too. I hope with time those friendships will take over.
Liz, mum to a girl, twelve, and a boy, eight

I think Alysha is starting to feel the pressure of peers now that she's at secondary school and starting to push her boundaries, mainly on curfews, which for most of her friends seem to be later than hers! I explain to her in our house I set the rules, and their parents set theirs. We've had a few set-tos over it: if necessary her phone or computer is confiscated, which seems to solve the problem.
Kerrie, mum to two girls aged twelve and one

Peer pressure can definitely be a good thing! Since starting secondary school, my twins have been in a close group with about eight other girls who are all academically focused, bright and articulate, and their influence has rubbed off. Although at home I moan about many things, like the state of their rooms, or their reluctance to do homework, their school reports have always been good and I'm sure their friends have played a part in that. I may not love all of their fashion choices, but the pressure to conform to a well-groomed group of girls is more effective than my nagging at them to shower and clean their teeth!

Natalie, mum to two girls aged fifteen

Our eldest fell in with the wrong crowd at thirteen. It wasn't so much that these kids were rough, but they all had parents who were busy with their own problems. Initially we made sure these friends were welcome in our house – as long as they followed our house rules, which they always respected. But then a friend told me she'd seen my son in an area known for alcohol abuse, which set alarm bells ringing. We tried to talk to him about it, but as we were both at work it was hard to keep a close eye on the situation. Things came to a head when one of his friends was found drunk in a garden by the police – they'd all emptied their savings to buy alcohol. We knew then we had to make a strong stand. So for three months we cut all contact with the children he'd been with, took time off work to be there for him, blocked his internet access, took away his mobile phone, asked his teachers to monitor him, and accompanied him to school and back daily. Then we gradually let him have his freedom back. It was tough, but it helped him realise how much we loved him.

Kathy, mum to two boys aged fifteen and eleven

Having moved to the UK from South Africa when my son was in his last year at junior school, everything was different for him and he didn't know anyone. The school really helped, but I also made an effort to go there every day and talk to other mums with children in his class (which was hard, because I'm not the best at talking to people I don't know). Once I explained that we'd just moved over and didn't know anyone, some of them invited us over after school, and we soon made friends with some really nice people.

Kirsty, mum to two boys aged thirteen and nine months

When friendships go bad

Tween friendships will inevitably involve rough as well as smooth, and lows as well as highs. Girls seem more at risk of fall-outs: although both boys and girls can be affected badly when friendships go wrong, parents of daughters tend to complain more of peer problems than those with sons. Whether this is to do with in-built gender characteristics, a result of socialisation, or something in between, is not certain. But what's evident is that girls are more likely to form 'packs'; to resort to cruelty and exclusion; and to care deeply about it when things do go wrong – they tend to 'internalise' problems with friends and feel it's their fault if there's a falling out, whilst boys are more likely to 'externalise', preferring to 'have it out' with a mate, maybe physically, so it's more quickly sorted and forgotten.

Very often, ups and downs in friendships during this period are mere blips: don't even think about getting involved in what seems to be a peer problem unless you've been expressly asked for help. Keep in mind that kids of all ages have great capacity to resolve their own conflicts.

Even when things seem more serious and distress has been caused, don't be tempted to jump straight in. Your main role at times like this is to offer lots of listening, and to gently help her work towards a resolution herself. It's almost never a good idea to get directly involved by approaching either the offending child or their parent, although, of course, if unpleasantness begins to develop into bullying then you will want to take firmer action. (There's more about bullying in the next few pages.)

You might have to help your child deal with rejection by her peers. Don't make light of it if this happens – it's probably a big deal to her. Offer to talk about it, listen reflectively, and perhaps share your own experiences of being hurt yourself, when you were younger. We've all been there. It may be that sometimes you have to step in, just temporarily, to help fill a hole left by a friend. Give whatever extra love, comfort and attention she seems prepared to accept right now. If getting through the school week is hard work for her because she's being left out, promise something good for the weekend: perhaps a movie or DVD together, a family outing, shopping or a special meal. And if finances won't allow for something like that, make a point of being around for her, anyway.

If you happen to know that your child has been guilty of unkind behaviour towards a friend, it's still a good idea to hang back a bit. Of course, if you feel the behaviour goes beyond the boundaries of your values, or it amounts to bullying, you'll no doubt want to talk to her about it. Try to invoke her sense of empathy by exploring how her friend feels about the situation, and how she would feel in their shoes.

Fall-outs among tweens may be over fairly quickly, and friendships patched back up again. On the other hand, it's not especially unusual for links to be permanently broken off. Don't be too concerned when this happens: it's a natural process that she is likely to go through more than once as she matures and begins to know her own mind. If she's upset about it, try to help her see it as a normal part of life's ever-changing pattern.

What the experts say

Crissy says: If there's a falling out, don't assume you need to be the trouble-shooter. Make sure your child knows you'll be there waiting in the wings with a cuddle and a non-judgemental listening ear, but bear in mind that in most cases, what seems the end of the world one day will have blown over by the next.

It takes careful handling when your child is feeling rejected. Don't push her to be the peacemaker when she's really the injured party. When she's hurting she needs to know that you really understand and that she still has value, even when a friend chooses not to see it.

When the shoe's on the other foot and your child is the instigator, take the time to sit down and talk with her. Respect her point of view and always make it clear your issue is with her behaviour, and not your child herself. If the problem originated at school, bring it up with her teachers. Never, ever confront the other child's parents, though. There are few things more humiliating for your youngster than the spectacle of her parents squabbling in public!

Elaine says: Conflict is natural and really useful for kids, because they need to learn about finding resolutions. We don't want our children to reach adult life never having solved a dispute. How will they cope in the workplace? The most important thing is not to be judgemental, of either side. You don't need to weigh in with your own opinion of the other child, but rather, empathise with how your child feels about what the other has said or done. Likewise, when your child is the one at fault we can convey lack of judgement by empathising first with how she must have felt to do whatever she did. Accept the feeling before moving on to say you expect she now regrets what she did, and help her to find ways of making amends if she's ready for that. Don't ask her how she thinks the other child would feel until her own feelings have been fully explored. For example, if she's sent an unkindly worded text to a friend you might say something like: 'For you to say something like that to Sara, you must have been pretty mad. I guess something happened that made you really furious with her . . . Oh, so you felt betrayed when she told Emily your secret? That's a shame; you and Emily have been friends a long time so you must be feeling rotten. Now that things are calmer, do you wish you hadn't put your thoughts in writing or phrased it a bit differently? I've sent emails late at night when I've been upset about something and regretted it later. Once it's in black and white you can't take it back, of course. My guess is you don't feel good about hurting her. What could you do now to make things better?'

Beating bullying

Sadly, bullying is not a particularly unusual experience, with more than half of kids estimated to be affected by it at some point, and many tweens pinpointing it as their main fear in moving up from primary to secondary school. Whilst it's not necessarily more widespread among older kids, they are undoubtedly more sophisticated in psychological bullying tactics; they are bigger and stronger and so more able to cause physical harm; and they are more likely to have the technical know-how and resources to dabble in one or other form of cyber-bullying.

In any case, bullying can be a damaging experience for victims of any age. Victims stand to lose self-esteem and confidence, may become depressed or withdrawn, and their general health and eating and sleeping habits could be affected for the worse. Schoolwork is very likely to suffer as a result, too. Once in a while, serious bullying leads to truly horrendous consequences, such as suicide or attempted suicide.

Bullying can take a number of forms. Direct forms of bullying may be physical, with punching, kicking, pinching, tripping or other form of attack; or verbal, with comments or insults, taunts and teasing made to the victim. It can also take a non-direct, psychological or emotional form, with a child being excluded from a group, gossiped or lied about, or simply ignored. And, increasingly these days, it may be linked to a modern form of technology such as the internet or mobile phones. This is cyber-bullying: there's more about it later, in the 'High-tech harassment' information box.

Although bullying incidents can be one-offs, it generally amounts to a sustained campaign against a victim, so incidents will usually occur repeatedly over a period of time. Victims often have something a little different about them: it needn't be much. Bullying can also, sadly, spring from racial or other types of prejudice.

Your tween won't necessarily let you know about it if she's being bullied – it's common for victims to be scared or ashamed and to want to keep it secret – so it's important to keep an eye out for clues. These could include her coming home with cuts, bruises or other injuries; torn clothing; spoiled schoolwork; or her dinner money, mobile, or other possessions missing. Alternatively she could simply be exhibiting an unexplained change of character – perhaps she is being moody, withdrawn, tearful, or picking fights with a sibling; she may have trouble concentrating on homework, or you might notice standards of her work at school slipping; she might not be eating well, or be comfort eating; she may have problems going to sleep, nightmares, or be waking in the night. Other signs to watch out for include a reluctance to go to school; not wanting to take her usual route to school, or seeming afraid of boarding the school bus; a sudden refusal to use the computer; or an apparent lack of confidence – and reluctance to talk about any of the above.

Whether or not she complains directly about bullying, or you have find out it's happening for yourself, do take it seriously, right from the start.

Don't wave it off with suggestions that she 'ignores it': take time to listen to what she has to say and, if it seems obvious the problem is more than a one-off incident, and an ongoing issue, pledge your support, and promise that you will help her find a solution. Don't promise to keep it a secret, though, or agree not to mention it any more. It will need tackling and in order to do that, you're going to need to talk openly about it.

Taking it up at school

If bullying is taking place at school, or involves peers who attend her school, don't hesitate to take the matter up with her teachers. However, don't consider it purely the school's problem: your own input is vital – there are some more ideas about what you can do to help overleaf.

All schools *must* have an anti-bullying policy and should be prepared to take action to resolve the problem. However, policies do vary: while some schools take a 'zero-tolerance' line, others prefer a 'no-blame' approach which usually involves getting bully and victim together to talk and find a resolution together, perhaps with other peers invited along too. For some parents of victims, this can feel a bit like a bully is being 'let off lightly'. However, if this is the case, try to be philosophical about it: it doesn't really matter how an end to the situation is brought about, as long as it is.

If you don't get much in the way of support from the school or the situation continues, keep calm, but stand firm. Keep a 'bully log' which details what happens, and when it occurs. (The anti-bullying charity Kidscape has a template for one of these, as well as tons more helpful, practical advice, on its website – you can find its contact details at the back of the book.) Be prepared to return to school and to ask to see a different member of staff if necessary – for instance, if a form or subject tutor has not been much help, you might approach a head of year, or anyone with a specific responsibility for pastoral care or student welfare. However emotional you feel, though, try to keep calm and avoid being defensive, as it won't help your case much.

If you are going into school, do discuss your plans with your child. If she's scared or embarrassed, she may dread the idea – however much she wants an end to the situation. If this is the case, you may decide to respect her wishes and concentrate on ways she can avoid or stand up to the bullying from home. However, if you're genuinely concerned about her safety or wellbeing and are determined to go in regardless of her reservations, you'll need to sit down with her and discuss your reasoning. Perhaps explaining that the bully or bullies are likely to make many more lives miserable, if a resolution can't be found, will help.

As angry as you are likely to feel if your child is being victimised systematically by an individual, it's worth bearing in mind that usually bullies are bullies because they are unhappy about something. It may be that they have a difficult home life, serious emotional or educational problems, low self-esteem or have been bullied themselves. As a general rule, it's not a good idea to approach a bully's parents yourself, however desperate you are – unless you happen to be on good terms with them, and you feel confident that things won't flare up into an almighty row.

If you can't achieve a resolution with the school's help and the bullying continues, or if the bullying involves very serious matters such as theft or assault, or it has a racial or sexual element, then take it further by writing to the school governors or local education authority, or, if necessary, the police.

Other ways you can help

It's not true to say that bullying victims are weak, but sometimes a sustained bullying campaign can leave a child with a victim mentality that locks them into a vicious cycle – her self-esteem and confidence is shattered, making it harder for her to stand up against bullying in the future. So, whilst it's not a good idea to advise retaliation against bullies – especially not physically, as this will only land her in trouble, too – you can and should help her to stand up for herself in the face of bullying.

Your aim is to help her be an assertive person. If you're a loving parent and you're generous with your praise, you're probably doing this anyway. But do keep pushing the message that assertiveness is a *good* thing: reassure her that it's fine to say no, and to keep saying no if that's what she wants to say. It's a really important life lesson for her.

Positive body language is a useful weapon in the battle against bullying, so teach her how it's done. It means standing up straight, and making eye contact when she's responding to a bully. She should aim to speak out firmly: perhaps, between you, you can come up with some short, snappy replies that she can throw back if necessary? However, let her know that if nothing particularly funny or clever springs to mind, a loud 'no' is a useful response. Although tempting, it's probably best not to encourage her to use strong swear words at this point, as that too could land her in trouble. You might also suggest she practises her positive body language and firm responses in front of a mirror.

Let her know that – wherever possible – she should strive not to show she's upset or angry in front of a bully. She might want to try a technique psychologists recommend, called 'fogging'. This is a tactic that allows you to 'swallow up' insults and switch off to them, by using short, bland, affirmative responses (such as 'that's true' or 'it's possible') to anything that's thrown her way. It disarms bullies as it gives them nothing to work with, unlike the normal defensive response ('I'm *not* fat!'), which simply lends itself to further taunts ('Yes you are! You're a pig!'). Linked to that is the role of humour in countering hostility: remind her that the best response might simply be for her to laugh off a rude comment or make a joke (at her own expense, if necessary) to defuse the situation, even if she's feeling very hurt inside, as it can be an extremely effective method to take the wind out of an aggressor's sails. Let her know, too, that it's always fine to walk away from a bully. If the abuse is physical, impress upon her that hitting back is not the answer: it's essential she gets herself away from danger and seeks immediate help from the nearest responsible adult.

As well as bolstering her mental responses, you could sit down with her and help her to thrash out any simple, practical ways that will help her to avoid the bully or bullies. So make sure she knows to avoid any areas where the bullies are likely to congregate and to be sure that there will be other students and teachers around if she has to go there. If the bullying is taking place on the way to or from school, can she make the journey with someone else, or can you or another adult accompany her for a short period?

Other, more reliable friends will be really important to her if she's being bullied. There's strength in numbers, so encourage her to enlist whatever support she can, even if it just means having company around. Help her boost the strength of existing friendships by suggesting social dates outside of school. If the bullying is a 'pack' activity, with one ringleader, she could perhaps approach some of the less threatening members of the gang and appeal to them.

As when friendships go wrong, it's vital to give lots of extra love, support and praise if your kid is being bullied. In particular, make sure that if she's behaved bravely or been assertive in the face of bullying, you give her plenty of credit for it.

You may also want to help your tween explore ways by which she can get advice and support for herself from some of the many great organisations and websites that exist to beat bullying – particularly if she's reluctant to accept help from you directly. Some web addresses and helplines are included in the back of this book.

What about the bully?

It's true to say that bullies are usually unhappy about something. However, it's quite possible for loving parents to discover their own child is a bully, or has been guilty of bullying behaviour. If your tween is in this position, it may be that she is going through a temporary phase of unhappiness or insecurity, or perhaps she's fallen victim to peer pressure and is bullying to fit in with behaviour that's expected of her. It may simply be an experimental phase.

Stay calm, and don't rush to come down hard if you discover your child has been bullying. Make certain she knows she has your support, come what may. Talk things through – get her side of the story, too, and gently try to find out what could be the cause of her behaviour: is she worried about something else that's going on in her life? Is she under pressure to fit in? Whilst you should offer support and help, don't let her imagine you are condoning her behaviour – make it clear it's not acceptable, especially if any kind of prejudice was at play, and do all you can to encourage her to make amends to the victim. Try to inspire her empathy by asking how she would feel if it were the other way round. If other peers are involved, then help her to find the confidence to remove herself from them if need be: sitting down and talking about what makes a good friend could be a useful exercise right now. Be sure to offer support and praise for any positive steps. Liaise with her school if that's required, and back them on any resolution or discipline that's been suggested.

Cyber-bullying

There's been a huge growth in the development of information and communication technologies in recent years, which means that chat rooms, social networking sites, instant messaging services, forums, emails and mobile phones are an increasingly important element in the social lives of today's tweens. One of the unfortunate consequences is a growing problem with cyber-bullying – any deliberately hostile or harmful behaviour carried out through these outlets – and it's thought as many as one in five children has been on the receiving end of it.

Cyber-bullying presents a potential nightmare for parents because it can so easily be anonymous, and can take place anywhere and at any time, including at home, which is the one place that ought to be safe. It's also harder to keep track of, because no physical scars are left and because parents don't always have a full understanding of the technology involved. Also, victims are more likely to keep quiet about it because they may fear losing the use of their computer or phone if it's found out.

There are tips for keeping on top of cyber-bullying in the box below – and more exploration of these and other issues surrounding new technologies in Chapter 5.

High-tech harassment: How to do battle with cyber-bullies

- Try to make sure the computer your child uses is in a family room so that you can always be around (even if you're not actually looking over her shoulder) when she's using it.
- Make it your business to know all about any websites or forums your child is using. Be aware of any age restrictions on these sites: they're there for a reason, so either be firm about asking your child to stick to them, or be prepared to always supervise when she's using them.
- Encourage her to let you know about any incident that has made her unhappy or uncomfortable, however small. Reassure her that you will always do your utmost to help out

and resolve the problem – and that it won't have to mean she loses out on her computer privileges.

- If she has a phone, make sure she only gives her number to family members and very close friends who she trusts. Where social networking sites are concerned, ask her to stick with contemporaries she knows well when it comes to chatting or making 'friends'.
- Warn her not to confide very personal information or post pictures or video clips which could come back to haunt her later. Talk through privacy issues and explain your views on what's suitable and what isn't: remember that her interpretation of this may be different from yours.
- Suggest she does not rise to the bait by replying to any negative or abusive texts, messages or posts – however tempting.
- Press home the importance of never forwarding abusive texts, emails or images of anyone else: this is not just colluding with cyber-bullying, it could be against the law and land her in serious trouble with the police. Insist she always has permission before posting a picture of someone: that way she can expect good friends to always return the favour.
- Help her to report any abuse by contacting the relevant mobile phone company, site moderator, or internet service provider. Most take complaints of bullying or abuse seriously and will help to remove offensive posts, or advise on tactics such as ways to block messages. If necessary, help her to change her username, email address or phone number.
- Advise her to save any bullying messages or images she receives, along with a note of the time and date sent and any details you have about the sender, in case you need to show them to teachers or the police.
- Bear in mind that serious bullying such as threats of a physical or sexual nature should be reported to the police, or to CEOP, the Child Exploitation and Online Protection Centre.
- Check out the wealth of information and support online

that's available to help parents guard against and deal with cyber-bullying – as well as other internet and technology-related concerns. Some are listed in the back of the book.

What the experts say

Crissy says: Sadly, the harmful effects of bullying can last into adulthood, so it's always important to be alert to any changes in your child's behaviour or manner, and to keep the lines of communication open. You need to be attuned to her moods in order to spot any sign that she's troubled or unhappy. This is particularly so once she moves up to secondary school, where the whole bullying phenomenon steps up a gear, since it's a far bigger environment which is less tightly controlled and monitored, and therefore there's more opportunity for bullying to occur out of sight of the teachers. Also, children don't have the secure attachments to staff and other pupils they enjoyed at their primary school and may feel unable to turn to anyone for help. This is where you come in. Your child needs to know that she can come to you without fear of being judged or criticised, and that you won't just storm in, all guns blazing, but will listen to and consider her opinion and what she wants to do about it. That said, schools will have particular policies you will need to adhere to, and your child should feel confident that the ultimate deci-sion on whether or not action needs to be taken lies with you.

You may need to be open to the painful possibility that your child is actually the bully herself. Emotions run high in situations like this so try to hang on to the knowledge that both sides need understanding and support rather than punishment and condem-nation. I've yet to meet a child who bullies because they are in a good place in life. Make it plain that your love is unconditional, and that nothing she does will change that. She needs to know she can come to you and tell you anything and that you will work through it together.

Building up her self-esteem is one of the best things you can do to protect your child against bullying. Make sure she knows she's fun to be around, and good company; that you enjoy hearing what she has to say, or just hanging out with her. The subject of bullying should be on the family agenda from the start. We all need to instil in our children the message that bullying is wrong, but that it can be overcome. We also need to reassure them that if they do tell, they will be heard and understood, and something will be done.

Elaine says: You'll need to work very hard at being empathetic if your child is being bullied. A lot of the time we just say 'ignore it', but that's very dismissive. And sometimes there's this old-fashioned attitude, that bullying takes place simply because 'kids will be kids'. But bullying always needs to be taken seriously – especially these days, with cyber-bullying so prevalent. You should always acknowledge how upsetting it is and, if she's come to tell you about it, praise her for her courage and honesty.

There's no point in fighting her battles for her. She has to be able to do it for herself: it's called dispute resolution. You need to empower her, and to arm her with solutions and strategies so she can stand up to bullies. One way to do this is to role-play situations and talk about how she might cope with them and what sort of things she might be able to say back – even if it's just 'whatever'. However, she also needs to know you're there if it turns out she does need you – so, whilst you want her to cope independently if possible, always make it clear that you're still available if required. The language you use will be important, so never refer to your child as a 'victim'.

I think it's also important to teach our youngsters that it's not acceptable to be a bystander when there's bullying going on. People who remain silent just perpetuate the problem. Whether or not the issue of bullying has appeared on her horizons, you might want to talk this issue through with her. Would she be brave enough to stand up for someone who was on the receiving end of bullying behaviour?

It can be completely devastating for parents who think

they've been bringing up their children well to discover that their child has been unkind or hurtful to another. It doesn't necessarily mean they've been parenting badly, but may have missed that their child is in some way unhappy, or underestimated her difficulties. And not all unkind or aggressive behaviour amounts to bullying – sometimes it's an impulsive response, not a premeditated act of asserting power. It will make matters worse if parents simply get angry and punish the child, as the reasons for the behaviour won't have been addressed. When trying to establish how this situation has come about, the child often won't be able or will feel too guilty to respond to direct questions, so the parent will need to take some educated guesses about possible reasons for the behaviour, and make gentle suggestions about how it can be remedied. Loving parents will want to help their child see that the behaviour isn't acceptable, without making her feel like a bad person. It often helps to ask, 'Why isn't this OK?' rather than lecturing. And, after you've explored fully the reasons why the behaviour arose, ask the child, 'How do you want to make amends?' The suggestion is implicit that wrongs need to be righted, but it will feel more like the child's idea than if the parent simply says, 'Now you'll need to make things better.'

What the netmums say

Friendship problems and bullying

My daughter makes friends very quickly, but being girls, they get very bitchy and fall out all the time, usually when one chooses a friend over another. One time, Charlie had fallen out with a girl who then went round telling the other girls they shouldn't go to Charlie's party. I was so unhappy about this, I went into school and they called a meeting. They spoke to all the girls, everyone apologised, and it was sorted out. It's definitely worth getting teachers involved if the problem takes place within school.

Nicola, mum to a boy, twelve, and two girls aged ten and two

We've had problems with online bullying. Luckily Alysha knows that she can come to me with any problem, and when she explained what was happening I went online pretending to be her – sure enough, she was sent some unpleasant messages. Then I told Alysha to let them know she was taking them off her friends list until they grew up a bit, which she did. She and I both got an apology from them the following day.
Kerrie, mum to two girls aged twelve and one

With this age group, it's inevitable that friendship problems occur. My daughter seemed to fall out with her friends almost daily at ten and eleven. She eventually settled into a nice group and one girl in particular became her closest friend and even came on holiday with us when they were both about thirteen. Shortly afterwards, though, the friend stopped coming round. I did ask why, but my daughter refused to discuss it. Some months later, the friend suddenly appeared again, but then a few weeks on I got a surprise visit from this girl and her mother, who I was quite friendly with. It turned out that they'd had another bust-up but this time the whole group had got involved and according to the mum they were now picking on her daughter. I could see how upset they both were so was furious with my daughter for being so horrible. Once I'd calmed down, I asked for my daughter's side of the story. It was completely different. So I singled out some of the other girls that had also been accused and so much came out, with evidence to back it up. It turned out that my daughter was more the victim than her friend, who had gathered a little posse to seek revenge on her for falling out over a boy, months before. I thought long and hard about how I was going to deal with it and decided not to approach the school because I wasn't sure that would solve anything. Instead I advised my daughter and her friends to stay away from this posse, and to let them know I would contact their parents if it continued. There was no more trouble, arguments or revenge plans, and it all blew over. That was the end of that friendship, though.
Ali, mum to a girl, eighteen, and a boy, eleven

Peer pressure made my daughter want to start social networking. We allowed her to go on MSN, but it caused endless problems with her friends, and it's now been taken off her computer. In my day, arguments with school friends ended at school. But with computers, problems can go into the evening and weekend, and really escalate!

Karen, mum to a girl, twelve, and a boy, seven

My daughter was bullied by a child from two years above her at school. Her behaviour changed but she wouldn't tell us what was happening. It all came to a head when the child turned up at our house, calling her names. I was able to get her to talk to me about what was happening then, and so the next day we went into school to speak to the head. He was very sympathetic about it and the child in question was suspended for a week. Unfortunately, the things she had said to my daughter – that she was ugly and stupid – continued to have an effect on her. She still asks, when she falls out with friends, if it's because she's stupid or ugly. We reassure her as best we can and just hope that as she gets older she realises she's neither of those things.

Emma, mum to a girl, nine, and a boy, four

My eldest son is generally very laid back but, aged thirteen, he came home from school in a rage one day. One of his close friends had been relentlessly winding him up on the school bus. By the time he got home, he was furious – I could feel him trembling when I tried to give him a hug. He refused to sit down and talk about it, but went into the garden with his baseball bat and took all his anger out on his swing ball, destroying it in the process. When he came in he said he felt much better – but it didn't make me feel better because I'd just seen him resolve his issues through violence! I realise it was better to take it out on a ball rather than another person, but I told him it worried me that he'd let the situation get to him so much. We talked about how he should deal with this 'friend', since he has no option but to get the same bus. He realised that when he reacted to what his friend was saying about him it made the situation worse, and the boy did it all the more, so he probably would have been better off sticking his iPod on and ignoring him. With hindsight, trying to talk to him straight away when he was so angry was a non-starter; he actually just needed me to listen.

Jo, mum to two boys aged fourteen and twelve, and a girl, ten

My eldest was bullied for many years, at primary school, and during the first two years at secondary school. Some schools don't like to admit they've got a bullying problem, and try to blame the victim. I was told my daughter was over-sensitive because she came home crying each day – hardly surprising given the treatment she was getting. It affected her badly. She was very quiet, insular, and had a complete lack of self-belief and self-worth. Her schoolwork suffered, as she didn't believe she was capable of doing it. In fact, for a while she didn't want to go to school at all, and it became so extreme our GP diagnosed mild depression.

Ruth, mum to two girls aged seventeen and eleven

When my son became a victim, I made a point of reading the school policy on bullying, then wrote letters to the teacher and made sure the head got copies as well. This seemed to force them into action because now they had it on record, and there were witnesses as well. As a result, the bully was moved into another class that day and their parents asked to come into school as an emergency to be given a formal warning. My advice is to get the facts and put it in writing. Don't be too emotional about it, although I know that's hard. It's better to appear rational.

Leila, mum to a boy, twelve, and a girl, nine

4 Puberty, sex and relationships

The process during which a child's body develops to sexual maturity – puberty – looms large for anyone entering the tween years. For a few girls, it will already have begun. There are huge physical and emotional changes in the pipeline, and it can be a pretty bewildering time. It's no picnic from a parent's point of view, either. In most cases, puberty kicks in when our kids are still kids, and it's tough coming to terms with those sprouting hairs and budding breasts – not to mention the knowledge that, some day soon, they'll be capable of conceiving, and thinking about sex. But get our heads round it we must. They're going to need our guidance, sympathy and practical help in order to get through this very important stage of life, and in laying the foundations for a healthy attitude to sexual relationships, when that time comes. It might help to look at puberty as an exciting and positive process, and to help your tween to see it as that. Perhaps, too, you can stretch your mind back to your own puberty, and recall the rollercoaster of physical and emotional change you found yourself riding at the time: reminiscing about it with your tween should help you both to feel better about what he's going through. And if all else fails, keep reminding yourself that it's a transition, and won't last forever (even if it seems like it at the time!).

Talking about puberty

There's no 'right' time for talking about puberty, as it's so variable when it starts. What's important is that your child knows what lies ahead for him and his peers, well in advance, so he's not confused, worried or downright frightened when it becomes a reality.

Your tween will learn the basics about puberty at school as part of the statutory science curriculum, usually in Years Four, Five or Six. But it's really important that he hears about it from you, too, because there'll no doubt be plenty of gaps he wants you to fill in – and because only a parent can provide that sort of information with sufficient support and reassurance. Try to bring the subject up in a natural way as part of the conversation, rather than announcing it's 'time for a chat', which is likely to cause embarrassment all round. And make the most of it if he comes to you with a question – perhaps inspired by a bodily change, a peer's experience, something he's seen on television, or heard in the playground – and use it to open up a wider discussion.

Ensure your other half pulls his weight on this. Dads may be even more reluctant than mums when it comes to nitty-gritty subjects, but it's better if the whole family can talk freely on the matter – siblings too. And don't forget that it's not just his own gender he needs information about: talk about what the opposite sex goes through, too. Hopefully it will help him to empathise with all his peers – and make the whole process less of a mystery.

Lots of parents find an illustrated book is helpful, although it's much better if you can look at it together and use it as a prompt for talking rather than leaving him to read through it himself. Of course, it may be that a conversation about puberty is something he simply can't face, and if that's the case, providing him with an appropriate textbook, or jotting down some helpful web addresses, is your best bet. Just let him know gently that you're around to answer questions, if he needs you to. There are some great internet sites aimed specifically at kids, for example the interactive Puberty Body Tour on the FPA site (formerly known as the Family Planning Assocation). Details for this and others are listed in the appendix at the back of the book.

If you have a tween daughter, do make sure she knows about periods well before she seems likely to start them. The subject of menstruation is also included in the curriculum, but for many girls, these lessons come too late. Packets of towels and tampons are almost always a good conversation starter. There's more on periods later in this chapter.

Of course, talking about puberty is very likely to lead naturally to the subject of sex and sexuality, since puberty is really all about the body gearing up to enjoy sex and to make babies. Your tween may seem to you to be light years away from having a sex life, but it's never too early to start communicating about this all-important subject.

What the experts say

Crissy says: It's entirely natural for parents to have mixed emotions as their child enters puberty. It can feel inappropriate, and even distasteful, to witness the 'child' who's still making Lego models or playing dress-up, becoming physically mature. The idea that your tween may actually now be capable of playing 'mummies and daddies' for real may be terrifying, but it's vital you don't pass your own fears on to him. After all, it's his body that's changing and he may well be feeling pretty bewildered and even scared about the whole process. Your tween needs to know these changes are absolutely normal, and that although we all go through them, everyone develops in different ways at different times: there's no master plan for puberty. By talking to your child about how you felt at their age, maybe recounting stories of your own tween years, you can encourage him to open up, ask questions and share how he's really feeling. Listen to the voice of your own experience and consider why you may be feeling a sense of dread as your child enters puberty. Were your own tween years racked with insecurity and self-doubt, or were you comfortable in your own skin? Is it difficult to reconcile memories of your own developing sexuality with the innocent child you put to bed each night? Perhaps, as your child grows older, you're simply feeling old yourself? This is a period of change and growth for both you and your child. More than ever, he'll be looking to you for guidance and support.

When it comes to teaching our tweens about puberty and sex, there's no perfect formula. Mums often enjoy a greater ongoing intimacy with their daughters and so may have more opportunities to notice and observe the physical and hormonal changes they're going through. However, not all mums feel they can talk comfortably and naturally about periods, breasts and hormones. Maybe you'd prefer to ask a trusted female relative or friend to help out. When it comes to boys, Dad's biological knowledge may surpass Mum's, but some dads find it more difficult to deal with the emotional side of puberty and sex, in which case it may be more helpful for Mum to tackle feelings while Dad sticks to the practical details. For single parents of both sexes, these can be difficult times without a partner's support, but again, if you're worried about getting it right, it's OK to rope in the help of another adult who your tween trusts and feels relaxed around. The most important thing is that whoever takes the lead makes sure they know their stuff. Do a bit of homework in advance and get your facts straight. This is where books come in handy. Read them through together and, no matter how embarrassed you're feeling, don't be tempted to rush or to gloss over the details. It may be helpful to begin by talking about feelings before moving on to the physical changes and then sex. Keep the whole thing laid back and casual and be careful not to overwhelm or scare him. If your child feels ambushed or pressured, he will run a mile. As embarrassing as this subject can be for parents, it's often doubly so for our kids. So let your child know you're relaxed and open to talk at any time. Don't make a big deal of it. If in doubt, do your homework and rehearse in advance. Try to plan for a series of age-appropriate talks rather than blurting out a barrage of information in a single conversation, then giving a sigh of relief that it's all over. The idea is to keep the lines of communication open so that he can come back to you again and again as life changes and his experience grows.

Elaine says: Puberty can creep up on parents ever so quickly – one minute they're children of primary-school age, and the next they're growing before your eyes into men and women! This is particularly true today, with puberty taking place earlier and earlier.

It's certainly important to talk openly about bodies from an early age, and to revisit the subject regularly. Body image is a key concern for tweens, particularly as they go through puberty, and particularly for girls. By ensuring our tweens are comfortable with their bodies, and creating a non-judgemental atmosphere of trust, they'll be better able to accept the changes that are occurring, and discuss them with you. Humour – as long as your tween leads the way on such an approach – can also be helpful during these discussions. When my own son, who has a wicked sense of humour, asked me if he was through puberty yet, we went through a light-hearted 'checklist' of bodily changes together. Had his testicles descended? Did he have pubic hairs? His conclusion was that yes, he had reached puberty, and therefore it was time to have a 'pube party'! Of course, he was only joking, but personally, I think a tween's 'coming of age' is something to be celebrated, quietly and privately. My daughter's not there yet, but we have a special pair of earrings put away, to give her when she has her first period. For my son, it may mean presenting him with a special watch. It makes the puberty experience a special one, and far from embarrassing.

When will it start?

Puberty kicks off when the body starts to produce sex hormones, although scientists aren't clear what exactly triggers the process. Over the years, the average age of puberty starting has decreased, particularly for girls. This is probably because of factors like better nutrition, and the increase in obesity, since body fat is linked to the hormonal release (although there are other theories, including one that environmental factors like harmful chemicals could be at play). In any case, you'll need to reassure your tween that there's a very wide range of normal ages for puberty to start. For girls, it usually begins between the ages of eight and fourteen

– with eleven being average – and for boys, between the ages of ten and fifteen – with twelve being average. The full process is a gradual progression, which takes anything from two to six years to complete. It tends to take place in phases, but the sequence can be very variable.

For both sexes, one of the first and most obvious signs of puberty is rapid physical growth. This may come in sudden spurts, or be a more gradual process, but it's not unusual to see a height increase of between 6 and 12 cm within the space of a year. Other parts of the body grow, too, but not necessarily at the same time – for instance, the hands and feet tend to get bigger early on, which is why at this age it's common to feel clumsy and gangly.

When a tween's body begins to change and mature, it's a good idea to talk about what a huge variation there is in the human form and give him loads of reassurance that – whatever he may think – he's normal. There's more about body image issues in Chapter 7.

Growing girls: The facts about female puberty

- Her breasts will develop. Initially she'll probably notice little lumps or 'buds', which she may complain are tender: you can reassure her it's simply the imminent arrival of her boobs and that they'll gradually develop into a more adult breast shape as puberty progresses. Of course, there's no telling what their eventual size and shape will be, and there's a huge variation. It's also normal for breasts to be different sizes.

- She'll probably notice an increase in vaginal discharge. It should be clear, off-white or white in colour and can vary in consistency. If she's worried, let her know these secretions are part of a healthy female reproductive system, and are there to help keep the vagina clean.

- Hair will start to grow in the pubic region, sparse and silky at first, growing coarser and more abundant with time. She'll also grow hair under her armpits, and it could also appear in areas like the abdomen and bikini line. Older female tweens may be self-conscious about certain areas of excess body hair, and press to be allowed to remove it. There's no medical reason why she should, but if it's a confidence issue for her, do consider providing a safe and simple way for her to do so, whether a razor and gel, wax or depilatory cream.

- Inside the body, her reproductive organs are developing and her hips will grow as the pelvic bone widens and fat is laid down in preparation for having a baby.
- Her periods will usually (although by no means always) come last of all. There's more about this below.

Her first bra

When will a female tween need her first bra? As soon as she's got something to put in it – or possibly even before that, if bras are the norm in her peer group and she wants to fit in. These days, bras are available for every breast size from 'non-existent' up – in fact, many parents feel this sort of underwear is pretty inappropriate for little girls of eight and under who are a long way from having real boobs. But if your tween really wants one, there's probably no harm in indulging her with a simple, comfortable design, even if she is still as flat as a pancake.

Once her breasts really have begun to grow significantly, a proper bra will offer support and comfort, so take her to a reputable store to be measured and steer her in the direction of something practical – stick with white for wearing underneath school blouses, and cotton, lace-free fabrics for comfort. For most girls, the excitement of this event will usually outweigh any embarrassment, and it can be a really enjoyable occasion for you both. Others may find it excruciating. If that's the case, don't force it: if she's really not keen to wear a bra, she shouldn't have to.

Bear in mind that young breasts can grow rapidly, so once she's on her way, you'll probably need to get her measured, and fork out for a new bra, fairly frequently.

Coping with periods

After years of having periods yourself, you might not remember what a big deal it was when they started. But it's a major rite of passage in any girl's life. She probably feels very excited about it – as well as a bit scared. When you talk about periods, stick to fairly simple biological explanations, and help her to understand *why* girls start to menstruate – essentially, that it's an indication that her body's ready to have a baby. You might be a bit hazy on the facts yourself, so a good book or website will be a boon: offer to go through it with her, or if she's very private, leave her to digest the information alone and then ask if she's got any questions.

Tell her about the realities of dealing with periods, and potential symptoms, such as sore breasts and crampy pains in the abdomen, back and pelvic region, in a matter-of-fact way. Be frank, but don't scare her. Let her know that it's normal and natural, but that she needn't ever suffer in silence. Reassure her that a painkiller and a lie-down will always be an option if she's badly affected.

Make sure she's practically ready. Buy her a packet of sanitary towels to keep tucked away in a drawer, explaining how they work if need be. (Tampons take practice getting used to, and flow often varies before settling down, so towels are a better bet at the start.) She may also want to keep one permanently in her schoolbag, or take one with her if she goes out – buy her a pretty, discreet little bag to keep supplies in.

Some girls start their periods as early as eight or nine, and if this is the case for your daughter, she may need a little extra support and sympathy in coping with this sooner-than-average start. Be sure to talk to her about what's happening and why, and stress that it's still normal. Make sure she's always got spare pads, a disposal bag and a change of knickers with her, particularly as periods are usually irregular at first and there's no way of knowing when her next will arrive. It's also a good idea to make sure a sympathetic teacher knows: primary school toilets don't always have disposal facilities, so she might need a helping hand, and if she suffers from period pain, she may need someone to provide her with a painkiller, or even to excuse her from lessons for a while.

If your tween's a boy, let him know all about periods, too, so he can get his facts straight. Explain that it's a normal part of life for girls, but they can be inconvenient and sometimes painful, so a little sympathy is required. Make sure he knows that teasing about periods is a definite no-no.

Blossoming boys: The facts about male puberty

- As well as an increase in height, he'll broaden in the shoulders and chest, and his muscles will develop.
- Hair will start to grow on his face, around his genitals, on his legs, under the arms, and perhaps elsewhere, such as the chest. It's soft and sparse at first, growing coarser and more abundant over time. Some boys are keen to start shaving off 'bum fluff' as soon as it appears, even though it's unlikely to be necessary. As with a girl's first bra, there's no harm if it makes him feel good about himself, so provide him with a razor and some shaving gel: one for sensitive skins will be a good bet to avoid soreness and shaving rash. His dad or the nearest alternative male role model may have some tips for him on this.
- His penis and balls will grow bigger (just like breasts, a boy's testicles may grow at different rates). He's beginning to produce sperm, and sometimes at night he'll ejaculate involuntarily during what's commonly known as a 'wet dream' – this could cause a little embarrassment if his sheets are soggy in the morning, so some discretion may be required. Although he may be no stranger to erections, since even very little boys can get these, he's likely to find he gets them more frequently (and often, quite spontaneously).
- He may feel lumps behind his nipples, or tenderness in the area, and wonder if he's growing 'man-boobs'. You can reassure him he isn't – they're caused by fluctuating hormones and they'll soon settle.
- The voice box (larynx) gets bigger and his voice will get deeper, often known as 'breaking'. This can happen quite quickly, or be a more gradual process during which the pitch and tone of the voice can suddenly change.

Skin and smells

Two potentially disagreeable aspects of puberty, for both boys and girls, are bad skin and body odour. Hormonal changes cause the sweat glands to produce too much sebum, or oil, as well as altering the levels of acid in the skin. This encourages the growth of bacteria, and the result can be spots and blackheads. The development of sweat glands around the armpits, breasts and genitals, means a natural increase in sweat, and in some cases, BO.

Personal hygiene will need to come further up his agenda now: let him know that washing daily will help keep the pongs at bay, and be sure to provide him with a non-perfumed deodorant. Keeping the skin clean with a gentle medicated facewash or cleanser, twice daily, will help fight spots. There are ranges available for both girls and boys. If acne becomes a serious problem, it's worth seeking advice from a GP, as there is medication that can help. Eating healthily and drinking water is helpful, too. There's more on diet in Chapter 7.

Boys in particular may need a bit of nudging to keep on top of personal hygiene, but as he gets older and more concerned with what other people think, he'll become more likely to take the initiative himself.

Emotional changes, too

As if all that freaky physical stuff isn't enough to cope with, your tween faces a whole load of emotional and psychological upheaval, as well: in fact, the emotional effects of hormone release often kick in before the physical ones. These factors are also driven by dramatic changes in the structure of the brain, as it begins a lengthy 're-wiring' process, in preparation for adulthood. So there really is a very genuine excuse for the mood swings, the tearfulness and the bad attitudes. Bearing that in mind might help to put things in perspective if you're struggling to cope.

Don't be surprised if your tween begins to look for privacy once he begins puberty – boys in particular are notoriously cagey about their changing form. He may want to lock the door to the bathroom, or be affronted if you walk into his bedroom without knocking. Maybe he's expressing himself by writing in a diary or perhaps via something else, such as music, and needs some time and space to do that. He might also become somewhat embarrassed by the sight of *your* body, so if you're a parent who's always been relaxed about nudity, it might be kinder to him to start covering up.

Girls too may prefer to get through puberty on their own as much as possible. Some, for instance, would rather be left to get on with it when it comes to having periods: as long as you're satisfied she's got all the information, as well as the sanitary protection she needs, there's no reason why she shouldn't be left to it. Just keep pushing the message home that you are there, if she needs you.

Whilst it's a good idea to remain casual and light-hearted on the subject of puberty, tread very carefully when it comes to teasing or making jokes. His mind, just like his genitals, is likely to be in a sensitive state right now.

What the netmums say

Coping with puberty

When my nine-year-old daughter complained about sore boobs, I thought she must have banged them. It was her dad who suggested that maybe her breasts were starting to grow – I wasn't expecting it until much later on, since I didn't get mine until I was fourteen. Now I'm expecting her periods to arrive. But I don't feel ready! She's growing up so fast and part of me wants to turn the clock back.
Linda, mum to two girls aged eleven and four, and a boy, nine

I talked to both my girls about puberty well in advance. I bought a book called *What's Happening to Me?* which we read through, and together we discussed the changes that happen. I've discussed the emotional changes too (like feeling moody, falling out with friends, attention from boys) as I think these are just as important as the physical changes. I went bra shopping with Maddie as soon as she started developing, and bought her some deodorant and some teenage sanitary pads to put away until needed, and a nifty little tin to store a couple of pads in her school bag – handy, but discreet.

Joanne, mum to two girls aged twelve and nine

My eldest son started puberty at around ten. It was more emotional than anything else at first. He couldn't understand what was going on and why one minute he'd be screaming and slamming doors, the next crying his eyes out. It hurts to see this change in your child, but I've begun to realise he doesn't understand half of the time why he acts the way he does. So I let him know that I understand what he's going through, and remind him that I love him but there's still no excuse to speak to me like that! As for the physical signs, he's really quite proud about them! He told everyone in the family he had his first pubic hair, which was quite funny – and I'm glad he felt he could be open about it. I noticed I was no longer allowed in the bathroom when he was in the bath, which I respect and understand.

Kate, mum to two boys aged eleven and nine

My son started growing lots of hair all over his body and face about eight months ago. He seems to be one of very few boys at school with this much hair, and he's very shy about it. He wanted to shave his legs (we persuaded him not to), and he's started shaving his face. We've had many long chats about it, trying to explain that the other boys will catch up. He wouldn't wear shorts this summer because of it. He is also so emotional – he's never been this way before now, but he gets stressed about too much homework or feels pressure at school and the smallest things will set off a full-blown meltdown. He has lots of spots too, no matter how many times he washes his face. It's hard to explain that it's just his age and hormones. We're expecting yet more issues over time, but for now we're just trying to address things as they turn up.

Kirsty, mum to two boys aged thirteen and nine months

Alysha started going through puberty at nine, and started her periods at ten. I've always talked to her openly, and before she started her periods I'd shown her what sanitary towels looked like, and practised with her how to use them. She was worried, and wanted me to reassure her it would all be OK, which I did. And because she was so young I made sure the school had made provisions for her. She does get tired and feels a bit low when she's on, but otherwise copes well. The worst part of her puberty for me is helping her to do her bikini line before she has to go swimming: I was concerned that she'd feel self-conscious about it at swimming, so I asked her if she wanted to do something about it and we discussed the different methods. We decided using hair-removal cream was the easiest and least painful for now. It's not something I thought I'd ever have to do, but until she's old enough to apply it on her own, I guess I'll have to.

Kerrie, mum to two girls aged twelve and one

Many people think my son is older than he is. At twelve, he's 5 ft 5 in, with size seven feet. He has pubic and facial hair and his voice is starting to break, and he's also rather stroppy and has become interested in the opposite sex! I feel a bit sad about it – I've lost my baby a bit earlier than is usual.

Victoria, mum to a boy aged twelve, and two girls aged nine and two

Sometimes, a first bra is required before a girl has any breasts! My daughter didn't have any boobs until she was in Year Six, but she did wear a little bra for about a year beforehand because most of her friends did, and she definitely didn't want to wear a vest any more. I indulged it because, at this age, other children can be cruel and take the mickey so easily if you don't fit in. And I remembered getting stick myself for not having a 'real' bra when I was her age. Our daughters are all individuals and I think we need to be guided by their feelings.

Sally, mum to a boy, seventeen, and a girl, fifteen

Just before her tenth birthday, my daughter got her first period. She dealt with it really well, as she'd read through a couple of books on the subject, and she knew what to expect. She's had hair 'downstairs' since she was eight, so in a way I was half expecting her to start early. That was a couple of months ago, and she hasn't had another one since. But bejesus, you would think she had PMT constantly, she is so moody. God help me when she does get them every month!

Helen, mum to two girls aged ten and four, and two boys aged two and nine months

I'd always been fairly open with my daughter about puberty and periods, and told her what to expect. Her body started to change around the age of nine, and she got her first period at ten: she's always been big for her age so we were expecting it to happen early. However, she was still extremely upset, and sobbed that she 'didn't want them'. It was really difficult to console her, because although she was quite well informed, she was still at primary school, and didn't want to be different from other girls. Knowing that her life had now changed for ever, there was no going back, and there was nothing I could do about it was unbearable. Now that she's in secondary school and many of her friends have also started, it's not as much of an issue. It still gets in the way of her doing things like swimming, and she avoids sleepovers when she's 'on'. But she's come to accept it and, while her periods do annoy her, she doesn't feel the same sense of embarrassment and solitude as when she first started.

Suzanne, mum to two girls aged thirteen and seven

My son is ten and has already started puberty. His arms and legs are really hairy, and one of the children in his school started picking on him because of it. His attitude is like nothing else. One minute he cries at the drop of a hat, the next he's arguing and sullen. I know this is a difficult time for these growing tweens, but it's also hard for their parents. Just when you thought the terrible twos, threes, fours, and fives are finished, along comes puberty!

Louise, mum to two boys aged ten and two

One is fun

If he hasn't already, your tween is very likely to discover the joys of masturbation before long. For both boys and girls, it's a very natural exploration of their bodies, and all the nice feelings that are to be had from touching yourself. Chances are he won't be much up for discussing it with you. But if the opportunity arises, it's good to let him know that it's a perfectly normal, safe and healthy practice.

What the experts say

Crissy says: There may not be much in the way of privacy on offer in the average family home, but whether your tween opts for the shower, the loo or his own bed, at some stage he will inevitably be looking for somewhere to be alone. Be respectful and discreet: if he's spending a bit too long in the bathroom, for example, avoid teasing and try not to bang on the door. To minimise the risk of embarrassment, you might introduce a new 'family' rule that everyone strips their own bed and puts their own washing in the basket. Resist the urge to place a man-size box of tissues in his room – and in the interests of your own sanity, avoid rummaging under his bed from now on!

Talking about sex

A tween is still a child, and may seem to be a long way off the need for information about sex, not to mention embarrassed or horrified by the prospect of any kind of conversation with *you* about it. And for many parents, it simply isn't an easy subject to broach – especially if their own parents were tight-lipped about it. But introducing the subject early on and in a natural, chatty way is all-important, because if you do, he's far more likely to grow up knowing that sex can be a positive, pleasurable and natural part of relationships. With your guidance, he can learn what is and isn't appropriate sexual behaviour, and – hopefully – be better equipped to resist pressure and make safer choices, when the time comes, and feel comfortable about coming to you for advice in the future. In fact, evidence suggests that children who have good sex education, early on, are more likely to wait a while before becoming sexually active themselves, and less likely to go on to have an unplanned pregnancy or to catch a sexually transmitted disease. Anyway, let's face it, if he doesn't get the facts of life from you, he's likely to get them from somewhere – and it may not be a reliable source.

A good general rule for this age group is to be guided by your child, and to exploit any cues that crop up to gently instigate conversation. So, always answer any questions he puts to you as honestly and appropriately as you can, and if something arises out of a television programme, for example, try to expand on it. It's quite possible he genuinely does want some advice, or the chance to chat, but just can't quite bring himself to say so – watch carefully, as his body language might give you a clue. Don't be surprised to find he already knows a surprising amount about sex – or thinks he does! Playground chat and snippets of information from the media may have informed him, and the picture he's built up may not be a very accurate one. Use reflective listening to find out what he knows, so you can expand on it where necessary, and gently put him right on anything he's got wrong.

When you're talking, or answering questions, stick with language and concepts you know won't confuse him, and keep it simple – in most cases you probably won't need to go into detail, unless you're pressed for it. Chances are you'll need to do a bit of research yourself, if you're hazy on the facts of life. If a tricky question comes up and you don't know the answer, you might suggest you look it up together online, or in a book. Looking through a resource like that together can seem a lot less pressured or awkward than a one-to-one conversation – in fact, if talking about sex is something you truly can't face, or if your tween really doesn't want to hear it, you could do a lot worse than leaving a suitable book around for him to dip in to as and when he feels like it.

Sex education: What your tween will learn at school

As things stand right now, the law states that both primary and secondary schools must teach the biological aspects of puberty and sexual reproduction, as part of the science curriculum. Secondary schools must also teach pupils about sexually trans-mitted infections (STIs) and HIV/AIDS.

However, as part of the non-statutory subject Personal, Social and Health Education (PSHE), many schools also teach the broader topic of Sex and Relationships Education (SRE), which includes a much deeper look at the issues surrounding puberty and sexual reproduction, including emotional and social aspects of growing up, relationships, sexuality and sexual health.

Plans to change the law to make SRE a compulsory subject were shelved in 2010; however, campaigners still insist it's the way forward and – at the time of writing – a new bill has been proposed.

All schools must have a policy on sex education that describes what they teach on the subject, and how they teach it. Parents have a right to withdraw their children from these lessons. Under the proposed SRE bill, they would no longer have this right, but children themselves could withdraw if they requested.

Love, etc

Of course, it's not just about biology. When you're talking about sex, discuss the feelings involved, too, and explain that sex is (hopefully) an expression of love between two people. Be sure to talk about relation-ships, too, and discuss how many different sorts there are – married, unmarried, straight, gay.

If you have values or beliefs that mean you feel strongly about certain 'rights and wrongs', talk about these, too. But try to remain neutral and open-minded, if you can: after all, tweens are people who are starting to form their own opinions and, before too long, they'll have the right to make their own choices. And do always be realistic. There's not much point in telling him that sex can only happen within marriage, for exam-ple, because in the wider society, that simply isn't true.

What the experts say

Crissy says: Some tweens would rather eat dirt than broach the subject of sex with their parents, so it's often up to you to open the discussion. Keep it casual and low-key. When the subject of sex comes up in a film, magazine article or conversation, try asking him how he feels about it, if he understands what's happening and if he'd like to know more, or to discuss it with you. If he says no, don't push it: respect his decision, but always leave the door open for him to come back to you at any time. It shouldn't be a case of a quick chat, a sigh of relief and it's all over. This is a subject to be revisited time and time again, over the months and years.

Ideally, I think we want to send the message that sex at its best is a loving and respectful act between two people. It's not just about making babies, sometimes it's just for fun, but the most important thing is that both parties feel ready for sex and want to do it together. You may feel tempted to send the message that sex is only good when you're in love or married, but this will seriously undermine your credibility if and when your tween later discovers for himself that sex can be pleasurable even outside a relationship. Perhaps the trick here is to stress that sex is *better* with someone you care about.

When it comes to talking about darker or more complex aspects of sex and relationships, take a leaf out of the Boy Scout handbook, and be prepared. You never know when your tween may throw a tricky question your way. Try to keep your answers well rooted in fact, but don't be too graphic: it's OK to soften the truth a little at this age. Relationships can be complicated and families take all sorts of forms these days, so you may have to answer some awkward and perhaps personal questions, such as 'Why does Daddy have another new girlfriend?' or 'Why does Mummy share a bed with her friend?' Kids can be incredibly blunt at times, but whilst it's important not to fob them off, don't feel you need to go into any great depth at this age. These sorts of questions are probably less about wanting a full run-down of your sexual history, and more about curiosity as to why one family is different from another.

Elaine says: It's vital that our tweens don't come to view sex as something naughty or dirty, but a healthy activity that they'll engage in as a young adult, when they're ready. Schools do play an important role here in delivering sex education lessons, but as parents we need to play our part, too. If we bring up our children in an atmosphere in which they can talk to us, knowing we will listen without judgement, then they won't feel anxious and unable to talk to us, and communication will flow. Be sure to respond to any questions he has: generally, if he wants to know about something, that's a sign that he's ready to absorb the information.

For this age group, conversations about sex really don't need to be too 'gritty'. When it comes to discussing pregnancy, for instance, I'd do so in a conversational way, rather than in a 'warning' manner. The chances are he'll know an adult who is having a baby, which may prompt questions. He doesn't need a lot of details about contraception at this point, but you might say that if couples don't want to have a baby, they can still have sex using some kind of protection. Always adopt a matter-of-fact tone, and don't suddenly adopt lots of clinical language if that's not how you normally talk.

I wouldn't set out deliberately to discuss difficult subjects like rape or sexually transmitted diseases with kids in this age group. Knowing too much before they're ready to absorb it could leave them confused and maybe scared. However if a child asks a specific question, I wouldn't avoid answering. It may give the idea that the topic is really scary if a loved adult isn't prepared to discuss the matter with him and it may mean he goes off to get the information elsewhere, which could be delivered in a less sensitive manner than you can. And if something comes up because of an article in the paper or on the news, or as a result of what he's learning at school, I would aim to talk about it at a level that seems right for him individually. There's no rule of thumb about how to handle these conversations. We know that nasty and unpleasant things happen in the world. We need to help our children to absorb that knowledge one step at a time, in manageable chunks, and without hysteria.

What the netmums say

Talking about sex

I've spoken to both my girls about sex. I believe in answering their questions as truthfully as possible, while being sensitive to their age and level of understanding. To be honest, I found the conversation a little embarrassing, but I know it's an important part of being a parent. Both girls thought it all sounded pretty gross, but they have asked occasional additional questions since, so they have taken it on board. I wanted to make sure they had all the facts from me, before the sex education and puberty talks they'll get at school. They may get the factual information then, but not the emotional and moral guidance that only a parent can give. I've stressed that a man and woman should love each other before they have sex, as I want them to understand that sex is something special and not just something to do because everyone else is doing it. We've also discussed what being 'gay' means: I just told them that sometimes two men or two women love each other, and want to have a relationship. I think the subject came up while watching an episode of *Four Weddings*, which featured a gay marriage!
Joanne, mum to two girls aged twelve and nine

We had our first sex talk with our son two years ago. He'd managed to get on to a rude website (despite all our protection methods) and we'd found out. It was a shock – when we asked him about it, he said he wanted to know what the boys at school were talking about. We then realised we needed to have 'the chat'! My partner took the honours and spent an evening

researching on the internet, trying to find out how to approach it. Kevin had lots of questions, from girls' periods to pregnancy and what a 'MILF' was, and my partner managed to stay calm and relaxed, and answer them all. It seems to have opened the door, as he comes and asks us whenever something is puzzling him now. I wouldn't say he gets enough correct information from school – most of it seems to come from his friends. Fortunately, he isn't too bothered with girls yet; sport and computer games come first! I'm sure there are tougher questions to come, though.
Kirsty, mum to two boys aged thirteen and nine months

We have a good open relationship with both our children and I've discussed sex freely with them. They're not afraid to ask questions if they need to know the answer to something, and I have also told them how important it is to use protection not just to stop pregnancies but also to protect against STIs. I feel it's important to be open and honest with children about these issues, otherwise it may become a taboo subject and something to be hidden, or ashamed of.
Gaynor, mum to a boy, fourteen, and a girl, twelve

We got a great book for my daughter when she was nine, as lots of her friends were 'discussing' sex and I wanted her to hear the 'truth' from me first. I know they will still talk, but at least I know she knows the facts. She wasn't too bothered. She asked if it hurt, and I said it sometimes does the first time. She then looked at me in horror and said, 'You do it more than ONCE?!' So the idea of sex being for pleasure has not dawned on her yet and I think that's great, as she's still very young to be thinking of things like that. It hasn't been raised again since, but she has told her younger sister that she can't see the book yet, as she's not ready and won't understand it. That did make me giggle!
Tanya, mum to two girls aged ten and seven

I have always been very open with my daughter. When I gave birth to her brother two years ago the hospital gave me some condoms, and I promptly passed them on to her . . . not because she is sexually active (she isn't), but so she could open the packet, see what they look and feel like, and so I could explain what they are for, and the importance of using them. There might come a time in the future when she does need them and I don't want her to be afraid to ask. I do think kids of her age are far more sexually aware than a lot of parents give credit for, these days. Her friend was over last week and was wearing one of these 'shag bands'. I know they all have different meanings so I asked what they were. I must admit they managed to shock me when they told me what one of them was for. My daughter wears some of these bracelets, too, sometimes. But they don't bother me because, although they're supposed to represent certain acts, the girls just seem to regard them as a slightly 'naughty' fashion. I also think they can actually be a useful tool to open up conversation.

Tracy, mum to a girl, thirteen, and two boys aged six and two

By nine, my daughter knew almost everything about babies except how they came into being. We had discussed pregnancy, birth, even Caesareans, but she'd never actually asked how you got to that point. My six-year-old then one day asked the 'big question' and I found myself giving a blushing, blustering answer about 'special cuddles', to which my nine-year-old listened avidly! I am not prudish at all, and we do talk a lot about relationships, changing bodies, being a mum, birth and so on, but the whole sex chat does make me feel a bit uncomfortable. Maybe it's because my mum never talked openly to me about it. (Thank heavens for friends and *Just Seventeen*!)

Karen, mum to two girls aged ten and seven

My policy is to talk to my daughter as and when things come up. I don't find it easy and if there's something I'm not sure about, I say leave it with me, and I will look it up. That then gives me some breathing space, and I can think about an age-appropriate way of telling her. We did have a situation that came up

recently, when a friend's daughter was being pressured by an older boy, which I used as a good chance to talk to her about how some people like to make things up, and tell you you're not normal if you don't want to do things, and that their friends were all doing it, when in fact, they are not. I made a point of saying she should not do anything unless she felt she wanted to, and also explained about the law, and what it meant. I felt really unsure about what I was saying, but I'm glad I had that chance.
Vickie, mum to two girls aged eleven and eight

I have always answered any questions my sons have, not necessarily offering the information but always replying truthfully when they do ask. As a result they both know where babies come from and what sex is. My oldest has asked about things in much more detail, however. He often hears words at school that he doesn't understand and so asks me for an explanation. The most recent word is 'wank' so we had a discussion about being erect, the pleasure that it may (or may not) bring by him touching himself and that it may end in him 'coming' (another word he's heard at school). It also led on to talking about the possibility of wet dreams, and that he's not to be embarrassed if something unexpected happens. His initial response was 'yuck', but he has since asked further questions so I know that he's thought about what was said. He knows what sex is and what it involves, although I always try to explain things so that he understands that it's something to be enjoyed between people who love each other and that it's a subject that's best discussed with people who he respects and trusts. Relatives have commented that he's too young to know things in such detail. I calmly point out that knowledge is power, and that being informed in good time means that he'll be able to make informed choices as he grows into a man.
Ann, mum to two boys aged ten and seven

Protecting his innocence

We live in an increasingly sexualised society, and there's no doubt that the tweens of today are more exposed to sexual language and images than in the past. Our kids don't have to look far to get the general idea: sex is everywhere, in music videos and song lyrics, on television and the web, in newspapers and magazines, and the overwhelming message is that it's a great thing – and everyone's at it. That's fair enough if you're a consenting adult, but confusing if you're still a child and a long way off ready for it.

You can't hope to shield your tween completely from this sort of influence – it's everywhere, whether we like it or not. But you can and should be vigilant about what exactly he is being exposed to and make up your own mind on what seems suitable and what doesn't. You might decide, for example, that whilst Lady GaGa's latest video is harmless, online porn is not. There's advice on how you can help protect your tween from consuming too much, too young, via technology in the following chapter, and more on the issue of growing up too fast in Chapter 8.

One positive thing to be said about this influx of images and messages, though, is that they should open up plenty of opportunities to talk about sex with your tween.

What the experts say

Crissy says: These days more and more marketing aimed at tweens seems to have a sexual content. From adult-styled tween clothing lines, to bump-and-grind idols in stockings and high heels, sex has now infiltrated the tween world in a big way. For girls, *Bunty* comics have been replaced by magazines offering free make-up gifts and advice on how to kiss, and what to do when your boyfriend cheats on you. There are still appropriate magazines out there, but it's not enough to check out the front cover: take a flick through before you buy to be sure the material is suitable for your tween.

It's the subliminal messages in the pop videos and the press that are most troubling. Images of super-slim, apparently sexually available young women and macho men can colour how our tweens see the opposite sex and also themselves. As parents we need to counter these by building up our tweens' self-esteem, and by teaching boys and girls to hold mutual respect and value for themselves, and for each other. Like it or not, eventually most boys will become fascinated by naked bodies. Whilst many parents find themselves turning a blind eye to the odd 'girlie' or lads' mag at some point, it's important to always draw the line at hard-core or sexually degrading, abusive or violent material.

It's often possible to turn the most difficult of tween experiences into something positive, so if something causes you or your tween concern, use it as a springboard for further conversation. When your daughter demands the latest crop top, or asks to watch *Glee* because everyone else is, don't just say 'no', take the opportunity to explain why you don't think it's appropriate – and make sure you've actually watched any contentious programmes for yourself first so you can back up your argument. And if you catch your son ogling Page Three, spend some time reminding him that all girls deserve his respect.

Elaine says: The early sexualisation of our tweens is a huge issue. The commercial exploitation of this age group means parents need to think carefully about the messages certain products give, and, if it's a message that's unsuitable, avoid buying them. Personally, for instance, I don't think g-strings, suggestive pencil cases and provocatively worded clothing are suitable for tweens – and yet these are all available in the shops. Comics, magazines and pop videos are often very sexually explicit, as are the lyrics in popular songs, and with increased access to media images there may be a real difficulty for tweens to divorce fiction from reality. The solution lies not in forbidding these things, but ensuring you keep talking to your tween about what he sees or hears and help him put it into context. Discuss marketing ploys and slogans, and how the advertisers use images and ideas to sell products. Fortunately, many tweens are pretty savvy and don't like the idea of being duped!

Early relationships

It may come to your attention that there's someone in your tween's social group that he 'fancies'. You'll perhaps find out he has a 'girlfriend', be asked to help facilitate a 'date', or to host an event at home to which only one rather special person is invited. An older tween of twelve or thirteen may even reckon himself to be 'in love'.

Try not to worry if your tween discovers the opposite sex. Girls and boys will usually start mixing socially during this phase – although for some, the opposite sex will remain a repellent species for a while – and genuine, platonic friendships between the sexes start to be formed. It's also quite normal for tweens to start feeling the first twinges of physical attraction. If this attraction is to someone of the same gender, it's most likely to be a developmental phase, or it may mean that he will be bisexual or gay when he's a little older. Either way, chatting openly about gay relationships and showing him that you have no prejudices about sexuality will help him work through any feelings he has without feeling there's something wrong with it.

If your tween is in a relationship and it seems to be fairly serious, don't dismiss his feelings. Hold fire before attempting to put a stop to it if you're worried it may become inappropriate, or you don't like his choice of girlfriend – as with friendships, you'll only make it seem more appealing if you show disapproval. Try not to jump to any conclusions: chances are, it's all pretty innocent. Meanwhile, keep talking and listening in subtle ways – you need your tween to know you're there if he needs you, but you don't want him to feel you're prying, otherwise you may push him towards secrecy.

It's down to you as parents to work out what your values are when it comes to those early relationships. You'll no doubt need to make some amendments to your book of golden rules, and let your tween know if you have particular expectations. You might be certain that you need to know where they are when they're together; or maybe you'd prefer it if they're only together alone in your house, or among a larger group of friends. No doubt you'll have strong feelings about a relationship with an age gap (and a very large age gap, at this age, will probably be downright unacceptable). It's your call. But lay the laws down gently, when you do so. If you make it out to be a bigger thing than it is, perhaps that's what it will become.

Beyond snogging

Hard as it is to think about as a parent, a minority of tweens do start experimenting with sexual behaviour, with a very small handful actually losing their virginity as young as twelve or thirteen. Even if he's in no danger of 'going all the way', it's quite possible that a child at the latter end of the tween years will discover the joys of snogging or petting – and this too might be something you don't really want to dwell on! But as parents, we do need to be aware, and to be realistic: in this modern world, our children may be facing these pressures from an early age. And the truth is that even if your tween himself is a long way off sexual activity, it's probable that one or more of his peers has indulged in it, is thinking about indulging in it, or talking about indulging in it. You should stay in tune to the possibility that it may not be far around the corner for your child, too.

Meanwhile, keep on talking openly about sex, love and relationships. Discuss the important fact that sixteen is the legal age of consent for both boys and girls (and that goes for same-sex relationships too) – but that even sixteen might be too early. Push home the messages that he does not have to have sex until he wants to; that whoever he has sex with should feel ready, too, and that when he does have sex, it will be a whole lot better within a steady relationship. Alongside that, make sure he's armed with all the vital practical information he needs, or might need in the future. In particular, fill him in on the basic facts regarding contraception and sexually transmitted diseases, which boil down to the mantra that a condom is always essential. If he's already learned about it all at school, back it up with conversation to make sure he really understands.

By the time he reaches the end of his tween years, a child is on the springboard to adult life – or he will be pretty soon – and he's likely to be dabbling in adulthood's pleasures before too long. You probably can't divert him from them, but you can help protect against the risks, and foster a healthy attitude towards them, by offering him tons of love, attention and stability, and delivering all the facts he needs as openly as possible.

What the experts say

Crissy says: Tween romance is nothing new. Kiss chase has long been *de rigueur* in the playground, and tweens really can and do fall in love. Just because their idea of love may not correspond to your own doesn't make it any less real or less intense, so take care not to dismiss or ridicule your tween if he announces it's happened to him. Any tween relationship is better conducted under your nose than behind your back, and unless you have serious cause for concern, you should resist the urge to interfere too much. Most tween love is short-lived, but while it lasts it can be incredibly precious for your child, so give him the respect he deserves. If it all ends in tears, make sure you're there with lots of hugs, then pick up the pieces and stand by for the next time.

In matters of the heart, as in all areas of tween parenting, ground rules are vital. Don't be too prohibitive, but it's worth taking time to consider what your immovable boundaries are when it comes to young romance. You may draw the line in terms of age difference, how much time they spend together, when and whether they spend it alone, in adult company or within a group of friends. Whatever your limits, make them clear and stick to them.

As you tuck your tween into bed at night, it may seem impossible that he could be even experiencing sexual thoughts and feelings, let alone acting upon them. The good news is that in most cases he won't be, but it does happen, and parents need to be alert to the possibility. Chances are the thought of your tween snogging or petting is disturbing to you, but don't be tempted to bury your head in the sand. Take care to create an affectionate, loving, supportive family environment where your tween feels celebrated and accepted for who he is, and he'll be less likely to go looking for self-value or intimacy from a sexual relationship. Instil a healthy respect in your child not only for the opposite sex but also for himself. Acknowledge the power of peer pressure and also how difficult it is when he cares for someone but feels pressured by them into doing something he isn't ready for. Make sure that boys and girls are clear that 'no' means 'no', and that it's always OK to say it if that's how they are feeling.

Elaine says: The reassuring reality is that most kids in the tween age group are not yet engaged in sexual activity. In fact, many will still see even the idea of sex as 'gross'! There should be no reason to feel suspicious if your child has a 'boyfriend' or 'girl-friend', as long as you have a relationship that's based on mutual trust and respect. Hopefully, you've talked about it, and laid the foundations about what's appropriate in relationships at different ages. Bear in mind, too, that the fact that he's referring to some-one as a 'girlfriend' doesn't necessarily mean much: nine-year-olds use those terms without the same meaning that a fifteen-year-old attaches to them. Personally, I'd be inclined to tell a twelve- or thirteen-year-old who claimed to be in an exclusive relationship that he was too young to focus on just one person – without actually prohibiting it – and encourage him to have lots of friends of both genders. I'd engage him in lots of family activities, too, to help him get the sense of belonging and approval he seeks.

'Hoping for the best' is not a good tactic for parenting. We need to be much more proactive than this. A child will be less inclined to look for substitutes like sex (as well as drugs and drink) if he has a good sense of self-belief and self-esteem. These things are at the core of whether they value themselves, so we need to keep on exposing them to experiences that demonstrate that they're worthwhile, unique individuals, that their opinions have validity, and that they're appreciated for who they are and what they can achieve, and not for matching up to someone else's ideal.

What the netmums say

Young love

My daughter has been asked out several times by boys in her class and asked me for permission to 'go out' with one of them. I said she couldn't (and also advised her on the most gentle way to turn the boy down). She is so young and has plenty of years of boy drama in front of her! Unfortunately she looks quite a bit older than her age, more like twelve or thirteen, and gets unwanted attention from older boys, which bothers me and makes me feel very protective.
Annette, mum to a girl, nine, and a boy, seven

My sport-mad middle son, who rarely had time even to acknowledge girls, suddenly fell head over heels for a girl in his year. Mostly it was pretty harmless – they spent quite a bit of time together at weekends and after school, she came round for tea a couple of times, and he went to her home. I didn't know the family, but talked to her mum on the phone to make arrangements, and we chatted after dropping them off. I took them to the cinema (with my other two children, although we sat a distance away from them!) and he was invited around for a sleepover, which did pose a dilemma, as I wouldn't be happy with them sharing a room, but the girl's mum slept in the lounge with them, so that solved that problem! This 'relationship' lasted about five months. Sadly, when they 'split up', her friends said some silly things about my son, and he felt he should retaliate, which led to a difficult week for us all. Now we've explained it's more important to value a good friendship than ruin it with silly labels that don't seem appropriate at this age. The key seems to be to keep things laid back and not get too heated about anything, or build it up into something it shouldn't be at this age. It's also essential to communicate well with the other child's parents.
Barbara, mum to two boys aged fourteen and twelve, and a girl, five

Both my older girls have had boyfriends and it all seemed very innocent. Evie wanted a mixed-sex birthday sleepover as she has both male and female friends (one of the boys being her boyfriend at the time). I agreed, as I trust my children implicitly and genuinely felt it was innocent. Then my mother pointed out to me that perhaps not all the parents would feel the same. So I telephoned each of them to let them know the situation and that I would be checking up on them from time to time, and most of them were fine with it. One of the girls, however, was not allowed to come, so I'm glad I checked. I always talk frankly and openly with my girls and no subject is taboo. I share little secrets and confide in them and I think they feel free to do the same in return. I also accept that they sometimes want to keep things to themselves and feel that a little of this is healthy, too.
Louise, mum to three girls aged thirteen, twelve and three

The other day my son, who's nearly ten, declared that there's a girl in his class that he has loved for years but he's not sure if she feels the same. He has three girlfriends, apparently, but it was this one he really liked. Then he asked me what he should do! I explained that he is very young and not to worry about having a 'girlfriend', but instead to value all of the good friends he has. I asked what he 'does' with his girlfriends – for instance, did they hold hands? He said, 'Eugh, no!' But he does help them with their work and when one of them fell over in the playground he was the first person to help her up! Although I don't want him to get wrapped up in it all, I also don't want him to be put off talking to me about love and relationships. So it's important to me that I explain to him what it's all about – but that he has many years to worry about girls and should enjoy just being friends with them whilst he has the chance!
Pippa from Oakham, mum to Alfie, nine, and Saffron, six

During the summer holidays, my eleven-year-old son was invited to his girlfriend's house for a sleepover with another girl and another boy. I allowed him to go, but did think at the time that it wasn't something I would have done. The mother said that the evening went very well and that she would maybe do it again! I have no doubt it was all innocent. The only times they saw each other were at school and playing out at the park, so I would hardly have called it going out together, as they referred to it. He's since ended the 'relationship' as they are now at different high schools. I believe many girls have asked him out since, but he's not really interested and would rather be out playing football! My daughter is fourteen and has never had a boyfriend, but she is rather shy. They both have lots of friends of the opposite sex.

Angela, mum to a girl, fourteen, and a boy, eleven

He's only nine, but my son is already noticing girls. One night he was swimming with his dad and sister and when they came home the first thing my husband said was, 'Oh, Ben pulled tonight!' It turned out a girl of the same age came up to him and said how much she liked him and she just asked him there and then would he go out with her?! Ben said he wasn't sure, so she should ask his younger brother Joe, which she did! It made me realise that kids now are so much more advanced than we were at that age. It also made me realise my husband is a lot more relaxed about the thought than I am, so maybe we will need to talk about it so we're both working from the same page. I do think girls are a lot more mature than boys. Ben has said that it's always the girls who make the decisions about who's going out with who; the boys don't get a say at all!

Amanda, mum to two boys aged nine and six

My eldest son, who's gay but only came out to us quite recently, tells me he began to have feelings for other boys when he was about eleven. Not surprisingly, it caused him a lot of confusion and worry at the time, because most of what he heard from his peers left him assuming he was supposed to like girls. Looking back, I realise I could have talked more to him about differences in sexuality, but it just didn't seem to come up much. If he'd told me then about how confused he felt, I could have helped him to understand it was OK.

Sarah, mum to two boys aged nineteen and twelve, and a girl, fifteen

I really hope my son isn't sexually active. But he's thirteen, and has been with his girlfriend for a year. I found some texts on his phone that suggested they were planning to have sex, and I was heartbroken. I felt like I'd lost my baby boy, and blamed his girlfriend for it all. When I talked to him about it, he cried and said they hadn't had sex, but he wanted to. I wanted to scream at him, and tell him he was grounded for the rest of his life, but of course I couldn't do that. And I desperately wanted to get across to him how significant losing your virginity is, for boys as well as girls, and that just because he felt ready it didn't mean they had to do it straight away. I told him that it was OK for him to want to have sex, that it was perfectly normal and if he really wanted to do it then we could get some condoms, but that his girlfriend had to speak to her parents too – or that I would. I'm not happy about it, but this is something I have to accept he will do. All I can do is guide him to make the right decisions for himself. Most of all I want him to know that I'm here for him if he needs me. I just hope I've taught him well enough to look after and respect himself.

Sarah, mum to two boys aged thirteen and ten

I was horrified the other day, when my son went to the park to meet a girl. I don't think he's ready for girls yet – I'm not ready for it, either! According to this girl's Facebook page, her interests include men! And he's gone with a mate who I know is more advanced. I know I can't really stop him going to the park to play, but that's my instinct. I just worry that she's going to jump on him, and 'teach him a thing or two'.

Katie, mum to a boy, twelve, and a girl, seven

5 Modern media

There's no getting round it. Computers, television and mobile phones are a fact of modern life – and it's usually during the tween years that the lure of all things technological really kicks in. Most families own at least one telly and a PC; games consoles are everywhere; and a majority of kids possess a mobile phone by the time they reach their teens. Information and Communication Technology (ICT) is on the national curriculum, so all tweens are expected to use computers and the internet as part of their studies. And many kids in this age group will, at some point, start exploring social networking sites and other ways of electronic communicating such as instant messaging: it's simply how you keep in touch with your mates these days. We need to remember that all these high-tech methods of communicating, learning and having fun offer fantastic benefits for our kids, and should be looked at positively. As adults, we all make use of modern media ourselves and, frankly, it's hard to imagine life without them.

With the undoubted benefits, though, come a variety of potential pitfalls. As parents of tweens, we need to be well informed as to what they are, and to provide whatever protection against them that's in our power. We need to be vigilant – a little nosey, even. And we need to keep on communicating with our tweens. That way, we can confidently trust them to make their own sensible choices, and become good 'digital citizens', even when we're not there to help them do so. Hopefully, our efforts will lay down the foundations for continued good habits as they move out of the tween years and beyond – at which point, our control starts to seriously dwindle, and how they use modern media is up to them.

Laying down the law

When it comes to your tween and all things technological, you'll no doubt want to have some rules in place. Not because you're hell-bent on making life miserable for her, but to protect her from those potential trouble-spots – and because it's not healthy for her to spend too much of her life in front of a screen.

Precisely what your rules will be is down to you. But most parents will probably want to start with a simple guideline about the amount of screen-time your tween is entitled to each day. There's lots of debate on the subject – with some experts more vociferous than others – but *everyone* agrees it's simply not a good idea to be staring at a screen, grasping a gamepad, texting endlessly or virtually chatting too frequently, for long periods of time. Physical consequences could include repetitive strain injury; eyesight damage, insomnia; and a negative influence on brain patterns; as well as an increased risk of obesity and a general lack of fitness. Then there are fears that it could affect literacy, learning and creative skills or, indeed – if it's happening at the expense of home or schoolwork – academic achievement in general. Others worry that too much screen-time could affect social development, because it detracts from actual, face-to-face interaction and proper conversation with friends and family.

Judgement on how much screen-time is reasonable is also likely to vary from family to family. There are no official guidelines for parents, so it's up to us to decide for ourselves. Some experts, including a team from Bristol University who carried out a study recently, suggest that no more than two hours of screen-time a day is a reasonable maximum to aim for. It's also a good idea to always stop and take a break after forty-five minutes of computer or gaming time. In any case, when you're adding up the total of her screen-time allowance, be sure to take everything into account: that's television, internet and gaming, too. Switching from the telly to the PC doesn't count as taking a break! (You might find it's hard to stick to a two-hour limit for screen-time on non-school days and that you need to be more flexible about these.)

Write your rules down if it helps, or consider drawing up a computer use or screen-time 'contract' which you can pin by the computer or in another obvious place. (You'll find a template for one on the Microsoft website. There's a link to the right page in the further information appendix at the back of the book.) Treat it as a bit of fun if you like, but make clear to your tween that it needs to be stuck to – or consequences will be dished out.

Of course, some families choose not to have rigid limits or set schedules for screen-time. That can work fine if your tween is good at self-moderating her screen habits for herself – and if you're confident, without counting, that the overall time she's spending in front of a screen is sensible.

It's up to us to help our tweens find a good balance. Some are pretty good at finding it for themselves, others need plenty of guidance. So as well as whatever she gets in the way of time spent on computers, tellies, games, or texting away on her mobile phone, make sure she's also doing lots of other stuff too over the course of an average week. That means some form of regular exercise; eating at the table and chatting with the rest of the family; meeting up with friends in person and having plenty of verbal conversations as well as virtual ones; reading books or magazines; indulging in at least one other 'old-fashioned' interest or hobby, whether sporting, creative, or social; and fitting in the less interesting but necessary other stuff such as homework, chores, good hygiene and enough sleep. If you know that's all covered, too, then you probably don't have anything to worry about.

What the experts say

Elaine says: I would strongly recommend that any family has rules around the use of screens. Our kids are exposed to an endless stream of media these days, and there has to be limits, for the sake of their health – and because otherwise nothing else would get done! I'd suggest that, as well as having rules around the amount of time the children may spend on the computer, gaming or watching television, it's also a good idea to have set times for sessions and agreements on what needs to be done first, for instance homework or chores.

It's very important that parents discuss with their children their concerns about screen-time, what their values are on the matter, and why those things are important to them. That doesn't mean that kids will like having their viewing, playing or surfing curtailed at that point, but it makes it more likely that they'll accept the values in the long term. If parents are clear about their reasons for the family rules they are more likely to follow through with them consistently. Aim to express the rule positively, so instead of saying, 'No TV until after homework,' it's better to say, 'Homework needs to be done first, before you get to watch TV.'

Limits on screen-time are a very personal thing. I know families who have no TV viewing at all during the week. My own view is that an hour a day on weekdays and two to three hours at the weekends is enough for this age group, and that it should come after (and is earned by doing) homework and other activities and responsibilities. I'd certainly be assessing whether the balance was right if my tween was in front of a screen for more than fourteen hours a week.

Crissy says: Computers, games, mobile phones and televisions can enhance and inform our children's lives, both educationally and socially. The key has to be moderation. If your tween is isolating herself, spending more time online than in the company of family and friends, or lying in front of the telly all evening rather than being active, then the balance is out of kilter and needs to be addressed. Time spent in this virtual world is time taken away from real human interaction, relationships and experiences, so by all means allow your tween to embrace technology, but don't let it be to the exclusion of everything and everyone else.

When setting ground-rules for our tweens, most of us could still benefit from taking a long hard look at our own leisure habits before we start laying down the law. Of course, I'm not suggesting parents should abide by the same rules they set for their tweens, but there's a definite whiff of hypocrisy in the air when we limit our tweens' screen-time, only to be found glued to the Xbox, Facebook, mobiles and trash television ourselves every evening.

Tweens and the internet

It's hard to imagine a time without the web: the internet is so much a part of all our lives now. Like many among our generation, you might feel a bit awestruck by how vast, multi-faceted and fast-moving it all is. But today's young people have grown up with it. For them, the internet is simply the main channel through which they can express themselves and communicate, and a one-stop shop for much of their entertainment and information needs.

For all its wonders, the internet does hold a great many potential worries for parents. Perhaps the most obvious one is that your tween will access websites – knowingly or otherwise – with inappropriate content. There are millions of destinations out there in cyberspace, accessible with just a few clicks of the mouse, and a great many of them are unsuitable for kids. No loving parent wants their tween to access porn online, for instance, particularly since it's so often extreme, degrading or violent: in other words, a view of sex you simply wouldn't want your child to see and imagine to be 'normal'. Other sites out there contain violent images, extremes of political or other opinions, and even 'instructional' videos that offer lessons in making bombs, concealing anorexia, committing suicide, or taking illegal drugs.

Thanks to the booming business of social networking, online gaming and interactive communities, the internet offers your tween many different ways of communicating with others. Used responsibly, they can be lots of fun and a great boon for friendship. But unfortunately they can also expose a child to contact with just about anyone.

On top of all that you have the risks of technical nasties such as viruses, the legal minefield that is downloading, inaccurate content, rampant commercialism, and all sorts of privacy issues to contend with.

In spite of such major worries, though, your best bet is to be positive about the internet. It is, after all, a pretty amazing resource. And besides, if you give the impression that you're neurotic and fearful about it, you may just give your tween a reason to set about finding out why.

How you can help

Practically speaking, there are many ways in which you can tap into technology in order to filter and restrict content, or to monitor your tween's internet use. Some are simple, and free. For example, most search engines will allow you to adjust settings so that searches are filtered, and there are child-friendly search engines such as www.yahooligans. com and www.askkids.com where filtering of unsuitable material is automatic. Your browser and operating system may also have parental control settings available, and it's always worth checking on individual sites and services, too. There's a huge range of commercially available software programmes to choose from. When you're buying one, look for the Child Safety Online kitemark logo for reassurance that it's a reliable product.

You may find it hard to get your head round the technological know-how required to make the internet a safer place for your tween. If you're struggling, take some time to read and research the matter. The website Getnetwise is a great place to start.

However, the bottom line is that all the parental-control software and filtering tools in the world will not give your tween complete protection: it's impossible to be comprehensive, and besides, she may be canny enough to defeat them. So, alongside whatever technical measures you put into place, you also need to employ good old-fashioned parental interest. It's best to always be physically nearby when a tween's on the internet. If you're 'shoulder surfing' – in other words, hovering never very far away, she simply won't get a chance to access something unsuitable, or at least, not for long.

With that in mind, the best place to locate the computer your tween uses is in the dining room or some other downstairs family space. If more than one family member needs to use the computer at the same time, or if she's pushing you for her own laptop because several of her friends have one, think carefully before you give in. Once your tween becomes a teen, the chances are you'll have to concede on this rule – but for now, it's a good one to stick with.

Of course, the internet is everywhere these days, so even if you put protective measures in place and keep a careful eye on your home PC, you still have to consider the possibility that your tween will find other ways to log on, whether it's via a mobile device like a phone or a games console, or on someone else's computer. You will probably have to accept that sometimes, you simply can't be there when your tween is in cyber-space – and that's why you also need to do everything you can to educate her, talk to her, and trust her.

Even if she isn't actually looking for it, it's quite possible your child will stumble upon something you'd rather she didn't while surfing the net. So bear that in mind if you catch her in front of something inappro-priate, before jumping to conclusions. Being open about this possibility and chatting with her about what she should do if she comes across something that makes her feel uncomfortable is a good policy. Make it clear that she should be upfront and let you know if this happens, and you won't take away her internet privileges as a result, since fear of this sanction can often push kids to secrecy.

Try to share some of her enthusiasm for favourite sites and services, and spend some time surfing with her. If you're trying to find your way round the net yourself, ask for her help in doing so. Help her find and bookmark her favourite websites. You might have a rule that she's only allowed to add something to her bookmarked list if you've given it the nod, first. You could also look together at an age-appropriate website aimed at informing youngsters about internet risk, such as Childnet International's Kidsmart, or ThinkUKnow, which was developed by the Child Exploitation and Online Protection Centre (CEOP).

Although you may not feel comfortable sneaking around behind your child's back, it's a good idea to keep an eye on her internet history. The same goes for checking out email and messaging inboxes and outboxes, and any profiles or pages she's got on social networking or other inter-active sites. Later on, when your tween becomes a teen and starts demanding more privacy, your entitlement to snoop becomes a greyer area. For now, it's in her interests that you do so. (Bear in mind, however, that it's not hard for a computer-savvy tween to hide or delete a browsing history, so it's by no means a foolproof way in itself of keeping tabs on her online experiences.)

Wise-up your tween to all the other potential pitfalls that a vulnerable internet user can fall prey to. Technical dangers such as viruses – malicious programmes that can cause a variety of problems – or spyware – which can be used to steal personal information from your computer – are spread in many ways, including through email attachments, instant messages, pop-ups, and downloads. Let your tween know that these things can lurk anywhere and teach her to be suspicious – instil the mantra, 'If in doubt, don't click!' Competitions, offers and all sorts of commercial lures are also extremely common, and these can be at best a nuisance and at worst, a con. Regularly remind your tween not to be tempted.

Another important message to pass on is that not everything on the internet is true. Help her to find authoritative sources when she needs them and to identify others that may not be so trustworthy. Although it's a fantastic resource for learning, don't let your tween get the internet to do all her homework for her! In particular, make sure she knows she can't just copy and paste chunks of text and pass it off as her own work. Apart from being cheating, there are copyright issues involved, which mean she could be breaking the law.

What the experts say

Elaine says: During the tween years, kids will still require supervision when they use the computer. Ideally it should be in a visible place in the home, ensuring it's a positive and open activity. Of course as they get older, they're more likely to access it in other ways, such as through mobile phones, and it then becomes impossible to monitor activity. Keep in mind that it's a fantastic resource: the hard part is to understand it, and help to teach our children to understand it. Certainly, one of the best things you can do as a parent is to educate yourself – get to know your way round all the sites she favours, and gain whatever technical knowledge you need to fix privacy settings, or install filter software.

One of the main worries is that tweens will come across images of a sexual nature online, boys in particular. Some good software protection will help ensure stuff of a really graphic nature is kept at bay, but it's not tween-proof, of course, and can only go so far, which means that the most important measure you can take is talking – about the benefits as well as the risks – and always keep communication open in order to promote an atmosphere of trust and respect.

If your tween does view such material, or indeed visit any site of which you don't approve, resist the temptation to deny internet usage but do sit down and reassess your rules. Removing PC rights as a punishment is likely to make her even more furtive about her use and then you won't be able to protect or educate her. In any case, even if she doesn't find unsuitable content for herself, it's quite possible it will be sent to her via her mobile phone, which you can do little about. So your best bet is to sit down and talk about it: was it clear that this was a site that was not allowed, or did you just assume that she would know? If the rule was clear then why did she want to access it? Empathise with her, and if possible acknowledge any reasonable intention of hers while still holding firm to your rule. It may be that she doesn't understand your concerns about this particular site, so you have to explain. Don't blame, but make clear your values for future reference. If she then *deliberately* goes against your rules and seeks out such material again, I think that removal of computer privileges for a time would be an appropriate consequence.

I also think it should be a rule that access to the internet is conditional upon you reviewing her history from time to time, knowing her passwords and being able to access her social networking profiles. It's not really about spying on your child, it's more about being familiar with what she likes to do on the computer and what she's accessing so that you can discuss it with her. As she gets older you'll need to step back a little, so make sure you've given her the ground rules and have built up trust. This means avoiding being judgemental, and praising descriptively any aspects of her screen use of which you approve.

Crissy says: Although your tween may be pestering for new freedoms, giving her too much responsibility for herself at this age may leave her feeling anxious and confused. Far from fostering a sense of autonomy, it might actually undermine her confidence and sense of independence. Tweens still need boundaries and the reassurance that you are waiting in the wings. Most lack the maturity and experience to self-supervise or regulate their computer activities and so although it's good to involve them in the decision-making process, ultimately the onus lies on parents to keep tweens safe on the internet. Simply put, the best way to do this is to monitor your tween's computer use.

Peer pressure inevitably means that by this age, your tween won't be quite so keen to tell you everything, so she needs to know that you're fully prepared to check her internet and chat histories, emails and texts at any time, and that if she breaks the house rules she'll lose her access. Be prepared to follow through on consequences, too. An empty threat carries no weight with your child. No matter how loud the protestations, it's still your job and a legal requirement for you to keep your tween safe. Work together to compile a list of approved sites, and agree who is and who isn't an acceptable email, IM or text pal. Then encourage your tween to come to you and ask if you'll sit with her if she wants to surf 'off-list'. That way she'll feel less restricted but she'll still be safe. Make sure she fully understands the dangers of internet use, and appreciate that you're doing this because you care and not as a punishment or because you don't trust her to make the right choices. But when and if you do decide to follow through and check up on your tween, do it with her rather than behind her back, which could leave her feeling spied on or betrayed.

As parents, we can at least minimise if not entirely avoid the vast majority of tween/parent conflict over the use or misuse of technology in the home by restricting computer and mobile use to common areas of the house. Of course this may not always be practical. Tweens need peace and quiet to do their homework and their bedroom may be the only option. Either way, showing you're interested and keeping the lines of communication open will hopefully mean that your tween will feel able to come to you for help should she run into trouble. Keeping the computer where it can be seen won't *necessarily* prevent your tween from breaking the rules – one way or another, curious tweens will often find a way. However, there's little doubt that they are more likely to stick to the rules when there's a risk of someone passing by and catching a glimpse over their shoulder.

What the netmums say

Screen time and computer use

My eldest two have a laptop and a PC between them. James uses a large number of search engines and sites for homework purposes, whilst Jake likes to play games or go on sites recommended by his teacher. Jake uses the laptop in the living room under my supervision, as there are no parental controls on it. The PC does have controls in place but I still like to sit with James whilst he's doing his homework. I need to override the controls sometimes and if this happens, I like to see what's on the site for it to have been blocked in the first place.
Claire, mum to five boys aged eleven, nine, six, five and one, and a girl, three

My oldest is twelve, and she loves using her laptop. She plays on a maths site that is for secondary schools, and pupils can play against other kids from all over the UK. She also plays an online role-playing game called *Guild Wars*: it's rated a '12', but she's been playing for three years now and I reckon it's good for her memory and maths skills. She also plays puzzles online, and has a Facebook account that she uses to play *Bejeweled Blitz*. Overall she has about sixty to ninety minutes per day online, as she's normally out after school playing football or netball, and this is her 'downtime' when she gets home. But she can't use the laptop until homework is done.

Naomi, mum to two girls aged twelve and five

We have a rule that there's no computer time an hour before bed so they can start to wind down. We also try and have one or two computer-free days a week, although admittedly this is getting more difficult as they get older.

Hayley, mum to a girl, sixteen, and a boy, thirteen

At home, my boys use the computer in my room. It's got controls set up on it so their access is limited to suitable sites. They tend to download music, look at funny clips on YouTube, and go on social networking pages where they communicate with their friends. They also use the internet at the public library sometimes and although I can't see what they're doing then, I trust them. I think the internet is a positive thing as long as it's used correctly. I guess there will always be people who will abuse it to their advantage and, as parents, it's our responsibility to teach our children about these dangers.

Caroline, mum to two boys aged twelve and eleven

Our children's computer use was beginning to get a bit out of hand, and overall screen-time was clocking up to quite a bit beyond two hours on some days, even in the week. We knew it was a habit that would be hard to break, so we tried to adjust it gradually, and we also made a big effort to offer something else as an alternative instead – for instance, we took to playing cards and had 'Gin Rummy' tournaments instead, which they loved. They still love their screen-time, of course, but we've got it down to two hours or less a day, which we're relieved about.

Rebecca, mum to two boys aged thirteen and eleven, and a girl, eight

I think the internet is a hugely positive thing, and really helps the kids with their learning. In particular, they know that not everything they read on it is correct, or that it may be just a theory or opinion. It's a great lesson in critical thinking – is the source reliable? I keep a vague eye on their browsing history but kids now are very savvy, and it's not hard to delete your history. All three boys have their own computer in their rooms, networked to one main computer downstairs. We did this for each of them as they started secondary school, as they do have a lot of homework that needs to be done on the computer or researched on the net. I also use the computer for work in the evening, so the logistics of the four of us fighting for time would be difficult.
Jo, mum to three boys aged seventeen, fourteen and eleven

Both boys head straight for the computer as soon as they get up in the morning. They get up about half an hour to an hour before us, and as long as they keep the volume down low and turn it off as soon as we say so, they are allowed to play. They don't always choose to do so, of course, it's just one of many activities they enjoy. Sometimes if the weather is bad after school or on a weekend they're allowed to go on the computer then, too. We try to limit it to about an hour before turning it off for a break of at least that long – by which time they've usually found something else to capture their interest anyway.
Lynn, mum to two boys aged nine and seven

Even though I feel really alarmed about what's out there on the internet, I try not to let my oldest daughter know it. She's only nine and has only just begun to explore the delights of cyberspace, and so far it's all innocent fun, which I'm happy to encourage. Recently we went through a phase of watching old episodes of *Paddington* on YouTube together, which I remember from my own childhood and which they all thought was brilliant! We have heeded all the advice, though, and the family PC is in the den – it's going to stay there, too.
Shelley, mum to three girls aged nine, six and two

Email and instant messaging

Your tween will probably want to use the internet to keep in touch with her friends and maybe family members (including you) via email or instant messaging. These modern methods of online communication provide free and speedy ways for her to have virtual chats with pals, and to share links, files and pictures. Again, there are great positives to these things – email can be a particularly handy way for your tween to make contact and share photos with her grandparents, for example, and instant messaging is a useful medium for consultation on school or social matters, without the worry of telephone bills.

It's easy enough to set up a free email account for your tween through a provider such as Hotmail or Yahoo. If you do set up an account for her, remember not to use her real name or any other personal details in the address. Better still, set up a general email account that the rest of the family can use, too, which will make it easier for you to monitor.

Having an email account means there's the risk of a variety of unwanted mail in her inbox. This might contain unkind or bullying messages (for more on cyber-bullying, see Chapter 3); unsuitable spam or junk; marketing ploys; or viruses and other security risks such as phishing (when an email that looks as if it's been sent from a genuine source asks for password or account details, leaving the user open to identity theft). As with internet usage, there are technology-based ways to add protection, including parental controls, spam-blockers and anti-virus software. But being there when she's emailing, educating your tween about the potential pitfalls and having a few basic rules in place is more important still. An agreement that she never opens a mail if she doesn't recognise the sender, and that she checks with you before opening any attachment, makes sense. Check her inbox regularly: be open about this, as you may lose her trust if you do it behind her back. And make sure that everyone in her address book is someone she knows well – help her set up an address book with a limited number of contacts, all approved by you. Her email address is something that she should be very careful about sharing. Make sure she never gives it to anyone, either online or otherwise, without checking with you first.

Similar rules apply to her use of instant messaging. These services, which allow her to chat in real-time with friends who also subscribe, include Skype, MSN, Yahoo! Messenger and Google Chat, and are usually free to sign up, without age restriction. Unfortunately, they can provide a portal for cyber-bullying and, sometimes, online predators. So, stick around whenever your tween is instant messaging; and drum into her the importance of getting your attention and help should she need it. Like email, instant messaging (IM) can also be used to spread viruses, so make sure she knows never to click on a link, or to open or download a file that she wasn't expecting, or which has been sent by someone she doesn't recognise. There should also be some helpful tools and settings on any IM service, such as ways to block someone she no longer wants to talk to.

Online socialising

The possibilities for communication and expression via the online world of social networking, virtual communities, blogging and interactive sites are endless. If your tween hasn't already begun to discover some of them, she probably will soon. As with all other sorts of digital entertainment and communication, it's massively popular and it's here to stay. So it's something we need to embrace as parents, whilst being informed about the risks, and keeping a protective eye on things.

You'll have heard of many of the social networking sites that are currently popular – you're very likely to belong to one or other yourself. Sites like Facebook, MySpace and Bebo typically allow users to set up a 'profile', communicate in real-time with friends, and post or share thoughts, messages, pictures, links and files. All of these (among others) have an age restriction of thirteen or more. However, this doesn't stop many tweens from using a false birthdate to register, with or without their parents' permission. There are also plenty of other interactive sites out there that are specifically aimed at younger users. Most are based around virtual activities and games but often they also offer opportunities to make online friends and chat – examples are Club Penguin, Moshi Monsters, Webkinz and Habbo Hotel. Gaming sites are also popular with many tweens, and virtual interaction between users is normal on most of these.

There are a number of worries about excessive social networking habits. Because it's easy to stay anonymous and create a persona that's not real, these sorts of sites can be hotbeds for unpleasantness. They're also likely to increase the risk of your tween being exposed to inappropriate chat or to content from elsewhere on the web, accessed through files or links from other people. And there are fears that too much time devoted to online relationships could come at the expense of 'real' relationships. There's even a theory that too much social networking could cause changes to the brain that could shorten attention spans and affect understanding and communication skills. It all sounds pretty worrying, but with a little attention paid to some basic rules, you shouldn't need to be concerned.

What you can do

Social networking age limits are there for a reason, so you'd be well advised to insist your tween pay heed to them, even if peer pressure to sign up is strong. Stand firm if it's important to you. If you do allow your tween to register underage, make sure you know exactly how the site or service works, and set out your conditions for agreeing to it: for instance, you might want to insist that you're always sitting next to her when she's online. Make sure you know her password and regularly access her profile page or files to keep an eye on all goings-on. Rather than making secret checks though, encourage openness, and try to get your tween herself to show you what she's been up to. Better still, sign up as a 'friend', too, or suggest you sign up together, as a family. Find out how the privacy features work – these will usually restrict who can access a user's account or profile – and ensure they're set. Rather than taking over when it comes to exploring privacy and help tools, it's a good idea to discuss them with your tween, and look into it together: that way, she'll know all about ways to protect herself when the time comes for her to use the internet independently. Make sure she knows how important it is, for her safety's sake, not to post personal details. She should always use a 'handle' or nickname rather than her real name.

Where sites aimed at younger users are concerned, don't make assumptions that these are 'safer' places because they require parental consent and boast tighter rules, moderation and approval processes for messages or chat. They'll still need checking out, and your tween will still need careful monitoring whilst using them: predators can and do infiltrate chat areas on these sites. However, they're probably a good place to start and, alongside education and guidance from you, they could help her develop good online behavioural habits that will stand her in good stead when she does move on to something a bit more sophisticated.

It's also worth being aware of the hidden costs that are sometimes involved. Social networking and interactive sites or online communities are usually free to sign up to, but in some cases there are extra features that come at a price. Make sure your tween knows she needs your permission before signing up for any.

Whilst social networking – used safely and closely monitored – can be a fun element of a tween's social life, it would be pretty tragic if a child's only outlet for friendships and socialising was virtual. Do make sure your tween gets plenty of real-life fun and face-to-face contact with her pals, too.

What the experts say

Elaine says: The idea that our tweens are making friends and keeping friends over the internet is worrying to me. Whether it's strangers or friends in chat rooms, both situations have the potential for danger. And when they're online, tweens may take on different personas that bear no relation to their real characters. I don't buy into the notion that we have to just accept it because it's simply modern life. I think we need to be very alarmed if our children aren't having much real interaction with other children. We need to educate them to pick up the phone and talk to people sometimes – and by that I mean the landline, not their mobile, since we can't be certain there aren't health risks in that. We need to be very vigilant that they're maintaining old-style friendships, too, by encouraging play dates and sleepovers, and getting them involved in groups outside school. There's got to be a good balance.

Crissy says: Like it or not, texting, social networking and instant messaging will almost certainly begin to appeal at some point during the tween years – cyber friendship is here to stay, and your child won't want to be left out of the loop. What's important is that these technology-based 'virtual' relationships co-exist with, rather than replace, real person-to-person, face-to-face communication. It's very much a question of balance. It's fine to hook up with your mates online now and then but it's always preferable to meet up face-to-face rather than sitting glued to the screen all evening. Everything in moderation makes a good mantra here. Of course there are also safety issues to bear in mind. It's fine to check out your tween's address books and limit who she can talk to and for how long, but make sure you negotiate and agree these ground rules in advance so she doesn't feel spied on. Show your tween that you respect her opinions. Take time to discuss the potential hazards of social networking and the risks of cyber bullying and always make it clear that you're just trying to keep her safe and not ruin her fun.

What the netmums say

Social lives online

Recently, Sam has asked to join Facebook. Apparently 'all' of his friends use it to chat after school. I'm on Facebook myself, so we used my account to search for them. In fact, only two were actually on there. We agreed there was no point him joining, but that we'd check again in a few months to see if there were enough of his friends to make it worthwhile. I'm hoping that it won't be for a long time yet, but if it's sooner rather than later, I will seriously consider letting him join as promised.

Anna, mum to a boy, nine, and a girl, six

My eldest son plays an online game called *SlashScape*, and he's on MSN and Facebook a lot, talking to his friends. I am on Facebook, too, so I can see what he's up to. He has his own laptop but he's only allowed to use it downstairs. There are no parental controls on it as I haven't felt the need to put any on – however, he knows that if he pushes the boundaries I will put them on. The same rule applies to my nine-year-old, although he doesn't have a laptop of his own.

Andrea, mum to two boys aged thirteen and nine, and a girl, two

I've connected my daughter's laptop to my own PC, which means she can't get online without me knowing about it. She had an account on a social networking site, but it caused problems after she logged into her account in someone else's house one day. Some other girls then accessed it and changed all her personal details, then wrote some very nasty things. They also sent unpleasant emails to other people from her account. It caused a lot of problems. So when she then wanted a Facebook page I said yes on the provision that no one from school gets added, only family and a few friends who don't live in this area. I have the password to the account and she knows if she starts adding unsuitable applications the account is gone. She knows what is and isn't suitable for her, as I've made it crystal clear.

Naomi, mum to two girls aged twelve and five

The only website my daughters have really got into so far is an interactive pet website. It seemed cute and age-appropriate, so I was happy for them to sign up. Then I took a look around the chat forum one day and realised there were some fairly dodgy postings there, asking about boyfriends and dating. I was immediately suspicious – why the moderator hadn't jumped in, I'm not sure. Online chat isn't something my daughters have discovered and they don't even know the forums are there, but even so, it brought home the risks to me. So even if they're only playing an innocent little game, I plan to always be around when they're online.

Julia, mum to two girls aged nine and six

My daughter uses the family PC, but she wants a netbook of her own for Christmas this year. She's been using MSN for a couple of years now, but only as a way of talking to family members, and always with me or her dad around. We let her join Facebook this year, and she does go on it quite a lot, usually only for a few minutes at a time. Her dad and I are both on her friends list, and we know her password and make sure that she always checks with us first before confirming any 'friend' requests. For the internet generally, I use parental controls to block unsuitable sites and, as it's the family computer, we're able to keep quite a close eye on what she does on there. If she does get her own netbook, I think I'll put more restrictions on it to control her browsing. Not that I don't trust her, but inappropriate things can pop up on the internet, even when you don't want them to.

Suzie, mum to two girls aged twelve and seven

Our PC is in our lounge so whenever my son is on it I have a clear view of what he is doing. He uses the internet to play Club Penguin, and I've also allowed him to browse Amazon, to put things on his wish list. Club Penguin has a social networking side to it, and up until last week he was only allowed to use safe chat, where you can pick from a range of things to say to another penguin, but last week I switched it to free chat so that he can say what he likes. The site is monitored and I tend to talk to him constantly – or rather, he talks to me – about what he's doing. He's learnt from school, as well as us, that he must not give out details online.

Mel, mum to two boys aged nine and two, and a girl, six

Carl, my eldest, plays a lot of online games. He joined in one once but must have been the least experienced, because some of the other players were unkind about his lack of speed and skill, and asked him to leave the game. Carl turned to me and asked what he should do. I asked him if people in the park were saying nasty things like that, what would he do? He replied that he'd either ignore them, or find someone else to play with. In the end, he just closed the game and played something else. By letting him experience this and helping him decide for himself how to deal with it, I feel that when something similar crops up (as I'm sure it will sooner or later), he'll have a good idea of what to do whether I'm there or not.

Menna, mum to two boys aged ten and seven, and a girl, two

I'm sticking to my guns with my eleven-year-old, who's not allowed a Facebook account until he's thirteen. It's caused a few debates, as his older brothers use it, but I've pointed out that he has his mobile for sorting his social life. I trust him not to just sign up behind my back!

Jo, mum to three boys aged seventeen, fourteen and eleven

My son uses the internet to talk to his friends either via Facebook or MSN. Personally I think it's a positive thing. He has contact with his friends, and he's learning new technology while having fun. There's a fine line between protecting your child and invading their privacy, and it's a hard balance to find. I've always told him that if he wouldn't talk to a stranger in the street, don't do it on the internet. He knows there are some dodgy people out there.

Ali, mum to a girl, eighteen, and a boy, eleven

Protection from online predators

Whilst it's not a danger of which we should be disproportionately fearful, the unsavoury fact is that online predators *are* out there in cyberspace. It provides a good place for them to hide, because of the anonymity of the medium, which allows them to lie and pretend to be people they are not. They may then chat with and 'befriend' youngsters, and extract personal information or photographs, for their own – and other predators' – sexual gratification. Ultimately, this contact can amount to 'grooming': in other words, building up enough trust to secure an actual meeting with a child. Although the risks of a situation going that far are low, our tweens need our protection, education and guidance to avoid becoming victims and, just as parents always warned children about 'stranger danger', we need to make them well aware of the risks of being approached by strangers on the internet. It's therefore important to have some basic rules in place – you might want to include them on your computer-use 'contract' if you have one. For example:

- The computer stays in a family room. Surfing in secret is not on: you reserve the right to 'shoulder surf' when she's online.
- Everyone she communicates with online should be someone that's (well) known to her. All requests for 'friends' should go through you.
- Keep personal information private: never post or give out details such as name, email or home address, password or school.
- If anyone gets in touch and asks her uncomfortable questions, she must tell you immediately.
- She must never, ever agree to meet anyone in person that she's met via an electronic source.

You should print off evidence of any illegal or inappropriate online approaches, and let the police know, or better still, report the matter direct to CEOP, the Child Exploitation and Online Protection Centre. Many sites now have a direct button that allows users to report abuse directly to CEOP: it has a clear red logo, with the phrase 'ClickCeop' on it.

What the experts say

Crissy says: In teaching your tween about staying safe online, the key is to keep things in perspective. These days few of us, your tween included, could get by without the internet. Indeed by secondary-school age, tweens without access to a computer may find themselves seriously disadvantaged in academic terms. So whilst we want to make our tweens aware of the dangers it's important not to overreact. Most parents' worst nightmare would be for their child to be targeted online by a predatory adult. Whilst it's important to stress that this is rare, it's equally vital that tweens are aware that stranger danger is as much of an issue online as on the street. The anonymity that the internet affords its users means that tweens can never be sure who they are actually talking to. Kids of this age often feel invincible and may tune out your warnings, believing they would never be fooled, so stand firm with your boundaries. You don't want to scare the life out of her, but it's vital you make absolutely sure that your tween knows the golden rules.

Elaine says: As parents of children in the twenty-first century, one of our main fears is that a crime will be committed against them because they are in danger from strangers. But what we really need to worry about is safety in the home, as ironically it is new technology used right under our noses that leaves them potentially more exposed to danger. It's critical that we equip ourselves and our children with the right information and skills so that they can protect themselves online. Try to ensure that their internet use is a positive and open activity, take an interest in the places and the people they come into contact with, and prevent any sense of secrecy and guilt that could be exploited by paedophiles.

Too much information?

There's no limit to what can be posted online these days in terms of information, thoughts, images and videos, via social networking services, blogs, and many other interactive sites such as YouTube. However, there are security and privacy issues involved in exposing your life to all-comers in cyberspace that we need to outline carefully to our tweens because, in many cases, it's just not a good idea to do so. Personal information and pictures can be exploited by predators or cyber-bullies, but not only that, it's horribly easy to post something you later feel embarrassed or regretful about, whether it's a photograph or a simple comment. Do make sure you talk to your tween about this possibility and urge her to always stop and think carefully before posting. Ask her whether she'd be happy for anyone to see it: she may be a good few years off worrying about prospective employers, but what about teachers, relatives, or her friends and their parents? Discuss with her what might constitute unsuitable, offensive, unkind, inappropriate or even illegal material.

When it comes to photographs, remind your tween that once a picture is posted, it could be copied or posted elsewhere, so even if she decides to remove it later on, it could still be online and accessible for anyone to view long into the future. It might be a good idea to have a clear rule about downloading photographs. Perhaps she needs to double-check with you – and anyone else who happens to be in the picture – before posting any image online?

Downloading and file-sharing

Among the many opportunities available to us on the web these days is a vast range of music and other entertainment, as well as software and documents that can be downloaded or streamed – sometimes free, sometimes for a cost. However, in many cases this content is copyrighted, and to download without permission, or paying, is illegal. Industries affected by illegal downloading are cracking down now, and if your tween does this, you could in theory be fined or sued as a consequence. Peer-to-peer file-sharing is another area of internet use that your tween may want to explore – this is when data that's been uploaded or downloaded is made available to other users – but it's risky for a number of reasons. File-sharing can put your computer at high risk of viruses and spyware, and also theft of personal information, as it allows others to view files on your computer. Some file-sharing sites also have chat opportunities, which means there's a risk of stranger contact, and it's also very easy to unwittingly download inappropriate content because a lot of illegal files are deliberately misnamed – and content filters aren't always effective in filtering the content that comes through file-sharing. Not only that, but sharing copyrighted material is illegal.

Your best bet with a child of this age is to select, together, a handful of sites that you know to be legal and to put them on her bookmarks, making it clear that she cannot download content from anywhere else. Talk to your tween about the importance of staying legal: quite apart from the possibility of being prosecuted, copyright laws are there for a reason, to make sure that people who've contributed are paid fairly for their work. Fortunately, there are masses of legal services on the web, so there really should be no need to download illegally. There are a couple of useful websites that list legal sites that you can use as a reference. There's lots more detailed information about this complex subject on the website of Childnet International. Details are given in the back of the book.

Playing the game

If your tween is gaming mad, she's not alone. And if it bothers you, *you're* not alone. Electronic and online games are massively popular with the tweens of today – it's a cultural swing we simply have to get to grips with. On the plus side, gaming requires a range of skills that includes concentration, hand-eye coordination, physical and mental agility, imagination, logic, maths and teamwork – so it's definitely not all bad news. However, none of us needs telling that too much gaming isn't great. As well as potential physical problems such as repetitive strain injury, eye strain, headaches and even seizures, there's a fear that gamers who refuse to put their handsets down will become anti-social, uncommunicative and sofa-bound. Some parents even fear it's an addiction.

What's in the box?

There's a lot of debate about whether violent games cause kids to be aggressive, but the evidence is inconclusive. Regardless, few parents of a tween-aged child would want them to be exposed to extreme violence, horror, swearing or sex via something that's supposed to be fun.

There's no excuse for not knowing whether a game is suitable for your tween or not: all games are given an age-related classification, either through the PEGI (Pan European Game Information) system, which rates games as '3+', '7+', '12+', '16+' and '18+', as well as a more specific symbols which indicate exactly what the content is. In the case of games with sensitive content, BBFC (British Board of Film Classification) ratings are given: as with movies and DVDs, these are either 'U', 'PG', '12', '15' or '18'. Some games are certified by both bodies.

If you do decide to allow your tween to play a game with a rating beyond her actual age, check it out yourself first. Everyone's got different ideas as to what's suitable and what isn't for their kids: maybe you don't mind so much about mild swearing, or maybe you think they can handle a bit of moderate horror. You could also check out a few online reviews, so you know what to expect.

Most modern consoles have settings that restrict access to certain games and functions. If you think it's possible your tween will go behind your back and play a game you've forbidden, you could take a look at these. But as with everything else, your best bet is to make sure you're never far away when you're tween's gaming – that way, you can see for yourself whether she's playing something suitable or not. Inevitably, you can't be there to monitor things when she's at a friend's house: there's probably not a lot of point getting heated about it if you suspect she's being exposed to unsuitable games elsewhere, but if you're really bothered, have a quiet word with the friend's parents – and stick to your guns in your own home. If it turns out she's played something inappropriate and it's worried her, avoid getting cross and make sure she knows you're available to talk it through, helping her put it into context by separating fantasy from reality if need be.

As with computer use, it's a good idea to write down an agreed 'contract' regarding any time limits or guidelines you're keen to stick to in your house. Since gaming can be physically intensive, it's really important to take regular breaks – fifteen minutes in every hour is what's widely recommended. You'll find a helpful template for a suitable contract on the website GetGameSmart. Make sure your tween plays in a well-lit room and doesn't get too close to the screen, and that the settings are neither too dark nor too light. Encourage her to take up a relaxed posture and to use a seat that gives her back good support. Don't let her play if she's tired, and make sure games are turned off well before bedtime to give your tween's brain a chance to slow down in readiness for sleep.

If you can't beat your kids when it comes to gaming, try to join them sometimes. When investing in a console, a sensible idea is to buy one for the whole family's use, and then pick some games that everyone can enjoy. Getting together on a Saturday night for an evening of digital entertainment means console-time is shared, and you can broaden horizons a bit by suggesting some tie-in activities: designing and creating a poster to keep scores on, for example, or whipping up some healthy snacks for fuel (and yes, experts tend to advise against snacking in front of the screen: but as an occasional treat for the whole family, it's not going to cause any harm).

What the netmums say

Tweens who love gaming

My son is a huge gamer, and I have many concerns about it. In particular, I hate how worked up he gets while playing. He likes mystery, fighting and monster games, but he will honestly play anything. He spends all his pocket money buying new games, which are ridiculously expensive. On cold days, he plays online with his friend who lives opposite us, rather than going out. He even tries to justify his time playing games as socialising, as all his friends are online too. I would hate him to be talking to just anyone, so we monitor which friends he's playing with, and he can't add people without asking us. Another thing that really angers me is that with every game there always seems to be some sort of add-on or extra that needs to be purchased, or you can play for free to a certain level, and then have to pay to go further. It's such a rip-off! Last year, we bought a Wii for the lounge so we could play as a family, even though we're not big gamers ourselves. Because of my concerns, we have rules in place. He can't go on until his homework and chores are done, and must be off an hour before bedtime. He does play out and takes part in some after-school activities, so he's not on for too long during the week. Weekends and holidays it's harder to get him off. I once caught him playing before he had even come downstairs to say good morning.

Kirsty, mum to two boys aged thirteen and nine months

Both my eldest boys have games consoles: James has a Play-Station Portable, and Jake a DSi. They enjoy a wide variety of games. I've put a limit of age twelve on the games I allow Jake to play, and fifteen on James, but even then I always have a go on the game myself first, to check suitability. They're allowed forty-five minutes on their consoles before they need to have a fifteen-minute minimum break from them. I usually make them use the time to do a chore!

Claire, mum to five boys aged eleven, nine, six, five and one, and a girl, three

We have a Wii, an Xbox, and an old PS2 dying somewhere in a box, but my older two have never really been that interested in them. The youngest enjoys the games consoles more but I've never had to limit time on it, so far – in fact, there are usually natural limitations because after a certain point it will be dinner time, or time to go to athletics or baseball. Also, the Xbox is on the TV in the front room, and there's a definite limit to how much his dad and I are prepared to put up with watching. Fortunately, when he's asked to finish, he does. Even on occasions when he does get a longer chance to play, he's never on it for more than an hour at a time, probably because he's a naturally fidgety child! All three of my boys play a lot of sport, so I wouldn't worry about them sitting and chilling with a computer game sometimes.

Jo, mum to three boys aged seventeen, fourteen and eleven

My son's outside most of the summer, but in the winter he would happily sit on his Xbox for twelve hours a day if I let him. I do place strict restrictions on him, and make him sit in the lounge sometimes, and spend time with us as a family. I always make him do something else after two hours on the console at weekends – if he moans and whines about this, I just ignore it. I've also stopped him going on the computer after school. He was coming in, running upstairs and turning it straight on until I put a stop to it. I now make him come home, have a bath, do his homework and sit with us and eat and chat. He's then allowed up to one hour on the computer.

Natalie, mum to a boy, ten, and a girl, two

As a family we have a Wii, but it was bought as a gift to *me*, so that they have to ask me for permission to use it, and as a result it's nearly always a family affair. My husband and I decided on a Wii over any of the other consoles because of the physical nature of many of the games . . . believe me, some of them give you a real workout! There are also many games where teamwork is essential, and it's been fascinating to see how they've learnt to interact with each other in order to complete goals or quests. They also each have a handheld console, but they're mainly used in the car to pass the time on long journeys.

Bethan, mum to two boys aged twelve and ten

I hate the fact that my nine-year-old is so obsessed with his computer games. We have a set rota for him so he knows when he can go on and when he can't, and this rota gives him an hour a day split over two sessions. He's also allowed his DS in the morning, once he's completely ready for school. However, he'll often ask for extra time and sometimes he pesters me so much when I'm busy or distracted that I give in. We created the rota because beforehand, he was switching on his DS the second he walked through the door after school, and would be gaming until bedtime. It got to the stage where he was wolfing down his food to get back to a computer, and he stopped wanting to go to his tae kwondo class. Both the PC and the Wii are in the lounge so I monitor what he plays, and it's only ever age-appropriate games. But if something happens to take his computer time, he gets really grumpy.

Mel, mum to two boys aged nine and two, and a girl, six

The small screen

Before computers, games and mobile phones became the main focus of parents concerned about screen-time, there was television. Now, the box is just one form of modern media among a whole load that we need to keep tabs on.

Most tweens become keen to start exploring the telly schedules beyond what's on CBBC or CITV, and naturally their bedtimes become later, so programmes such as soaps and comedies start to have a pull. That can mean a need for vigilance about the content in some cases – but this is yet another matter for individual parents to weigh up. Broadly speaking, nothing screened before the 9 p.m. watershed should cause any major offence, but that doesn't mean your tween won't be exposed to all sorts of adult themes before then, so vet anything you're not sure about in advance. With so many digital channels and view-on-demand services, it's a harder job these days for parents to monitor their tweens' telly consumption. Keep control of the remote, and agree in advance what's on her viewing schedule – in writing if need be.

DVDs are easier to assess because they all have a BBFC certificate and these days that also includes a brief summary of content. But even so, it's down to you to decide what your tween watches, according to your own values, and also perhaps, how mature your tween is. Maybe you'll feel a '12' certificate still isn't really appropriate for your ten- or eleven-year-old, or maybe you think your thirteen-year-old is not going to be fazed by a little adult language in a movie that's rated '15'. If in any doubt, watch it beforehand.

Aim to sit down and watch the telly with your tween whenever possible. As well as being a fun thing to do together, it means you can also chat about what you're viewing, which will enhance what she gets out of it and also gives you a chance to discuss any issues that worry or confuse her. In fact, lots of parents feel this is a good way of tackling thorny subjects that might not otherwise come up in the conversation.

As with all other modern media, it helps to see the positive side of things. Curling up in front of the television for a while is – as any adult will tell you – a great way to relax and unwind, which is something every busy tween needs to do regularly. And television programmes of all types can be a brilliant resource for learning – not just via the more obvious sources of general knowledge like factual TV, quiz shows, documentaries and the news, but also from soaps, dramas and comedies too, from which there's much to be gained in terms of social development, language skills and critical thinking.

Turn-ons and turn-offs: Some telly time guidelines

- Have clear, set 'television times'. It shouldn't just be on in the background. Get to know the telly schedules and when your tween's favourite programmes are on. Look at the TV guide together in advance and agree what she can watch and when, factoring in any other stuff she needs to get done either before or afterwards, or other scheduled events such as dinner.
- Don't ask her to switch off midway through a programme she's enjoying. (How annoyed would you be if someone told you to turn off your favourite soap fifteen minutes before the end?)
- Give descriptive praise when she does turn off.
- Try to avoid eating in front of the telly. The occasional TV dinner won't harm, but it's healthier all round if there's a rule about screens being off in good time for tea. Snacking in front of the telly isn't generally recommended by experts – however it can be a useful way to get some nutritious nibbles down her while she's distracted!
- Consider a 'no telly on a school morning' policy. Time is usually pressed then and once it's gone on, it can be hard to get it off.

- As with computers, it's a good idea to make sure televisions are turned off with plenty of time to spare before bedtime, to allow brains to wind down and relax in preparation for good sleep.
- Think carefully before allowing your tween to have a television in the bedroom. All the experts agree it's not a good idea.

What the experts say

Crissy says: There's been much discussion in recent years as to whether watching violent material (online, via games or on the box) influences our tweens' behaviour. In my personal experience, tweens are generally capable of differentiating between fantasy and real-life violence, but to be safe, talk to her if she's been exposed to something that bothers you. Make sure she understands that real people don't bounce back if they're hurt. Try to instil a sense of respect for others in your child and an awareness that violence is not the way to settle disputes. If you find certain material distasteful, trust your own judgement and try not to be swayed by your tween's assertion that she's the 'only' child on the planet not playing that particular game or watching '12'- or '15'-rated movies. Certificates exist for a reason and a little research on your part will often reveal whether you feel a game, programme or film is age-appropriate or not.

Elaine says: I think it's important to review film and game ratings, and to be aware of the TV watershed. I personally don't, for instance, think tweens should watch anything with a '15' certificate, which may contain scenes of a sexually graphic nature, violence, swearing or other adult themes, and I would recommend sticking with the age limits the film censors suggest. I can remember my daughter complaining about not being able to watch *EastEnders* as all her friends watched it and she'd have nothing to talk to them about the next day! I empathised, but stuck to our rule and explained why. My children thought I was entirely unreasonable for denying them access to *The Simpsons* when they were very young. I just didn't think it offered them the values I wanted them to absorb around family life. They seem to have survived the deprivation.

What the netmums say

Small-screen habits

With Jake still having an eight o'clock bedtime, he's in bed before the television watershed. Even so, there have still been times when he's been watching and references to drugs, sex or alcohol have come up, so we've used it as an opportunity to discuss those things. He understands I won't let him watch anything more than moderate violence, as I just don't think it's a good thing for young children to see. James' bedtime is 9 p.m., which means he gets to see a little more, although it's still pre-watershed.
Claire, mum to five boys aged eleven, nine, six, five and one, and a girl, three

Even though my boys have computers in their bedrooms, I firmly believe they shouldn't have television in there. I think that watching television should be a social thing, and is a great way to teach us all to negotiate and share. So we have a TV in the main room and also one in another room downstairs, so there are other options if people really want to watch two different things at once – although I can't really remember the last time that happened. I hate the thought of the kids shutting themselves away in their rooms and spending their evening alone watching who knows what. Now and again I have to grit my teeth and sit through something I hate with Kester. On the plus side, there are plenty of things we both enjoy!
Jo, mum to three boys aged seventeen, fourteen and eleven

Kevin is a bit of a geek when it comes to TV. He loves the Discovery network and the History Channel and has picked up all sorts of random bits of information from watching documentaries. He's not interested in anything else. It's almost become a study aid.
Kirsty, mum to two boys aged thirteen and nine months

I've never imposed a rule of turning the television off or allowing only certain screen times, as I don't feel I've needed to. They would both prefer to do other things than watch TV most of the time. My son mainly loves to watch sport, such as football and wrestling. He also still watches the Disney Channel too and likes to watch films when he gets the chance. They both love *The X Factor*!
Angela, mum to a girl, fourteen, and a boy, eleven

My daughter has always been more interested in adult 'sitcom' and soap-opera-type programmes than children's TV: things like *Friends*, *Ugly Betty* and *Hollyoaks*. I don't mind her watching stuff before 9 p.m. but if certain programmes are on after that then there's a reason for it, and I don't let her tune in. She'll then say it's not fair because all her friends watch it! She recently asked me if she could stay up on a Saturday night to watch *Celebrity Juice* which, although funny, is also rather suggestive. Now she feels left out, because apparently other kids in her year are walking round school shouting out the catchphrases. One night she stayed over at her friend's, and the next day, she asked if she could watch *Hollyoaks Later*, the more adult spin-off series. It turned out she'd watched it the night before! So now I wonder if I'm being too strict? Is she actually more grown up and capable of handling adult issues than I think she is? Her friends don't seem to be affected in any way by it. I'm sure she hears more bad language and filth in school than I'd like to acknowledge. But that still won't change what I let her watch. There are some things that are meant for adults and should stay that way. Things like internet 'catch-up' players and YouTube also worry me. It's easy to control what they watch on the television, but the internet doesn't have a watershed.

Suzanne, mum to two girls aged thirteen and seven

My daughter is very eclectic in her TV watching. She still loves kids' cartoons but also likes dramas such as *House*, *ER* and *Bones*, and comedies like *Friends* and *Scrubs*. There are some things she's not allowed to watch that are too graphic, such as *CSI* and *Criminal Minds*. I don't think she needs to see the more adult-themed things yet. She also joins me to watch lots of the documentaries that I love, and enjoys discussing them me – everything from *Edwardian Farm*, to programmes about the Second World War.

Nicky, mum to a girl, eleven

My youngest loves telly but I sometimes have to stop her watching rubbish just for the sake of it – if she had her way she'd probably have the Disney Channel on a loop. She also loves *Dr Who*, *The Sarah Jane Adventures* and *Glee*, and is mad for *EastEnders*. She loves *Animal Planet*, too, but gets upset when anything dies so has to sit there with the remote in her hand!

Jackie, mum to two girls aged seventeen and twelve

Emma does have a TV and DVD player in her room, but she doesn't watch a lot, probably only an hour a week. At weekends she likes to sit in bed on a Saturday night and watch a DVD. Generally she prefers listening to music instead.

Nicola, mum to a girl, eleven, and a boy, four

Mobile phones

If your tween doesn't have her own mobile yet, chances are she'll soon be pressing you for one: research suggests around half of kids aged eight to eleven and eighty-two per cent of twelve- to fifteen-year-olds have one. There's no doubt that mobiles can be a reassuring piece of technology when an increasingly independent tween is out and about without you. But there are a number of downsides to weigh up, among which which could be potential health risks. Although there's no clear evidence that the small doses of radiation emitted by mobile phones are danger-ous, no one knows for sure yet. And children would certainly be more vulnerable to any harmful effects as their brains and immune systems are not fully developed. Experts now advise that it's best to err on the side of caution, and not to give your child a mobile until she's twelve. If you do, encourage her to keep calls short and to a minimum – or urge her to stick with texting.

Other worries over mobile phones include unmonitored access to the internet and chat rooms, the risk of malicious or unwanted calls or texts – and big bills. There are tips on countering all those things in the box below.

Phones and the web

These days, many modern mobile phones offer access to the internet, making it hard to keep constant tabs on your tween's surfing habits. If you're worried about this, you could simply plump for a second-hand or basic model that doesn't have internet access. Otherwise, bear in mind that all UK mobile networks must provide free filters on it to restrict access to unsuitable sites – however, these aren't automatically applied so you'll need to specifically request that it's activated. Remember though, that filtering is not foolproof. The best thing you can do to help your child use the internet via her mobile is to educate her, as outlined earl-ier.

Many mobiles have Bluetooth these days and it's an extremely popu-lar feature with kids. Phones that are Bluetooth-enabled (as well as computers and consoles) can be used to share messages, music, videos and pictures via radio waves, free, to any other users within short range. Unfortunately, this can easily include material that's unsuitable, and you can't restrict incoming messages or downloads from mobiles using Blue-tooth. For peace of mind, you might be better off avoiding Bluetooth as a feature, or de-activating the option. If your tween objects, explain the safety issues involved and let her know it's for her own protection.

Hanging on the telephone: Tips for tweens and mobiles

- Don't give your tween an expensive or flashy mobile phone. It's likely to get lost or damaged – or worse, it could leave her vulnerable to being mugged. Give her an old one you no longer want, or one that comes free with a package deal.

- If your tween's phone has a camera, drum into her the importance of privacy issues: she needs to be very circumspect about any images she takes and shares.

- Make sure she knows she should come to you if anyone sends her an image, link, file or message via her mobile phone that's offensive or unwanted. Let the mobile operator know if this happens and if necessary, inform the police. Watch out for 'text' chat rooms, which are offered by some providers, and may not be moderated.

- Pre-set your own number so your child can reach you easily if she needs to, and make sure all numbers listed on her mobile are approved by you.

- Shop around for a child-friendly tariff that will help you prevent spiralling bills. Pay-as-you-go deals make it easier to keep costs capped, and there are deals that offer emergency reserve funds, so your tween can call you if she needs to, but has run out of credit. Encourage her to keep tabs on her credit status – and perhaps insist she pays for any costs racked up above and beyond the limits you've set.

- To prevent your tween being tempted by expensive extras like ringtone downloads and sport or celebrity alerts, ask the network if they can activate call barring on premium-rate numbers.

- Treat texting time as screen-time: make sure your tween's use is monitored and restricted, and don't let her text late in the evening. You might want to make a rule that her phone is always turned off at least an hour before bedtime, or even that you look after it for her until the morning.

- Check out her school's rules on mobile phones and make

sure she sticks to them. It may be OK for her to take it to school, for instance, but it's likely she'll be asked to keep it switched off or locked away during lessons.

What the netmums say

Mobile phones

Both older boys have a mobile: Jake to speak with his father and James so that he can contact me about pick-up times. He's just had a new one bought for him for Christmas, to keep up with the friends at his new secondary school. James plays a lot of sports with late finishes and weekend games, so I need to know when he's finished so I can come and pick him up.
Claire, mum to five boys aged eleven, nine, six, five and one, and a girl, three

I put Alysha's mobile on a £10 monthly plan, which means she can't afford to download music, or make expensive calls to premium-rate numbers. It's purely for getting in touch with friends and family. She's only had it a short while – I didn't see the need until she went into Year Six and was walking home from school on her own. I felt as she was becoming more independent she needed one so I could keep track of her.
Kerrie, mum to two girls aged twelve and one

Emma has a mobile phone and has done since she was eight. I bought it so her dad could contact her direct on it. She has a small allowance to pay for it and when she went over it recently I deducted it from her pocket money: it turned out she was letting all her school pals use it on the way home from school. Although it was supposed to be only for emergencies and to contact her dad, she has 100 texts a month to use and enjoys texting her friends. She's asked for an iPhone this year, but I've said no.
Nicola, mum to a girl, eleven, and a boy, four

Both my kids got mobiles of their own in Year Six, when they started to go out to play with their friends and walk to school without me. I felt safer knowing they could contact me if necessary. However then, as now, I never let them have the latest models as I think it's a huge risk to their personal safety to have a good phone. Imagine a nine-year-old whipping out an iPhone – what an easy target for a mugging! They're not happy that they have rubbish phones, but as long as they can make a call and send a text, what else do they need?

Julie, mum to two girls aged seventeen and four, and two boys aged fifteen and two

I have relented and bought my ten-year-old a phone for her birthday. I really didn't want to but she's started cycling to the local shops and going to the green behind our house. Now I know she's able to contact us if need be. This did happen the other day when she went to buy a loaf of bread for us and fell off her bike. She called and asked if my husband could drive over and 'rescue' her! We've also opted for a 'bottom-of-the-range' phone for her but she was just so happy to have the phone she didn't care.

Tanya, mum to two girls aged ten and seven

My daughter started to use her phone quite a bit during the summer before starting secondary school. Not only was she using it to call and text her friends, but as she was starting to go out more on her own, we insisted that she take the phone everywhere and call or text us to let us know where she was and when she'd be home. She did what we asked. The problem was I had to top the phone up every week, and during one month alone I ended up putting £60 on it. After that we got her a £10 per month contract that has 200 minutes and unlimited texts. Some people might think that's a little extravagant, but it's actually cheaper than pay-as-you-go, and I know she'll never be stuck somewhere with no credit and no way of getting hold of us. So far, she hasn't asked for a top-of-the-range model. If she

did, I must admit I'd be worried, and probably wouldn't let her take it to school. I work in a secondary school, and I know that mobile phone theft is a big problem.
Sarah, mum to a girl, twelve, and a boy, eight

Originally my daughter's phone was bought so she could say 'goodnight' on her own to her dad. He's a truck driver, and she thinks it is great when Daddy texts her. Now she's in secondary school, it's become a godsend. She gets home twenty minutes before I do, so she texts me to say she's leaving school and then again when she's home. It has also helped when rehearsals for her school musical have finished early, and I can go and pick her up. I have a bolt-on tariff which means she can text and ring me and her dad for free whether she has credit or not. She then pays for her own credit herself from her pocket money.
Nicky, mum to a girl, eleven

All three of my boys got a mobile phone when they started secondary school. Mobiles for kids of this age are great in some respects, as it really takes a lot of worry away when you can always text them to see where they are or what they're doing. (Never phoning – that would be far too embarrassing!) We've always insisted on a cheap phone, as they do tend to lose them, or tread on them when their blazer happens to be serving time as a goal post, and an expensive phone makes your child an easy target to be pushed around and have their phone taken. Obviously it has to be a balance as a really cheap phone won't help your child's social status. It's very tricky getting that balance right. Another downside is that sooner or later you will receive a text from them during the day – and you suddenly realise that your little darling is actually texting you during a lesson!
Jo, mum to three boys aged seventeen, fourteen and eleven

6 Good health

You've probably worried about your child's health and wellbeing all his life: what he eats, how much sleep he's getting, whether he's active enough. Nothing much changes – now he's a tween, you may well fret about all these things still. Feeding him continues to be a bit of a minefield, and couch potato tendencies can creep in, giving rise to more worries about his general state of health and fitness. Getting him into bed at a decent hour, and for the optimum amount of sleep, can become a challenge all over again. And, now that he's older, there may be new health risks on the horizon, with the lure of a range of unhealthy habits like smoking, drinking and taking drugs coming into view.

It's important to keep all these worries in perspective. Your tween's ever-growing push for independence means you can no longer hope to (and neither should you) take complete control of his life. He can probably reach the high cupboards in the kitchen now, and may have the resources and opportunities to 'shop' for snacks without you around. He can't very easily be *forced* out of the door for fresh air. And even if you send him to bed at 8 p.m., he may still attempt to play with his console under the covers for a while. So, as parents of tweens we should aim to be flexible and reasonable about issues like food, exercise and sleep – whilst maintaining sensible boundaries as much as possible.

Feeding tweens

You may no longer be responsible for actually putting the spoon in your child's mouth these days, but it doesn't mean you don't continue to worry about everything he eats as he grows older. It's instinctive for us as parents to have concerns about our kids' diets. After all, food is fundamental to survival. And tweens are – *literally* – growing children. They need plenty of fuel to make all that vital physical development possible, as well as feeding their busy brains, and it's up to us to make sure they get it. On top of all that, there's huge pressure these days from the media and authorities for parents to heed messages about the importance of healthy eating, which can leave you feeling a bit of a failure when you know that, in spite of your best efforts, you've fallen short.

However, if we worry too much about feeding our tweens, and if we *show* them we're worried, we could be passing on some unhealthy messages. So make it an aim to stay relaxed about food, as much as you can, while offering as sensible a diet at home as you can get away with.

Meanwhile, as ever, setting a good example is probably the best thing you can do to help put healthy eating habits into place. Encourage your tween to take a healthy interest in food of all sorts by getting him in the kitchen or asking him to help plan menus and meals. And try to sit down as a family for meals – if it's just not possible in the week because of differing schedules, make a point of doing so as much as possible at the weekend. Try to make mealtimes a happy and relaxed experience for your tween: keep the conversation light and chatty, and don't nag him to eat up, or hassle him – unless really necessary – about his table manners.

Fussy eaters

If your tween was a fussy eater as a small child, you probably hoped he'd have grown out of it by now. Don't bank on it. Much like toddlers, tweens are often anxious to assert their independence from parents and push the boundaries a bit. And food is one of the few aspects of life kids can take total control of, so it's great way to exert power and wind up parents. You may even have ended up with a tween-aged fussy eater when you never had one before.

Try to ensure there's a good balance in your tween's diet – later in the chapter is an outline of what an ideal day's intake would include. But remember, this is *ideal*. If your tween seems to you to be a long way off hitting the mark, try not to fret: it won't help matters much. Don't feel you must bend over backwards to accommodate your fussy eater, either. Cook the same meal for everyone in the family, making easy adaptations where possible to suit his whims and allowing him, if necessary, to fill up later with a bowl of cereal or some toast.

Above all, never try to force anything down him, or get into any kind of deadlock over food: it's the worst thing you can do. Remind yourself he'll survive, and stay chilled. He'll almost certainly grow out of it – eventually. If you're really worried, you could consider giving him some dietary supplements, and if you're concerned his health's really being affected, a trip to your GP for some basic health checks should help put your mind at rest.

Going veggie

If your tween begins to take an interest in environmental and animal welfare issues, or if he's influenced by someone else who is, a previously carnivorous tween might decide to give vegetarianism a whirl. It may be an experimental phase, or it may be the start of a lifelong commitment, but either way, try to show respect for a decision like this and give him the support he needs, however much of a nuisance it seems. Don't go to pains to create entirely different meals – try to make simple adaptations or swaps to your usual meals or, better still, try to get everyone to eat veggie, at least sometimes. (Health experts say we should all eat less meat than we do, so maybe the whole family could benefit.)

Swot up a little – and encourage him to do so, too – so you both know what he needs to consume to stay healthy on a vegetarian diet. If he hasn't already, he'll need to develop a taste for alternatives such as beans, nuts, pulses and soya products – as well as vegetables, of course. If necessary, strike a deal with him: if he wants to go veggie, he's got to do it properly, and that means being prepared to try all the alternatives, and helping you to source, shop for, and cook vegetarian recipes.

The website of the Vegetarian Society is a great place to start if you're looking for further information.

Healthy eating

Most tweens are big fans of junk food, and it's not really hard to see why: sugar and fat taste great, after all. Not only that, but peer and commercial pressures are likely to be mounting for him right now – what his mates eat is likely to be an influence, and exposure to advertising and marketing of unhealthy foods is simply unavoidable.

Clearly, too much junk isn't good for a tween's health, and as a loving parent you'll no doubt want to keep some limits on his consumption of it. This is by no means just about beating obesity, which you might need to make clear to your tween if you're trying to steer him in the right direction diet-wise. Regardless of how 'skinny' he is, sensible eating is important for his general health, too, because too much junk could affect a range of things, including his concentration, energy and fitness levels, bowels and digestion, and immune system.

It should go without saying that it's a bad idea to attempt to ban junk food outright – you'll just make it more desirable. Making his own food choices is part of growing up and becoming independent from you, and naturally he's more likely to choose rubbish when he gets the chance. You can give him a healthy packed lunch and even rely on school meals being a reasonable option these days, but you might not be able to stop him buying sweets on the way home, or making a beeline for fast food when he's down town with his mates at the weekend. Neither can you do much about it if he eats at a friend's house where healthy eating is not especially high on the agenda. Make what's on offer at home as healthy as possible, and then try to relax about the rest of it.

Look to provide regular meals and healthy snacks for your tween. Always get a breakfast of some sort down him, make sure he's getting a good meal at school or is taking in a packed lunch, and try to offer a hot meal every evening – preferably consumed whilst sitting down with the rest of the family. Your tween will need to snack between meals to keep his blood-sugar levels regular – in particular, he'll probably be raven-ous when he gets in from school, so keep a stock of snack foods that are reasonably nutritious, such as fruit or smoothies, wholemeal toast, plain scones or flapjacks, yoghurts and mini-cheeses, for example. Don't let him snack too much, though, or too soon before dinner.

Home cooking is always likelier to provide the healthier option for your family but if you're working long hours you'll no doubt have less time to devote to preparing meals. If necessary, go for the healthiest pre-packaged foods you can; and look out for nutritious ingredients you can sling together easily, whilst endeavouring to keep the number of take-aways and pre-packed foods your family relies on to a reasonable minimum. There are loads of ideas for healthy family meals and tons of other nutrition tips on the food pages at www.netmums.com.

An apple a day: A healthy tween's daily diet

- A couple of portions of protein, essential for growth and repair, enzyme and hormone production. Sources include meat, fish, eggs, nuts, soya products, beans and pulses.
- Plenty of carbs, vital for the provision of energy. Sources are spuds, pasta, rice, cereals or bread. Unrefined and wholemeal varieties are the healthiest.
- Some calcium, essential for strong bones and teeth. Dairy products are the most obvious sources, so three daily portions of cheese, yoghurt or milk – or anything containing them – is a good aim. If your tween doesn't like or can't tolerate dairy, alternatives include white bread, nuts and seeds, dried fruits, pulses, and fortified cereals and juices.
- Lots of fruit or veg, vital for the provision of essential vitamins and minerals, and a healthy digestive system. Five portions a day is recommended, so stick them in wherever you can – on top of pizzas, whizzed up in smoothies or blended into sauces – but try to avoid them always being 'hidden'. Don't push it, or be tempted to offer unhealthy foods as a bribe for eating his greens. They'll lose their appeal even further! Some iron. Stats show that lots of tweens don't get enough of this due to rapid growth and poor modern diets, and

girls in particular need lots of iron because supplies can run low during periods. Red meat's the main source (so that hamburger is not such a bad thing, after all) but there are plenty of other places to find iron including fortified bread and breakfast cereals, leafy green veg and dried fruit. Vitamin C aids the absorption of iron, so a glass of orange juice is a good accompaniment to meals.

• Plenty of fluids, essential to aid digestion and functioning of brain and body in general. Six to eight drinks a day is recommended – more if the weather's hot or he's been exercising. Water, milk and diluted fruit juices are the healthiest options. Try to keep firm limits on canned or fizzy drinks that are high in undesirable ingredients such as sugar, acid, caffeine, artificial sweeteners or other additives.

• Only limited quantities of 'bad' fats (such as hydrogenated fats and saturated fats), sugars and salt. Commercial pre-packaged and convenience foods in particular can contain lots of these things, so be label-aware when shopping.

Overeaters and weight loss

It's natural for tweens to gain weight as well as height as they grow. Girls, in particular, develop layers of fat during puberty that are part of the body's preparation for bearing children. However, sedentary lifestyles and exposure to junk food does mean that many modern tweens gain more weight than is healthy: recent research shows that a third of ten- and eleven-year-olds in England are overweight or very overweight. Medical experts are pretty worried, because being overweight increases the risk of serious illnesses like type 2 diabetes, cancer and heart disease. Overweight kids are also more likely to be bullied, have fewer friends and to suffer from low self-esteem.

As a parent, it can be easy to overlook it when a child has become an unhealthy weight. After all, giving him the food he loves – especially if you love food yourself – is one sure way to show you care. It's also common to pass off extra weight during this period as 'puppy fat', but in fact, many experts stress that there's no such thing, and that tweens who are overweight are likely to remain so into adulthood – particularly if one or both parents are overweight, too.

So, it's a good idea to keep subtle tabs on your tween's eating habits if you suspect he's bigger than is normal. Don't guestimate his weight if you're worried: the only way to tell for sure is by measuring his Body Mass Index (BMI), which involves a calculation that takes into account his age, gender and height as well as how much he weighs. You can use the online NHS healthy weight calculator to do this, or ask your GP for help. In England, the weight of all Year Six pupils is measured as part of the Child Measurement Programme.

Don't be tempted to put your tween on a 'diet', unless your GP or a dietician has specifically advised it. He needs plenty of fuel for his increasing energy needs – and besides, telling him in no uncertain terms that he needs to lose weight is likely to make him feel pretty bad about himself. Instead, just pay a little attention to making his diet more healthy generally, whilst boosting the amount of physical activity he's getting. Don't single him out for these health improvements, either: make it something the whole family has to do, as you'll all benefit. Now is a good time to start getting the message across – if you haven't already – that we *all* need to be a bit careful about what we eat, and we all need to stay active, in order to burn off the excess.

If your tween announces he wants to diet, but really doesn't seem to need to, it may be that he's got a body image problem which you should offer to talk through with him. Sadly, this is a common story among tweens of today, for girls in particular – although boys too can be affected as images of slim, muscular young men are also prevalent. There's more on body image and eating disorders in the following chapter.

What the experts say

Crissy says: Your tween's eating patterns – for better or for worse – were probably set out in early childhood. But the tween-age years are marked by a new hunger, one for freedom and independence. So it may well be that the previously confirmed meat-eater tries vegetarianism, or vice versa, or that a child who could once be relied upon to eat the varied and healthy diet you offered now seems to crave nothing but junk food. The journey to and from school, increased pocket money and time on his own offers new opportunities for a tween to decide what he wants to eat and when and where he wants to eat it – so don't be surprised if you find pockets full of sweet wrappers, or discover he's been hanging round outside the bakers after school. This is all part of growing up and experimenting with making choices and decisions, and that includes the novelty of feeding himself, as well as the pull to fit in with his peers, so take a deep breath and keep your cool. Lecturing him on healthy eating will only cause him to tune out, so for the time being turn a blind eye (within reason), make sure he eats well at home, and try to get your message across by modelling your own (hopefully) healthy relationship with food and exercise.

Tweens are developing and growing at a phenomenal rate and their bodies need certain key nutrients, but of course food is more than just fuel and there's an emotional side to your tween's eating habits too. There's no denying the attraction of junk food, not just for tweens but for most of us. You may be tempted to try cutting it out altogether, but if your child doesn't get it at home, chances are he'll get it elsewhere – it's not so much *if* he'll be tempted by it, as *when*. However, nothing will drive a tween towards junk food quicker than a total ban. Prohibition is often counterproductive, and can leave them squaring up for a fight and desperate for something to which they previously had a 'take it or leave it' attitude.

You will have food rules, of course, but be flexible, not unconditional, and make sure your rules make sense and that you can back up your argument with fact. So, it's OK to say, 'I know sweets taste good but it's not good for you to have them all the time,' and rather than issuing an outright ban maybe burger and fries can become an occasional indulgence rather than a regular occurrence. Wherever you set your goalposts try to stick with them. I personally don't have a problem with calling sweets and junk food 'treats', because no matter how hard you try to deny it they do taste good, and most kids (and adults) love them. An outright ban is more likely to cause your tween to become a secret junk-food junkie, so keep things in the open and make it more a case of 'everything in moderation'.

To a certain degree we all have an emotional relationship with food. We use it to celebrate when we're happy and to comfort us when we're low. But for some young people, caught up in the turmoil of the tween years, manipulating their food intake can give them the illusion that they can exert control over at least one area of their life. So beware of attaching too many emotional messages to food, or using the provision and/or the prohibition of food to bribe or punish your child. The key at all times is to work towards normalising healthy eating and appropriate levels of regular exercise and not to present them as a punishment or a chore.

Avoid associating food and exercise with appearance – talk instead in terms of health, energy and general wellbeing. Never put your tween on a diet unless specifically advised to do so by a health professional. If you're concerned about his weight don't use the 'D' word or talk in terms of weight loss; instead let your tween know it's about taking care of his body and caring for himself. Aim to keep your child at a steady weight by surreptitiously adjusting the whole family's eating and exercise levels rather than singling him out. Let him have his 'treats' too. You don't want him to feel guilty about eating a bit of junk food now and then.

Elaine says: Often, as parents, we end up being over-controlling around food and inadvertently set things up so that our children realise early on that food refusal is a way to exert influence, show emotions and get attention. We then often fall into the trap of labelling our children as 'fussy eaters', and before you know it your children are viewing food as a source of difficulty rather than as a pleasure. But we also have unrealistic expectations of perfection, often, and then fret that we are hopeless parents if our children will not eat their 'five a day'. The relatively recent trends towards a more healthy approach to eating can put tremendous pressure on parents, so that we feel that 'the Food Police' will be on our case if we haven't put together a nutritious and imaginative lunch box that our child will actually eat. This pressure that parents feel gets passed on to the children and we nag and criticise out of our belief that we're failing.

When you're dealing with a fussy eater, try and achieve a balance between being in charge of mealtimes and maintaining a relaxed approach. Offer choice within a set of acceptable boundaries. You decide what he gets to choose from, where and when he eats. He decides how much to eat, and what to choose. Don't give in to junk food if he won't eat anything else. You set yourself up for failure if you're not clear of your own values in this area. The best policy is just not to have food in the house that you're not happy about him eating. If there are foods that you're happy for him to have in moderation then buy these on an *ad hoc* basis once a healthy intake has been achieved. And do allow your child to genuinely dislike something after he's tried it many times. After all, adults have preferences too. Introduce new foods in very small proportions constantly, alongside the food he loves, so he can get used to the idea of trying new things. He may not like it, but it's important to praise him for effort and attitude.

Above all, try and have times in the week when you get your children involved in preparing the meal and then sit down to enjoy it as a family together, with good conversation. If you take an honest look at mealtimes and conclude that they've become unhappy occasions, with you nagging and your tween digging his heels in, then you need to make changes. Try swapping where everyone sits, or your placemats or crockery, so it's clear things are different. Draw up some rules, including several that you know will be easy to follow, and make sure you give praise, specifically and frequently. If your main problem is that your child is reluctant to sample new foods, then make sure you praise him elsewhere in his life for taking risks, being brave and trying things.

As parents we have to balance encouraging healthy eating and exercise with not making our children feel pressurised about their bodies, especially during the tween years when puberty begins and their bodies starts a process of change that will continue for a long time ahead. The key is not to distinguish between fattening and non-fattening foods, but to talk about the importance of balance – why some foods need to be eaten in moderation and some can be eaten in abundance, and why that is so. Rather than talking about 'good' and 'bad' foods, talk about tastes and textures; what we like about food; and how particular foods contribute to our nutritional needs: for instance, chicken has protein which is good for building muscle, milk has calcium which is good for bones, and the omega-3 fatty acids in oily fish are good for our brains. Discuss, too, the less desirable effects of salt, sugar and fat. If you're not sure yourself about these things, then do a little research into the matter. Help your tween to understand when he is full, and when he is hungry. And don't make him finish a meal if he says he is full. Often, we're not really hungry when we want something to eat, but bored or looking for something to do with our hands, or in need of emotional fulfilment.

What the netmums say

Tweens' eating habits

My son consumes a large amount of food, including lots of fruit and veg, but there's not much variety. I'm not overly strict on what he and his sister consume as snacks, as I believe everything is OK in moderation. They have a bag of crisps and a small chocolate bar every day. At the weekends, they're allowed sweets. George is rarely ill and is a healthy weight, so I must be doing something right. At least he eats plenty, unlike my daughter! I don't stress about food, though. If they don't want it, then they don't have to eat it. But we do have a rule that they can't ask for snacks later if they leave their dinner.

Natalie, mum to a boy, ten, and a girl, two

Kevin will eat anything you put on his plate, but given a choice, he would eat junk food all day. If he knows he likes something, he'll have it over and over and over again. Ask him what he wants to eat and he'll say spaghetti or pizza, without fail. We try to cook with him, and do something different every other weekend. His favourite thing to make from scratch? Pizza.
Kirsty, mum to two boys aged thirteen and nine months

I hoped my girls would grow out of their fussy eating habits, but it hasn't happened yet. I've never tried to force things upon them, but I often end up cooking separately for them, and they eat more junk than I'd like. Lunch times became more of an unknown territory once they started at high school: at primary I'd either know what was on the lunch menu, or I'd get to see the remains of their packed lunch. Now they prefer to make their own choices in the canteen as that's what their friends do, but it's not very healthy. I've worried in the past that they're underweight, but they're full of energy and will eat when they're hungry. I think making a big issue out of it would make them self-conscious and make their relationship with food and body image more complex so I'd rather let them work their own way through.
Natalie, mum to two girls aged fifteen

Food is purely functional to my son; it's just fuel to him. My daughter, on the other hand, has an emotional approach to food. She says she's constantly hungry, but only for snack foods and the things she loves. If I offer her something healthy it turns out she's not that hungry after all. The things she loves are mostly high in carbs – plain pasta, crisps, bread and butter, jacket potato with butter – and she refuses most protein except for revolting things like processed cheese or frankfurters. I do bang on about nutrition because it's one of my pet interests, and we have a five-a-day rule, but she says she has 'ultrasensitive taste buds' and can't stand many flavours. I don't think it can be all my fault, because my son is so different, but their

tastes are so at odds, I usually end up catering to the lowest common denominator.
Katy, mum to a boy, fourteen, and a girl, eleven

I have a daily battle with my twelve-year-old-daughter, who won't eat breakfast, but will happily go to McDonald's on her way to school. She won't eat what we eat for dinner, with a few exceptions. And she says she's always hungry, but only for crisps or sweets. She's like me and puts on weight easily, but unfortunately she will not listen to our advice.
Kirsty, mum to a girl, twelve, and a boy, four

My daughter has turned into a very fussy eater in the last couple of years and I'm sick of hearing 'I don't like that'. She's active, but she has the same metabolism as me so she puts weight on easily. I try to make sure she doesn't have massive portions and cook as healthily as possible. However, we do have some junk food and treats because I think removing them completely makes them more attractive. My girls do a three-hour disco dance class on a Friday evening, and are always starving when they come out, so we always get a bag of chips to share at home afterwards. I don't want to stick her on a diet as I think she is too young and needs to be eating well to grow properly.
Naomi, mum to two girls aged twelve and five

Alex rarely has breakfast at home in the morning, but he does have a bacon roll from the shop at school during morning break. It used to worry me but now I think, I'm not going to force him to eat when it doesn't suit him. He eats in the school restaurant at lunchtime and I have no idea what. He's aware that too much junk and sugar is bad for him but he has a very sweet tooth and, if allowed, he would eat chocolate all day. So apart from the odd treat, I don't buy chocolate, biscuits or junk. I cook every night, so I know he gets one reasonably healthy meal a day. As for fruit and veg, he knows he should eat five a day but two or three is probably average for him. At ten, he did start eating anything in sight and put on quite a bit of weight – but then he suddenly shot up in height by about two inches. He's far from skinny, but I don't worry because I don't believe he has a problem, or want to make an issue of it. Equally, there's no way I'd allow him to munch his way through crisps, pizza and chocolate all day.

Ali, mum to a girl, eighteen, and a boy, eleven

My children can be fussy but I try not to worry too much about it. I like them to get their five a day and eat a varied diet, but I'm also happy for them to have treats every day. I try to lead by example, and always have plenty of healthy and easy snack options available like fruit, cheese and homemade muffins. I believe in picking your battles carefully with tweens: if their diet is reasonable, then don't rock the boat!

Hayley, mum to a girl, sixteen, and a boy, thirteen

Getting lively

Staying active is as important for tweens' health as what they eat: in fact, sedentary lifestyles tend to be cited, along with the increased availability of junk food, as the main reason for the nation's growing obesity rates. It's true that kids these days aren't generally as active as they used to be, probably because of busy lives, keen screen habits, routine reliance on cars and fears over safety, which mean they're less likely to be allowed the freedom and time to let rip outdoors. Helping your tween get into good habits is important for his general health right now – and for the future, too. And like healthy eating, staying active is about much more than just maintaining a healthy weight: it will also increase strength and stamina, build strong bones, boost energy levels, keep heart and blood pressure rates healthy, improve the immune system, promote good sleep and enhance emotional wellbeing, too.

Keeping active is something to aim for as a family. But resist selling it as 'exercise' – instead try to make it a normal and enjoyable part of your everyday lives. According to the experts, tweens should be getting an hour's moderate exercise every day: hopefully they'll be getting at least some of that during PE sessions and playtimes at school, but don't assume it – make sure they're active during home time, too. Look for easy ways to encourage activity – walking anywhere that's a reasonable distance rather than taking the car, for instance, taking the dog out if you have one, or doing jobs around the house. Encourage your tween to take up at least one active pastime after school and help him to get there on a regular basis. Not all kids enjoy sport, it's true, but it doesn't have to be competitive and there are so many choices out there, you should be able to find something he thinks fun. If you do some kind of sport or regular exercise session yourself that will help set a good example, but even if you don't, make sure your kids see you walking rather than taking the car, choosing stairs rather than lifts, and getting stuck in yourself when you're out and about enjoying the fresh air with them.

The importance of play

Lots of people worry that the current tween generation is growing up too fast, and if that's something concerns you, too, perhaps you could find ways to encourage more informal playtime, preferably outside. (There's more discussion of this issue in the final chapter.) Make it a goal to always get out and about at least once at the weekends, for a brisk walk or a run around in your nearest bit of parkland or forest – and make a pact with yourself that you won't care about consequences like dirty clothes or minor injuries. If you and your tween haven't explored them for a while, try to rediscover some simple, old-fashioned ways to have fun such as skipping, kite-flying, hide-and-seek, tag, or just chucking a ball around. And don't let bad weather put you off – wrap up and take on the elements.

There are loads of ideas for ways that families can maintain a healthy lifestyle together on the Change 4 Life website (see the appendix for the web address).

What the experts say

Elaine says: Most of parenting is about modelling, so if you as an adult are inactive and don't illustrate how important a healthy lifestyle is, don't be surprised if your children don't develop healthy lifestyle habits. It's vital for health and wellbeing that our tweens find an activity they can partake in and most importantly enjoy. Do listen to him, to find out what he likes and what he feels capable of. There are parents who force their children into a sport they don't enjoy, often because that sport is too competitive, but not everyone can or wants to do sport at a competitive level. Choosing an activity to be enjoyed by all the family can be a challenge, so start with the simple stuff of having the routine of a family walk or bike ride at the weekend. And be willing to try out things that can involve the whole family: it may take a good few years of practice and support, but there's deep joy to be had if you can find something you can all do together. If your tween's a bit of a couch potato by nature, you may have to be firm about encouraging physical exercise, perhaps restricting sedentary activities like computer games or TV watching until after he's done a few circuits round the park!

What the netmums say

Keeping active

Kevin's a total couch potato. He does judo twice a week but I sometimes have to push him to go. We're close to a canal and river, so we head out at the weekends to walk the dog – I do think it's important to be out in the fresh air and to get him away from his computer and console. We may have to force him to leave the house, but he does enjoy it once we're out.
Kirsty, mum to two boys aged thirteen and nine months

My husband and I are both into fitness – mainly because we'd much rather exercise than diet! We hope our girls will grow up wanting to be fit and healthy, too, so we're doing our best to make it a normal part of our lives. We go to school and every-where else that's in walking distance on foot, rain or shine, and at the weekends we always go for a long walk in the forest or cycle along the canal. It's lovely being out as a family, with the added bonus that we're all boosting fitness levels, too.

Julia, mum to two girls aged nine and six

We live in a second-floor flat and I'm a little wary of letting Gemima out to play in the winter when the dark creeps in early. But she enjoys PE at school, and is often to be found on her Just Dance or Wii Fit games. She loves music, and is always dancing round the flat like a crazy person. I also try to take her swimming once a week.

Emily, mum to a girl, ten

Exercise is not something I worry about. Sam and Adam are both active boys – they can't even sit still! We have a big garden and live very close to a park, both of which they spend lots of time in. They regularly go on bike rides with my husband, as well as den-building and tree-climbing with one of their uncles, and then there's all the wrestling and fighting they do with each other! They also have lots of sports at school, including football, and we make a point of walking to and from school every day, whatever the weather.

Peta, mum to two boys aged nine and seven

My son plays for a football team, which involves training every Saturday and a match every Sunday – and although all the transporting and spectating can be a bit of a drag, especially in the winter, I think it's really important to encourage it.

Hayley, mum to a girl, sixteen, and a boy, thirteen

My daughter is naturally active and will seek out activity if she
feels stressed. So, if she's doing her homework and gets frustrated,
for example, then she'll go in the garden and jump on the tram-
poline for a while. In fact, she can become grumpy if she has
had a day or two with no activity. She swims once a week, dances,
and begs me to cycle everywhere. I tell you, there are days that
the constant movement makes me tired just watching it!
Tanya, mum to two girls aged ten and seven

Sleep, rest and relaxation

No doubt your tween's sleeping habits are changing somewhat these
days. He probably wants to stay up later, because there's more in the
way of homework, socialising and other pastimes to fit in to his evening
now – and also because that, no doubt, is what all his friends are doing.
All of which is likely to mean he also wants to lie in bed for longer in
the mornings – making it a challenge in the week, sometimes, to shift
him up and out in time for school. But regardless of how his patterns
have shifted, the fact remains that your tween needs to get a good night's
sleep: nine to ten hours is what's recommended for this age group.
Sleep's vital because it allows us to rest, repair and grow – and particularly so during puberty, when a major reorganisation of the brain is
taking place. Lack of sleep could cause concentration and attention problems at school, affect his general health, and trigger or exacerbate
emotional problems such as stress, anxiety and depression (for more on
these, turn to the next chapter).

Bedtimes

Although the days when you put on his pyjamas, read him a story, and
tucked him in may be long behind you, it remains a good idea for your
tween to have some sort of regular bedtime routine. Make sure he gets
a period of time that's calm, quiet and relaxing before bed: so try to make
sure homework and chores are complete, and that tellies, computers and
phones are switched off well in advance. Instead, encourage quiet reading
or listening to an audio CD. It's probably sensible to suggest the winding-

down is done in his bedroom, so make sure it's a room that's warm and comfortable, and somewhere he enjoys spending time. Ensure he's had a substantial supper earlier in the evening, and that if he also needs a drink and a snack a bit later on, there's some time to digest it. Steer him away, too, from anything that might keep him awake, such as caffeine or lots of sugar. Food and drinks containing the amino acid tryptophan are a good bet as this aids the production of melatonin, the sleep hormone: examples are milk and other dairy products, poultry, eggs and bananas.

Your tween might like a little privacy at bedtime, but he will probably feel pleased if you're hovering nearby. Bedtime stories can still be a good source of comfort, even for this age group. Offer him the chance to chat if he seems preoccupied: a few words of reassurance from you may be all he needs to offset a concern that could otherwise keep him awake.

Weekends and special events are bound to involve later nights, and hopefully the chance for a morning lie-in, too, but even so, try to keep to sensible limits whenever possible.

Don't forget to relax

Tweens have busy lives these days, and it's important to make sure yours gets some form of relaxation. Sometimes, this means just doing nothing for a while: perhaps lying on his bed, listening to music, or watching a movie. If it seems as though his life is just too full to fit a bit of 'nothing' in, then it might be time to reassess his schedule and cut back on some of his formal activities.

You might want to suggest some simple relaxation exercises, particularly if your tween finds it hard to wind down and settle to sleep at night. He could try breathing slowly and deeply, then clenching and relaxing each bit of his body in turn starting with fists, toes and hands, and finishing with the muscles in the face.

What the experts say

Elaine says: Relaxation is as vital for tweens as it is for us adults and it's important that they learn *how* to relax as children. Most tweens tend to have very full-on days in the week with school, extra-curricular and social activities, and of course homework.

Try to help your tween establish at least one time in the week when there's nothing to do but relax. In our house, we call it the Sunday Magical Moment – it's the one time when I know I can truly connect with my kids and help them relax without dreaded questions like, 'Is your homework done?' You could have a movie and popcorn night, or plan for a special meal that everyone's had a hand in cooking. Old-fashioned board games like Scrabble or Monopoly are great, as is curling up on the sofa together to watch something entertaining on the TV. If you're feeling energetic, take an afternoon bike ride, or go for a walk. Doing stuff like this together is a wonderful way to practise 'connective' parenting. Don't be surprised if your tween resists you at first, saying it's uncool to hang out and relax with parents. Persist with it and, trust me, he will come to treasure and value those moments. We also need to encourage our tweens to have some down-time on their own – ideally without always resorting to screens – whether it's listening to or playing music, pursuing a hobby, or reading.

Crissy says: When it comes to sleep, tweens need more than they think, but convincing them of the importance of a good night's sleep is often easier said than done. An early bedtime is likely to mark him out as a geek and it's not something he'll brag about to his peers, but the fact is that if your tween is staying up too late it will almost certainly have an effect on his ability to concentrate, his mood and his academic performance.

Do be respectful of the physiological and social changes that mean his timescales are naturally changing. Consider putting bedtimes back as he grows, and allow him lie-in time at the weekend where possible. But bear in mind how important his sleep is and remember, you're the adult, so you're in charge. Make bedtimes non-negotiable other than in exceptional circumstances and you'll save on a whole lot of nightly grief. Be clear about your values: establish a lights-out rule, allowing for some time before it to relax and read a bit, and be consistent about sticking with it. Just as when he was very young, it will pay for a tween to have some structure to his sleeping habits – too much sleep late into the morning, for instance, may be to the detriment of the sleep he needs later that night, so it may not be such a good idea to let him lie in bed indefinitely on a Saturday morning. Sleep isn't a bankable commodity: it's not something you can catch up on later in the week, and being over-tired becomes a vicious circle with tension and anxiety making it difficult for your child to unwind even when he's genuinely tired. And do make sure he isn't doing more than is good for him. While exercise and physical activity during the day can help burn off extra energy and release soothing endorphins, too much after-school activity can have the opposite effect, leaving him feeling wound up and frazzled.

Don't expect your tween to just 'switch off' in the evening. Build in some transition time when screens are turned off and he can simply slow down and unwind. This may be a good chance for some one-on-one quality time as he talks through his day with you. A warm bath or shower, catching up on a good book, (nothing scary though!), chilling out in his room, playing music or pottering around can help him unwind, and if his head's still buzzing, why not suggest a spot of diary-writing? It's a great way for him to get things off his chest before bedtime.

What the netmums say

Sleep, rest and relaxation

Emma goes to bed at 9 p.m. during the week and is up at 7.30 in the morning. I know if she stays up any later, she'll be tired in the morning. I have to ask her a couple of times in the morning to get out of bed, but if she's gone to bed early enough, she's usually good at getting up. She goes to Guides on a Tuesday night, which means she doesn't get to bed till 10 p.m. then, but

I reason that it's only once a week. She's allowed to stay up later at the weekends, and she'll have a morning lie-in to make up for it.

Nicola, mum to a girl, eleven, and a boy, four

I'm very strict on sleep routines. My ten-year-old goes to bed at 8.30 p.m. on a school night and 9.30 p.m. on a weekend. If he goes to bed any later then he's unbearable the next day – really grumpy and tearful. The trouble is he refuses to lie in. Even on the rare occasion that we go out or to a party, he still gets up at 6 a.m., and has done since he was born. He's up and dressed before me on a school day, and I've never had trouble getting him to school. At the moment he gets plenty of rest and relaxation time: whether that will change once he reaches high school, I do not know.

Natalie, mum to a boy, ten, and a girl, two

Since he turned eleven, Alex doesn't seem to have needed as much sleep as he used to. He usually goes up to bed about 9 p.m. during the week and about 10 p.m. at the weekends, sometimes later. I don't wake him in the morning – he has his own alarm and it's his responsibility to get up. In the summer, he doesn't stop from the minute he wakes up to when he goes to bed. He does get plenty of relaxation time during the winter though, and near the end of the day we usually snuggle up and watch a bit of TV together.

Ali, mum to a girl, eighteen, and a boy, eleven

It can be a struggle getting my boys out of bed in time for school, but they know that they have to take responsibility for getting themselves ready. They have a bedtime of around 9–10 p.m. on a school day and the weekends are not usually that different. I might be a bit more lenient if there's something on television they want to watch, otherwise I will put my foot down, although that does not always make me popular!

Caroline, mum to two boys aged twelve and eleven

Zoe goes to bed about 9.30–9.45 p.m. during the week and gets woken at 7.45 a.m. in the morning. She does moan about getting up, but she always does so within ten minutes, so it's fine. Her relaxation time is normally from 8–9.30 p.m. every night. She does a lot of activities after school and also outside school clubs. It can be a struggle trying to fit everything into the week, though.
Naomi, mum to two girls aged twelve and five

I can always tell the difference in my kids' behaviour if they overshoot their bedtimes – my daughter usually goes to bed at 9 p.m. and my son at 8 p.m. Trying to get them motivated is a nightmare! Once a week we try and have a completely relaxing evening, be that a trip to pictures, or a take-away meal and a DVD, so there's no rushing around getting tea made, pots washed, or homework done.
Emma, mum to a girl, eleven, and a boy, nine

My son needs his sleep but loves reading at night, and often struggles to get up at 7 a.m. His twin sister is worse: she goes to bed at half eight but is often awake at 10 p.m., and then she's a nightmare in the morning too. Regardless, my husband likes them to be in bed in the evening – whether it's the right thing to send them, even when they are not sleeping, I don't know. I suppose at least they are resting.
Jennie, mum to a girl, twelve, and two boys, twelve and ten

Although we are strict about him getting to bed by 10 p.m., Kevin fights it every night. I personally don't think he gets enough sleep – he often falls asleep on the way home from school. At the weekend he can sleep until lunchtime easily, if we leave him. Once his homework is done he can relax and do what he wants so he gets enough chill time – though we do make him turn off his computer or console an hour before bedtime so he can wind down from his games. He'll watch telly with us or do some drawing. Maybe even some reading!
Kirsty, mum to two boys aged thirteen and nine months

Unhealthy habits

Statistics suggest that a significant number of youngsters first experiment with smoking, drinking and drug-taking whilst still in their
tweens. In a major recent survey, twenty-five per cent of eleven- to
fifteen-year-olds admitted they had tried drugs at least once, thirty-three
per cent had tried smoking, and more than half had drunk alcohol.
Even if you're confident your tween is one of the majority *not* tempted,
it still makes sense to be realistic: like it or not, these temptations may
not be too far round the corner, if they're not already a possibility.

It's really important to talk openly to your tween about alcohol, smoking and drugs, sooner rather than later. These issues are discussed at
school as part of the national curriculum, but it's vital that you also talk
at home about the risks involved in these dangerous habits. Don't get
heavy, or you might just increase the mystery and appeal, but do chat
naturally about the fact that they're not good for your health, and make
sure your tween knows about where you stand, values-wise, on things
like alcohol, cigarettes, and other sorts of drugs.

Of course, the best way to show how you feel is by example: if you
hope he will only ever drink moderately then only drink moderately in
front of him; and if you would hate for him to smoke, don't be a smoker.
If you used to smoke or took drugs in your youth, you don't have to
make a major confession, but it's best to be honest in response to any
questions you get about it from your tween.

Try not to freak out if you do discover your tween has been indulging
in either underage drinking, smoking or drug-taking. If you know because
he's confessed, do credit him for it: he may feel scared about what he's
done and needs you to reassure him it's OK. Calm down before attempting to talk to him about it, and don't panic: it's not *so* unusual for a
child this young to dabble, and it doesn't necessarily mean it's going to
develop into a serious problem. Do talk about it though, and make sure
he knows you're concerned. Reiterate, assuming you've been through
them already, what the risks are.

If you've done all the right things at home, the most likely reason
for your tween to be tempted by unhealthy habits is because of peer
pressure. And you can't be with your tween all the time – especially as
the tween years roll on and he becomes more independent. That's all

the more reason to openly discuss the issues with him, educate him, and pass on your values on the matter just as best you can.

Your tween and booze

Unlike many drugs, alcohol is legal, and unlike smoking, it's widely regarded as socially acceptable, which means that booze is probably the foremost temptation to be placed under your tween's nose. For most, it's likely to mean nothing more than a brief tipple – and perhaps this will even be at home, under your supervision. However, there are fears that serious misuse of alcohol is a significant problem for this age group: in one recent study, one in five fifteen-year-olds reported that they had first been drunk when thirteen or younger.

The official recommendation of the UK's chief medical officer is that young people should not drink alcohol at all until they're at least fifteen years old. That's because their growing bodies and still-developing brains are particularly vulnerable to the health risks, and because of fears that starting young increases the risk of serious alcohol-related problems later on. There are also major concerns that alcohol misuse is linked to risky sexual and antisocial behaviour, mental health problems, drug use and accidents.

Along with information about the dangers of smoking and drugs, your tween will learn about the damaging effects of alcohol misuse, and be taught basic skills for making responsible choices, as part of the national curriculum whilst still at primary school. The subject will be explored further still at some point during his first few years at secondary school. Don't assume this covers the subject, though. Just like sex, it's best if it's a natural and ongoing conversation-piece at home, as well. Use what you see on television and elsewhere in the media to spark chat – encourage your tween to ask questions and if you're not sure of the answer, look it up together on the internet. He may also want to discuss the exploits of peers that he has heard about. Let him chat freely if that's what he wants, listen carefully, and don't react strongly, however shocked you may be by what you hear.

Try to emphasise that drinking alcohol is something that's best done in moderation, and help your tween understand that it's fine to say no if he encounters peer pressure to try booze – and that if he does, it's OK to come to you to talk about it. When it comes to discussing the risks of booze misuse, you might have more impact if you talk about the immediate effects rather than the long-term dangers such as liver cirrhosis, which may seem light years away. For instance, too much alcohol can make you overweight, your skin look ropey, your breath smell, and, of course, cause a hangover from hell. Try to help him understand that being drunk can lead to a change of temperament and a loss of control that's no fun.

If you're a drinker yourself and your tween regularly sees you indulging, there's not a lot of point in trying to claim it's a terrible thing! For many people, drinking moderately is relaxing, sociable and enjoyable – it would be hypocritical to suggest otherwise. But it's fine to explain that drinking is something *you're* allowed to do, and he's not; that alcohol has far more risks for him because of his size and because his brain and other organs such as his liver, as well as his general growth, are still in development. Chat about what constitutes sensible drinking: knowing your limits, for example; never mixing drinks; alternating alcoholic drinks with water; and being unit-aware. And do avoid drinking to irresponsible levels when he's around: apart from it being somewhat dangerous to be drunk in charge of kids, it's pretty obvious that this isn't setting a good example. (Although, if your tween ever witnesses you suffering a bad hangover, perhaps that's no bad thing!) If you're regularly drinking more than the recommended daily limits for adults (three to four units for men, and two to three for women) then maybe having an impressionable tween in the house is the incentive you need to cut down? Be wary of drinking secretively, too: most tweens aren't daft and it's likely the empty bottles and smell on your breath will give you away. If your tween comes to believe drinking is a forbidden pleasure, it could just increase its appeal.

There's lots more information about booze on the websites of Drinkaware and FRANK. Details for both are given in the back of the book.

Underage drinking: Is 'wine weaning' a good idea?

Although official advice is that alcohol should not be offered to children, it's not illegal for parents to do so at home – and quite a lot do. Many feel the 'continental approach' (i.e. allowing a small amount of experimentation within the safe confines of home and under adult supervision) will remove the lure of 'forbidden' booze, and prevent a tween from trying it out in more dangerous quantities or circumstances whilst alone or with friends. Only you can decide if this is the right approach for you, or not. If you decide it is, bear in mind the following tips:

- Offer a drink only very occasionally, and as part of a special meal or social event.
- Stick to low-strength brands – they vary a lot, so check the percentage on the label if you are not sure – and offer diluted versions: wine with water, or beer with lemonade. Alcopops are best avoided: they can taste appealing to tweens, but at an average 1.5 units a bottle, that's not a taste you want to encourage.
- Don't let him drink on an empty stomach – only with a meal.
- Allow no more than one small glass of anything at a time: tweens' bodies are smaller and they are likely to get drunk far more easily than an adult.
- Don't be tempted to provide alcohol to tweens at a party. Even if you've decided it's OK for your tween to take a sip or two at home, other parents may not agree.

What the experts say

Elaine says: This is an area steeped in hypocrisy as many parents may drink and smoke and even perhaps dabble in drugs, but lecture their children about the dangers of doing so. Depending on our values here, it's very unwise to forbid our children to indulge in the above if we're partaking ourselves. Sometimes, it means curbing our own bad habits – or at least being conscious of not parading them in front of the children.

Tweens will experiment. It's a rite of passage for them, and as long as we encourage them to talk about their experiences and make sure they understand some of the dangers and implications, we can confidently hope they'll be able to make sensible decisions and judgements about what's good for them, and come to adopt our values for themselves. If you forbid your child to go to a party because you know alcohol may be available, you'll just be giving your tween the message that you don't care and you don't understand, which makes it more likely he'll choose to experiment behind your back. It's much better to engage in a conversation that states your concerns, but that will only work if you've always been good at noticing and praising when your tween exercises good judgement, and empathising with him if he does want to do what the 'in crowd' are doing. If your child knows you respect him, he's much more likely to respect you and your values. Sometimes, children rebel in the moment and flout the rules we're trying to impose but actually adopt the values encapsulated in those rules in the long term. A child engaging in booze or fags behind a parent's back has breached the parent's trust and an appropriate consequence could well be a restriction on freedoms. But such a consequence would have limited effect and may even backfire if not accompanied by empathetic discussion that makes clear that it is the behaviour that's inappropriate, not the child who is bad.

On the continent, many families give their children alcohol at a very young age, usually mixed with water, and the statistics for teenage drinking are low. Experts in the UK are divided about this approach. I personally think that as parents we need to be careful not to give mixed messages about the consumption of alcohol. If you wish your children to be law-abiding citizens, and this is an important value to you, then providing them with alcohol under-age could undermine that value, unless you are careful to explain that the limited amount of alcohol you allow them at home – and we're talking sips here – is for educational purposes only. This is something that will be decided upon differently by individual families, but if as a parent you decide to give your tween small amounts of alcohol then you also need to educate him about the importance of drinking in moderation and the effects of alcohol on his body. Kids at this age tend to love to learn facts, especially strange ones, and are eager to learn how things work. So it's a good time to discuss openly some facts about alcohol: its long- and short-term effects and consequences, its physical effects, and why it's especially dangerous for growing bodies. Be aware that ads about alcohol show people having fun, surrounded by friends, and give the message that drinking alcohol is super cool – and at the moment there is no pre-watershed restriction on alcohol advertising. If your tween is seeing such ads, the messages need to be balanced with information about the downsides.

Crissy says: A common assumption is that tweens who experiment with drink or drugs do so because they have serious problems or are 'off the rails'. But in fact, it may simply be about curiosity, boredom, opportunity, isolation or peer pressure. Taking risks is often part and parcel of a tween's growing need for greater autonomy. As well as challenging you, he's also pushing his own boundaries, trying behaviours on for size, and exploring the unknown and the forbidden. The good news is that most kids will successfully negotiate this tricky developmental period in their lives, emerging changed, but relatively unscathed.

Don't wait until it happens and tempers are running high before talking to your tweens about smoking, drinking and taking drugs. Remember that 'taboo' can often equal 'irresistible attraction' for your tween, so aim to normalise the whole business. Talk about why people do and don't partake of these substances, and give your own opinions, by all means, but take care also to listen to and respect his point of view. Invite him to consider how he feels about the long-term health implications and any possible legal ramifications of such behaviour, and above all be approachable and encourage a casual and relaxed approach towards such discussions. If something is regularly discussed in the car or over the dinner table it somehow demystifies the whole business and makes it less likely to appear exciting or glamorous. Keep the lines of communication open and make sure you always know where your tween is going and who with.

Before talking to your tween do the research and make sure you know your stuff. Don't be afraid to admit ignorance and ask for help yourself. Resist the temptation to fall back on scare tactics. There's no point telling him alcohol tastes foul or makes you sick and then pouring yourself a large glass of red, or suggesting that the very whiff of tobacco causes cancer when he can plainly see his sprightly grandfather puffing away on the patio. Treat your tween like the bright young thing he really is and give him some credit. Be honest, but be realistic. Of course cigarettes, alcohol and drugs do present a serious long-term health risk, but kids of this age often feel pretty invincible so you might be better off flagging up the more short-term issues: ciggies make your clothes and breath stink, for example, and falling over drunk and throwing up won't impress the girls. Of course, you can talk to your tween until you're blue in the face, but at the end of the day actions do speak louder than words – so think carefully before you use alcohol, tobacco or any sort of drug in front of him.

There's always the risk you might find yourself put firmly on the spot by your tween asking about your own youthful habits, so it's a good idea to plan for such eventualities. Remember it's less about what you did and more about what you learned from it. So if you decide to confess all, remember to let your tween know how powerful addictions can be and that looking back now as an adult you can see how risky your behaviour was and that's why you're just trying to save him from making the same mistakes you did.

If you do find out he's experimented with alcohol, cigarettes or drugs, try not to overreact: chances are he'll just tune out and shut down. Instead, talk to him. Show him you care, and are concerned. And, rather than rushing to impose sanctions or punishments, encourage him to consider the potential consequences of his actions so that – hopefully – he'll make a more sensible decision next time he has the opportunity.

What the netmums say

Horrible habits

I talk to George a lot about smoking and drugs and alcohol. I am the biggest anti-smoker ever and I've discussed why I hate it at length with him. I hope I've also explained the dangers of drugs to him enough to try and make him stop and think before he ever took any. I do think though, that to an extent it's out of your hands once they reach their teens. You can be the best parent in the world and your child could still get into a bad crowd and choose to take drugs, or be pressured into it. All you can do is try and steer them in the right direction and hope to God it works. I hope he would come to me if he did ever come under pressure. He's never tried alcohol as I don't like the taste of it myself, and don't have it in the house. I see no reason to let him try it.
Natalie, mum to a boy, ten, and a girl, two

When my oldest was in Year Eleven, he told me, sadly, that well over half of his year group were regular smokers and some were even experimenting with soft drugs. My husband and I both smoked as teenagers for a few years and experimented with drugs – it was the done thing where we lived and among the people we mixed with. The boys know this and I think in some ways it makes them more likely to ask our opinion. We drink alcohol socially and often have wine in the evening, but I would not allow a tween to try alcohol, as I think it's just too young.
Jo, mum to three boys aged seventeen, fourteen and eleven

I haven't really brought up the subject of drinks, alcohol and booze. One of her school pals recently posted on Facebook that she was drunk. She is twelve! Emma told me she has no interest in getting drunk, which I believe. She's quite naïve in this respect, and also very honest. She hasn't grown up in an environment where people have smoked and I'm hoping she will

follow my example by never trying it. She has tried sips of cider and wine in the past from my glass, but didn't like the taste.
Nicola, mum to a girl, eleven, and a boy, four

We were horrified to discover our son had been smoking whilst in the park with his friends. It was pretty obvious – I could smell it on his breath. Neither of us smoke now – although we both did in the past – and we can't bear the thought of our kids taking it up. My immediate reaction was to rant, but thankfully his dad managed to step in with a calmer approach and was able to talk to him about it. As it turned out, he'd tried it because he felt he should – and he hadn't enjoyed it that much. He promised he won't be trying it again in a hurry. I just hope he sticks to that.
Bella, mum to a boy, twelve, and two girls aged ten and seven

I don't think lecturing is the way to go a lot of the time. I know my parents told me not to drink but the minute I was able to get my hands on some alcohol, I drank. My daughter's quite sensible. We recently travelled back from the city centre at night, by bus, and of course, there were drunk, loud people everywhere. My daughter looked horrified and I told her, 'That's what drink does for you.' I don't think you can ever stop your child from experimenting with anything – we're naïve if we think otherwise. We know what we did when we were that age and know how easy it is to get away with things. I think educating them about the risks of doing these things and explaining the consequences of such behaviour is more effective than just telling them never to do it.
Naomi, mum to two girls aged twelve and five

Smoking is a hard one, because I'm guilty of smoking about five a day. Obviously he knows I do it, even though I go outside. Fortunately both of my children tell me I'm disgusting and stink, which may sound disrespectful but I cannot really argue with it! My daughter has never smoked but my son is probably more easily led so it wouldn't surprise me if he does try it in the future.

However, I believe that peer pressure is more likely to encourage him than his stinky mother. As for alcohol, we drink wine occasionally and my husband has the odd beer. We believe in introducing alcohol to children early, in moderation, in the home, where we can keep our eye on them, and we always offer them the chance to try it. My son doesn't like the taste at all so declines and at eighteen my daughter likes to drink but, as far as I know, she's never yet been drunk.

Ali, mum to a girl, eighteen, and a boy, eleven

I don't think my girls will ever smoke because they don't live in a house where people smoke and when they visit their dad, who does smoke, they find it disgusting. I like a drink on occasion and so they see me drinking in moderation, which I think is a good example to set. I have let them have a sip of my wine, and I think that's OK. Drugs, however, is a difficult subject for me as I experimented with lots of different drugs myself when I was young, and it really worries me that they might too. I put myself in some very dangerous situations, and I can't stand the thought of them doing that. Usually I'm honest about everything with my children, but I don't want them to know what I've done, in case they think it's OK. I hope my children will always share what's going on in their lives with me, whatever it is.

Louise, mum to three girls aged thirteen, twelve and three

My other half recently had a night out with some other dads who don't get out much: the children were appalled at their uselessness the following day – something the mums were keen to point out was the result of too much alcohol! And a recent trip to town where they were shocked by the drunks they saw in the streets also raised a lot of questions, and illustrated what can happen when things get out of control. It was a very educational trip. Using opportunities to reinforce the messages as they come up seems to work, without going on and on about it.

Jo, mum to a boy, eleven, and a girl, nine

7 Emotional issues

Tweens are highly vulnerable to emotional problems like stress, anxiety and depression. It stands to reason – after all, life's throwing a lot at them right now, with all the mental, physical and social upheaval of the transitional years between childhood and teens. They're old enough to *feel* emotional difficulties, but not yet mature or experienced enough to cope with them. And whilst it's probably never been any picnic getting through the tween years, many experts reckon it's harder than ever today, with commercial, peer, and academic pressures spoiling the latter years of childhood, and even threatening emotional wellbeing. Family breakdown and hard economic times mean that for many there are also other background difficulties to cope with, too. So it's hardly surprising if the emotional going gets tough, sometimes, for this age group.

It's important to be alert to the possibility that your tween is struggling emotionally in some way. It won't always be obvious – especially since mood swings are part and parcel of life for this age group – but looking out for major changes in her usual behaviour or attitude is something worth doing. Don't forget, too, that emotional worries can manifest themselves in physical ways with headaches or stomach pains, so if your tween seems to be suffering a lot and there's no clear medical reason for it, try asking if there's anything on her mind. Never underestimate any emotional problem your tween seems to have, however minor it may seem to you. It may be a seriously big deal to her.

Boosting confidence and self-esteem

Self-esteem is the way we feel about ourselves, and having plenty of the positive sort is essential for good mental health. With high self-esteem, it's easier to make and keep friends, to solve problems or find help to do so if necessary, to respect ourselves and in turn gain respect from others, and to generally behave in a socially acceptable way. Low self-esteem, on the other hand, makes it harder to mix socially or to deal with failure or new experiences, can lead to feelings of inadequacy or being unloved, and makes us vulnerable to more serious emotional disorders.

As parents, we need to do all we can to nurture self-esteem and confidence in our tweens, since these things can really take a nosedive during this challenging time. Some kids already have a good supply, others need plenty of stoking – and it's not always obvious which is which. In any case, it may not be a permanent state: they can move in and out of different phases. In particular, a period of low self-esteem or loss of confidence may follow a specific trigger such as a family crisis, or an experience such as bullying.

Look for ways that you can boost your tween's confidence and self-esteem by giving praise and encouragement whenever it's due, as well as listening to her and allowing her to express herself whenever she needs to. Make sure she knows your love is unconditional – that you won't ever withdraw it, whatever she does, or whatever happens. Don't feel bad if your love and praise seems sometimes to be rejected. She almost certainly cares more than she lets on.

It goes without saying that it's a bad idea to pile on pressure for your child to achieve in areas like exams, schoolwork and extra-curricular activities. It's fine to give positive encouragement, and even to help her set goals for herself, but do be realistic about what these should be – and don't ever show you're disappointed if and when she fails to reach them. Don't force her to try and take up an activity she clearly doesn't want to do, or doesn't have an aptitude for: just look for something else that suits her better.

When your tween fails to pull something off or something doesn't go according to plan for her, try to find something to praise anyway – effort or attitude, perhaps. Don't forget to be specific in your language, though. If it's just a general 'well done', she might feel merely patronised. If she's being self-critical, don't brush off or deny those feelings, but acknowledge them, and offer to talk about how she could change things. Don't let her wallow in it, though: help her see the things about her that are good, instead. And reassure her that it's fine to fail or make mistakes sometimes; it's absolutely normal, and we all do it. Try to avoid criticising your tween. Even if you have to pull her up for bad behaviour, emphasise that it's the behaviour, not her, that you're unhappy about. And if your tween is not your only child, remember to give plenty of praise to both, or all your children. Don't ever be tempted to hold up comparisons among brothers and sisters (or other friends, for that matter).

Giving your tween some of the independence she's no doubt looking for, and allowing her scope to find her own solutions to difficulties – by questioning, as well as listening, when you're discussing problems – is also an important step in building her self-esteem. Allow her to start making small steps away from you and praise her for it when she copes well. There's more on independence issues in the following chapter.

What the experts say

Elaine says: Self-esteem is all about having a core belief in one's own value. It comes from a tween having many experiences that demonstrate that her life has value, that she's a worthwhile person, and that her opinion has validity. Tweens need to be accepted as unique individuals, appreciated for who they are, and not who we'd like them to be. Self-esteem comes primarily from parents' approval, and the key to it is ensuring she feels understood, respected, heard and valued for who she is. Aim to build a strong relationship based on 'three pillars' – listening, praising, and positively reinforcing boundaries. Listening to tweens' feelings, thoughts, ideas and opinions without judgement and without offering too much advice is vital. By the time many children approach their teens, they've developed a strategy of not talking to their parents, for fear of being nagged or told what to do, or being judged or criticised for what they share. Active and reflective listening is a really important skill to make sure we're building rapport with our children. Praising her descriptively will motivate her, and ensure she knows she's valued. And clear, consistent boundaries give tweens the security from which they can develop their increasingly independent lives.

Our tweens will often make mistakes and won't always succeed in all areas. How we talk to them has a huge impact on how they view themselves. If your child has made a mistake, it's vital not to bang on about it or be critical or it will inevitably result in her feeling very unsuccessful or even seeing herself as useless. We need to help our tweens view failure as part of life, and something to learn from rather than something that diminishes them. If they get the idea that failure is to be avoided, they will become risk-averse and unable to grow. We also need to stay calm and non-judgemental in the face of their mistakes, while ensuring that some learning comes out of the incident. And we need to model positively how we handle our own mistakes: not beating ourselves up over slip-ups, but letting them see us take steps to remedy the situation, and learn for the future.

If you're talking to a child who has experienced failure, voice your support carefully. When my own daughter, then aged eleven, failed to make the netball team, my words to her were: 'I know how hard you've been working at it and I'm impressed by how dedicated and committed you were. Getting up early every Tuesday morning to get to training took a lot of effort on your part. I'm guessing this must feel very unfair.' It's amazing what happens when tweens feel heard and are able to let go of the feelings – they can then start looking for solutions. After her disappointment, my daughter picked herself up and looked for other opportunities within the squad. Eventually, she became goalkeeper.

Crissy says: A strong sense of self will stand your tween in good stead when it comes to facing all the challenges that the tween years bring. Feeling valued by you will encourage your child to value herself and go some way towards nurturing her sense of self-worth. Building self-esteem is not the same as spoiling or over-indulging your tween. It's about showing her that she matters, that you care and believe in her as the unique and capable human being that she is. Tweens who demonstrate a healthy level of self-esteem and self-worth tend to be happier and more successful at school, in relationships and in life generally. They're more likely to have the confidence to take on new challenges and explore new activities, and are less likely to suffer from depression or other emotional disorders.

No matter how well developed your tween's self-worth may be, life will still tend to give it a knock from time to time, so it's important that in traumatic periods we make sure our children feel especially loved, supported and valued for who they are, and not for what they may achieve or who we might like them to be. If your tween is lacking self-esteem, make sure you take time out to really listen to her viewpoint and to show that her opinion matters, and that you are willing to consider her choices as viable options. Practise positive parenting, appreciating what she does well rather than resorting to criticism when things go wrong. But resist the urge to mollycoddle. What your tween needs now is the confidence to pursue greater autonomy, not parents who are unconsciously reinforcing her own feelings of inadequacy or failure. I would add, though, that it's important to be realistic in your praise! If you build her up to believe she's better at something than she really is, she could end up expecting everything in life to come easily to her with minimum effort – and that way bitter disappointment lies.

Stress, anxiety and feeling blue

So, it's not unusual for tweens to suffer sometimes from emotional difficulties such as stress and anxiety, or to feel down for short periods. Just like us adults, individual tweens will cope differently with these problems, some better than others. It may be that a specific cause or event has triggered these difficult feelings – which could be something that seems quite trivial to us, such as falling out with a friend, or difficulty with a particular subject at school – or it may just be general feelings that she's struggling with. In most cases, these difficulties will be temporary phases which you can help your tween through with lots of love and a little extra attention.

Talking about it

Try to get your tween to talk if she seems stressed, worried or low, and when she talks, be sure to listen. Use reflective listening – repeat back what she's saying, so she knows you're taking it all in – and try to help her work out for herself what might make her feel better, or if there are any practical solutions you could look at together.

Of course, she might not want to talk much – it's normal for tweens to 'internalise' difficult feelings. If you can't get her to talk face-to-face, you could try and instigate a conversation while something else is going on, to relieve the pressure a little – perhaps in the car, or whilst she's helping you with the washing up. You could also suggest that she puts her thoughts in writing, via a letter, email or text. Or perhaps she will more happily talk to another trusted adult instead. If she's determined not to talk, make sure she knows you're there for her, should she change her mind. Allow her privacy and time to mull things over alone, but don't be tempted just to let her get on with it, either – she may secretly really need you to butt in, so check back regularly to see if she's changed her mind about opening up.

Try too to help your tween understand that it's normal and OK to feel a bit rubbish sometimes. Life isn't always a bed of roses.

The big chill: How to de-stress your tween's lifestyle

- Is her agenda too full? Kids do a lot these days with all that schoolwork, socialising and extra-curricular activities. If you suspect she's suffering from a bit of 'burn-out', it may be time to take a look at her schedule and readjust if necessary.

- Sleep is vital for good emotional health. If your tween isn't getting a good nine hours a night, she should be.
- Find time for fun. Keep screen-time limited and make sure she's getting plenty of play and relaxation. Sometimes, it's good to do absolutely nothing.
- Make sure she's getting regular exercise – and some fresh air, too. These things can also boost sleep.
- Encourage her to eat well. Turn back to Chapter 6 for more tips on this.
- Help to counter 'education stress' as best you can. Give help with homework (see Chapter 2), and offer to speak to her teachers if anything's worrying her. If you're supporting your child through SATs or a major project, do your utmost to reduce pressure, rather than increase it.
- Art, creative writing, diary-keeping and music can be good ways to prevent or release stress and unhappiness, so provide your tween with the equipment, time and privacy she needs to express her feelings in these ways if she wants to.
- The company of good friends can be a tonic, so make sure she gets to spend plenty of time with pals who you know can be relied on to make her feel better.

Your mental health

If you're worried about your tween's mental health, don't forget to pay some attention to your own. As adults, we often struggle to deal with stress ourselves and when that happens, it's likely to rub off on our children. You don't have to hide how you're feeling from your tween if you've got problems, but you should try not to burden her with the very worst of them: turn to an adult for the support you need in times of crisis.

If you have a diagnosed mental health problem such as depression, it's really important you get the best professional help you can to cope, because evidence shows your children will be more at risk of developing problems, too.

Could this be serious?

All tweens will have ups and downs, and periods of stress, worry and feeling blue are usually just phases that come and go. But if your tween seems persistently low, worried, weepy or anxious and it's been going on for a month or more, or if it's significantly affecting other aspects of life such as interest in her schoolwork or usual activities, sleep and eating, relationships with friends or family, behaviour, or her general health, she may be suffering from depression, and in need of some professional help. Although depression tends to be considered an adult problem, kids can suffer, too: according to the Royal College of Psychiatrists, it affects one in 200 children under the age of twelve, and two to three per cent of teenagers. There's more about how to get help later in this chapter.

What the experts say

Elaine says: I believe a key cause of the stress and anxiety experienced by our tweens today is pressure from parents, schools and society. We all need to redefine success for our children, so we create a nation of critical thinkers and problem solvers, and a society of happier and motivated children. We want our children to be able to recognise their strengths and weaknesses and appreciate who they are and what they can offer, and not strive for perfection or perfect grades, nor to view success in terms of beating others. Instead they should see it more in terms of their own best efforts. The more we do to build strong self-esteem and foster resilience the less likely it is that our children will succumb to stress, anxiety or depression.

As her parent, you're the expert on your tween, and hopefully you will notice any signs of these problems by changes in her behaviour – although, of course, as they get closer to adolescence, tweens may be naturally moody, unresponsive and intensely private. Parents need to be observant, which means spending time with their children, and they need to foster communication. Kids are more likely to listen if what we say to them is more often positive, and they are more likely to talk if we adopt an open, non-judgemental attitude. Again, we have to make time to listen. It's hard enough for an almost-teenager to talk to parents about some issues, let alone if she has to make an appointment to do so. Doing activities with our children – both fun ones and routine ones – means the opportunities for conversations are maximised.

I feel the best thing we can do for our kids is to support them from within the home, and establish a connective relationship between parent and tween. However, there are times when outside help can be incredibly useful, if indeed she's receptive to talking to someone else. Family therapy can help, in that it doesn't make the tween the problem but looks instead at how the whole family interacts. If the issues are complex or harmful, I would always urge parents to seek help from within the medical profession.

What the netmums say

Emotional problems

Kevin gets very stressed about nothing. Sometimes he says he has too much homework and sometimes he says he's stressed, but doesn't know why. My theory is that most of it is fuelled by hormones. We talk to him about how he's feeling, but more often than not he can't really explain what's wrong. Schoolwork certainly does seem to be part of the problem, and keeping up with his friends on some of his computer games is a big worry – one seems to have unlimited time and access to a game as well as help from his dad, which means Kevin is quite far behind. This friend brags about being so far ahead, and it really worries Kevin that he can't catch up.

Kirsty, mum to two boys aged thirteen and nine months

James and Jake have both suffered from emotional problems, caused by being bullied. I found that lots of encouragement to get on with the things they enjoy and a positive attitude at home seemed to help. We had a fantastic family support worker at their school and she helped the boys a lot by talking over the problems they were having, and helping them to find their own ways to resolve it.

Claire, mum to five boys aged eleven, nine, six, five and one, and a girl, three

Because he has Asperger's Syndrome, my son suffers from constantly high levels of anxiety in everyday life. To help him to cope with these super-stressful times, we plan things to the nth degree, and include him in all the planning. He can also be prone to brief bouts of depression, possibly because he finds the world so confusing. We're getting very good at explaining life's mysteries in a way that helps him make sense of them! Every child has their own emotional make-up and every child needs support tailored to their individual needs. As parents, we need as much reliable information as possible on emotional health and wellbeing, so we're equipped to help our children cope. The tween years are the hardest because they're going through so many transitions, both physically and in their education, so the more support we can give them, the happier they will be.

Julie, mum to a boy, nine

As a mum of five kids aged from eight to twenty-four, I often feel I've 'been there, done that and got the T-shirt'! But this meant that by the time my third child had got to the tween stage, I was quick to dismiss the daily angst he was going through, rather than get too involved in the rollercoaster of emotions he was feeling. Sadly, he felt that I was dismissing his concerns and was not there for him, causing him real emotional pain, and he was unable to share his very real concerns to me. He struggled with his emotions and developed an eating disorder, requiring medical and psychological support from professionals. So I've learnt that

the 'normal' angst that comes during this time should be individually acknowledged, the child supported and the drama
dealt with, rather than dismissed as just the same thing that you
or their siblings went through.

Pam, mum to two girls aged twenty-four and eight, and three
boys aged twenty-two, seventeen and fourteen

He's normally a happy and quiet lad, but my eldest went through
a period of being very emotional a little while ago. We had
frequent bouts of tears and self-deprecation, violent anger, defiance and indifference. Our home life is good and there were
no obvious reasons for it. I arranged an informal meeting with
his teacher but was told he was a model pupil and there was
nothing untoward going on. Then my son told me, in a fit of
tears, that nobody loved him and he wanted to kill himself. I
took this seriously, and went to see my GP, who referred us to
our local Child and Adolescent Mental Health Services. Through
them, we had a couple of counselling sessions, during which we
talked about ways of coping with his extreme emotions, and
then he undertook a one-on-one art therapy course. Ultimately,
they could not find anything to explain his outbursts. I was
told they were probably just part of his personality. As we both
re-learnt how to deal with these potentially explosive incidents,
the situation improved and the outbursts lessened. He's now
been discharged and, most of the time, back to normal. There
are still occasional outbursts, which I do my best to deal with.
But at least I know he's a normal, healthy child – and I know
what to look for in the future, so will hopefully be able to avert
further problems. The advice I would give is that, if you want
help, it is available. Never be afraid to talk to school or to your
GP about your child. They're professionals, and want your child
to be happy as much as you do.

Peta, mum to two boys aged nine and seven

My son is going through problems with self-esteem at school right
now, having been singled out for bullying by one particular boy.

He now tends to bring all his anger home, and has become quite unruly, so me, his dad and his younger brother have to endure the frustration he's kept in during the day. He's constantly asking to be hugged – which is hardly typical for a nine-year-old boy – and asking how much we love him. It just shows that it only takes one event or one person to bring your confidence down. As a family we're constantly reassuring him. His brother has a hearing problem and also confidence issues. We just make sure that no matter what happens we are there for them, and also make time for them separately so they can talk about anything they want to.

Amanda, mum to two boys aged nine and six

Feelings about their bodies

Sadly, many of today's tweens are unhappy about their bodies. As well as quite natural worries about how puberty is changing the way they look, there's now intense social pressure, fuelled by peers and the media, to match up to physical ideals that aren't actually that realistic. There are also concerns that, for some tweens, the drive to combat obesity – although well intended – has put too much emphasis on the issue of weight loss. A recent survey by Ofsted found that more than forty per cent of girls and a quarter of boys have become worried about their body image by the age of twelve.

The best way to ward off feelings of inadequacy and distorted self-image is to talk openly around the issue. Experts say there's little doubt about the significance of media images when it comes to unhealthy body-related behaviours, which include eating disorders and exercise obsession. You can't shield your tween from these images because they're everywhere, but you can educate her about the realities. So, chat about those glossy adverts, celebrity photo-shoots and pop videos. Make sure she knows the images she sees have little to do with reality because the people in them have benefited from personal trainers, plastic surgery and photographic re-touching, and help her compare this catalogue of perfection with people you know in real life. Discuss the fact that there's huge natural variation in body shape, due to factors beyond our control, such as genetics. It's also important she knows that gaining weight and changing shape is totally natural at this time of life.

If your tween seems worried about her body image, let her know she looks fine as she is but avoid specifically praising her simply for looking good. Instead heap credit on her for the more important stuff like kindness, empathy and sharing, and other talents too.

Never be negative – even in jest – about the way your tween looks. Even if she really is carrying a bit of extra weight, don't comment on it, or make a big deal about it. Just help her towards a healthier lifestyle by making some subtle adjustments to the whole family's diet, and upping the amount of exercise she does (turn back to Chapter 6 for a bit more on this subject).

Think carefully about your own body image, if you have a tween who seems to have a problem in that area. If it's something you worry about, keep it to yourself – and if you tend to obsess over what you're eating or you're often trying to lose weight, be very careful about the messages you're passing on. Don't let her hear you say your bum's too big, and don't let her know you're 'dieting': trying to achieve a healthier lifestyle would be a better way to put it. Keep your ears open, and pull her up if you hear her making negative comments about someone else's appearance. If she tells you she's been subjected to bullying comments herself because of the way she looks, help her to work out some appropriate and assertive responses.

Kids who suffer generally from low self-esteem are more likely to have a poor body image, so keep on boosting this prize commodity whenever you get the chance.

When it goes too far

Although it is still pretty rare for an eating disorder to develop in a child under thirteen, it does happen – and medical experts are concerned that it is on the rise within this age group.

Whilst eating disorders are inevitably linked with weight or body image issues, they're usually far more complex than just that, developing as a way of coping with broader emotional problems such as low self-esteem, stress, anxiety or boredom, or specific issues such as abuse, loss, family breakdown or bullying. High-achieving kids who strive for perfection are also among those prone to developing eating disorders. Taking control of food and eating is a way to feel in control of difficult feelings.

According to BEAT, the Eating Disorders Association, there are three main types of eating disorder: anorexia nervosa, which involves skipping meals, and rigid control of what's eaten; bulimia nervosa, which involves a cycle of bingeing and vomiting; and binge-eating disorder, which involves overeating. Boys are affected too, although eating disorders are more common in girls. And naturally, all of these can have serious and even dangerous effects on physical and mental health.

A tween with an eating disorder is very likely to be secretive about it. Signs to watch out for include weight loss, baggy clothing, hiding or picking at food, trying to avoid meals, eating in secret, talking about being fat continually, vomiting after meals or exercising excessively.

If you do suspect your tween has fallen into a pattern of potentially damaging eating habits, try not to panic. Let her know you want to help, but don't get into any battles or try to force healthier eating habits on her. And seek professional help as soon as possible: the earlier eating disorders are treated, the better the chance of a full recovery.

BEAT is the main UK charity dedicated to helping people with eating disorders. Helpline and website details are included in the back of this book.

What the experts say

Crissy says: Our tweens are constantly soaking up media images of super-skinny women and tall, muscular men, which are presented as the ideal way to look. It's our job as parents to try to redress the balance by moving the emphasis away from the physical form and teaching our children from an early age that all types of body are beautiful. If you comment on how a child is pretty, handsome, tall or slim, it suggests a preference on your part, which may impact upon the self-esteem of any tween who considers herself to be none of these things. Hearing gleeful praise lavished upon Mum's weight-watching friend inevitably sends the message to your tween that thin is good. Make your tween aware that the images she sees in magazines and on television are manufactured. Models are chosen precisely because they are thin, and make-up, lighting, editing and air brushing add to the illusion.

Children watch and learn from us, so never tease your tween about her looks and discourage them from judging others based on their outward appearance. Look carefully at your own attitudes and behaviours around body image and try to instil in your child the idea that beauty is skin deep and it's our inner qualities that really matter. Avoid talking to your tween in terms of weight or dieting and try to set up healthy eating habits from an early age. When we label foods as good or bad we inadvertently create taboo foods, so opting for the 'everything in moderation' approach may be preferable. Similarly, try to foster the idea in your tween that exercise is a fun daily activity rather than a chore or a means to an end.

The onset of puberty can be a scary time for your tween. Huge changes in her physical and emotional development can leave her feeling out of control. Tweens need to be informed and feel involved, so make sure she knows about and understands these changes before they occur so that she doesn't feel frightened by or disconnected from her body. To a degree, the combination of cultural pressures and puberty itself means that a general preoccupation with how their bodies look is pretty natural for kids at this stage, but if your tween seems overly focused on her body image and seeks to alter or control it through food or exercise, that should set alarm bells ringing. The words 'eating disorder' can instantly provoke anxiety, but no matter how fearful you are, try not to be seen to panic. The fact that your tween's worried about her weight or eating too much or too little, doesn't necessarily mean she's headed for a major problem. At the same time, you shouldn't just assume it's a phase that will soon pass. Talk to her about it.

Those tweens who develop eating disorders do so in response to a complex combination of psychological, physiological and social influences, and generally not purely as a response to a single traumatic event or experience. Research suggests that some are actually more likely to develop an eating disorder because they are genetically predisposed to do so. The presence of certain triggers in their life such as divorce, bereavement or bullying, a family history of anxiety or depression and/or issues around sexuality or abuse also increase the likelihood that an eating disorder could develop. Sufferers often have low self-esteem and may have issues around perfectionism and failure and a poor or distorted body image – but sadly there is no fail-safe checklist we can use to determine why one tween succumbs and another doesn't. As with many tween-age issues, there's a school of thought that automatically blames the parents, and although there is evidence to suggest that possible triggers include exposure to the disordered eating of a close family member and over-controlling parenting styles, we can see that the issue is far more complex than simply pointing the finger at Mum and Dad. To my mind, time spent feeling guilty is probably time squandered and would be better spent making sure your tween gets the support and treatment she needs. Whatever the root cause of eating disorders amongst tweens, what is clear is that positive parental involvement and support has a profoundly healing affect and can be a huge aid to recovery.

Tweens who hurt themselves

Although it sounds like an extreme problem, self-harming is not so unusual in kids and young people – according to the mental health charity Young Minds, between one in twelve and one in fifteen deliberately self-harm, for example by cutting, burning, scratching, and pulling out hair, as a way of dealing with difficult feelings or experiences.

Self-harming is not the same as feeling suicidal – the majority who do it don't want to end their life, but rather are just struggling to cope with some aspect of it and cannot find the words to express themselves, or ask for help. Self-harm can be a way to release feelings or to be distracted from them, to self-punish, to feel in control, to communicate, to seek comfort or care from others, or to feel 'alive'.

Chances are you'll be shocked and horrified if it's something that affects your family, but it's important to realise that it may not be your fault or caused by anything you've done. A tween with a problem that goes this deep will probably need some professional help to get her through it, so don't hesitate to seek it.

Coping with traumatic times

Tweens are at a tricky age when it comes to getting through traumatic times. They're old enough to understand the complexities of a relationship breakdown, or the finality of death, but still immature, vulnerable and sensitive enough that dealing with it is going to be difficult. Trauma can lead to self-destructive behaviour in tweens, or can make them turn in on themselves and become silent and self-critical, so if your tween is going through a difficult phase of life, she's going to need loads of love, support and attention to get her through.

There's no set way that a tween will respond to a major trauma – grief and distress can present itself in different guises. Anger is a common response, and this could manifest itself in a variety of ways, including bad behaviour, aggression, sulkiness or problems at school. Anxiety is also a likely outcome: if something's gone badly wrong for her, she may well worry that something else will go wrong, too. And guilt is another common possibility – she may feel what's happened is her fault. Her feelings may also show themselves in one of a number of physical ways such as trouble sleeping, nightmares, bed-wetting, refusing food or overeating, headaches or stomach upsets. But don't be particularly surprised, either, if your tween doesn't show much in the way of obvious emotion during times of trauma – it's common for children of this age to prefer to grieve privately. It may also be that her feelings fluctuate wildly, moving in between unhappiness and what appears to be indifference. She might regress during difficult periods, reverting to childlike characteristics you haven't seen in her for a while, like clinginess or attention-seeking. She may also be concerned about trivial things that don't seem important: who's going to take her to school; will she still be able to celebrate her birthday; is she going to get her pocket money that week? As far as you can, try to see the situation through her eyes, as well as your own, and indulge her responses, whatever they may be.

Experts stress that we should try and make life as normal as possible for kids during and after times of trauma. So, sticking to familiar routines and patterns can really help. If this is a struggle for you because you're feeling grief or pain too, then enlist whatever help you can from willing friends or relatives to try and keep life on as even a keel as possible. Make sure important people such as teachers and friends all know what's going on, so they can help with this process.

Talking it through

When it comes to supporting tweens through major difficulties like death and divorce, there's no question that honesty is the best policy. Where possible, you should protect her from really worrying details, but you do need to let her have the basic facts, and you need to answer any questions she has truthfully. Chances are, your tween *will* have some tricky questions for you: at this age, she is likely to want to explore the 'whys' as well as the 'whens, wheres and hows' of a death, or be told precisely what factors have contributed to a marriage breakdown. Be as honest as you feel you can be; say if it's something you don't really have an answer for. Listen reflectively to anything she has to say, and ask for her take on the matter, too. Make sure she knows she can talk about it, and ask questions about it whenever she wants, for as long as she wants.

Don't go it alone

Do draw on whatever professional help is available when you need to get a tween through a trauma – if you're also affected and are struggling yourself with grief or pain, then a neutral third party will be invaluable in sharing the load. Your GP can refer you to an appropriate counsellor, either from a relevant support organisation or from your local Child and Adolescent Mental Health Service (CAMHS). Lean on friends and relatives, too, if they're willing to help. It may be that your tween doesn't want or can't cope with talking to you about what she's going through, but she might be able to talk to another adult she trusts. You could also consider exploring books together: there's a wide range of titles written specifically to help children through all sorts of difficult situations.

Living with loss: How to help your tween through bereavement

- Be truthful with your tween, and don't use flowery language or euphemisms. Kids of this age start to understand that death is final, and that someone who dies is not coming back. If you have religious or cultural reasons to tell them otherwise, that's fair enough. But otherwise, be upfront: it won't be helpful for your tween to hear that a dead person is now a star, or an angel, or in a better place.
- When talking about death, or someone dying, avoid having a big 'sit-down' discussion, which may feel awkward to her. Try to bring it into conversations frequently, and as naturally as you can.
- Don't feel you need to keep your own grief in for your tween's sake. She can and should see you cry, so she understands this is an OK way to release grief and difficult feelings. Don't close up when emotion overspills, though: if you're crying, you will need to explain to her why.
- It's very normal for children to feel guilt when a person close to them dies. You may need to help her understand that what's happened is absolutely not her fault.
- Saying goodbye is an important part of the grieving process. Make all efforts to ensure your tween attends the funeral – if this isn't possible, consider holding some alternative ceremony or another way to remember them.
  Holding on to memories is all-important when someone dies. A bereaved tween should be helped to do this by talking about the person that's gone as much and for as long as she wants – even long after the death. Keeping photographs and other precious mementoes, perhaps in a specially created 'memory box', is a good idea.

Get professional help if you need it. Relevant organisations are Winston's Wish; The Child Bereavement Charity; and the Grief Encounter Project. Details for these are included in the back of the book.

What the experts say

Crissy says: Your tween's emotional antennae are acutely attuned to your current state of mind, so in traumatic times – no matter how hard you try to hide it – she will often instinctively know something is wrong. If an explanation is not forthcoming from you, tweens' imaginations may run riot and it's possible they will blame themselves. Ironically at the very time they need us most, mid-crisis parents are often emotionally unavailable, fragile, volatile or even physically absent from the home, and so your tween may find herself bearing not only her own distress, but the brunt of yours, too. Tweens don't generally respond well to secrecy and most will be mature enough to handle at least the bare bones of the issue at hand. So be upfront, and be sure to keep talking.

Unresolved trauma can have a profound long-term effect on children, leaving them feeling fearful and helpless. Tweens need to be able to share their fears, to have them validated, and to feel they are being taken seriously. Sweeping things under the carpet doesn't make them go away. Allow your tween time and a safe space to grieve, to be angry or sad. Giving yourself permission to show emotion lets your tween know it's OK for her, too, and if the words won't come, offer her opportunities to express herself creatively or physically through writing, art, music, dance or sport.

By this age tweens will probably have more awareness and understanding of the emotions they are experiencing than younger siblings, but they are also more capable of thinking outside the box, and so you may find your tween not just dwelling on the crisis at hand but also speculating on how the trauma might affect her life in the long term. Generally, children are very resilient and with ongoing support from parents or other trusted adults can emerge from traumatic times in good shape. Parents may worry that encouraging a child to talk about problems will keep reopening old wounds and make things worse, but open and honest two-way communication will actually tend to make a child feel safer. Just remember to take things at your tween's speed, and to stop if she calls time on the talking.

When assessing the level of emotional fall-out for your tween, be on the lookout for emotional responses such as anger, anxiety or sadness, nightmares, behavioural difficulties or a tendency to avoid certain people, places or subjects of conversation. Responses like these may be immediate or delayed, fleeting or long-lived. And, as ever, if you're feeling out of your depth, don't be afraid to seek professional help.

What the netmums say

Coping through crisis

My granddad died a little while ago, and it upset Gemima enormously. She cried for several days afterwards. I found that for her, the best thing I could do was just tell her that if she wanted to talk, then she could come to me. They were good at her school, too, and her teacher said the same thing. For a day or so she just kept to herself, and she then came to me with a couple of questions: where was he when he passed away, who was with him, what time had it been? The question I found difficult to answer was, 'Has Granddad gone to heaven?' I'm not religious, but my granddad was. So I explained that he was a good man who always believed in going somewhere nice. We talked about heaven, which I've always thought was whatever you believe it to be. She seemed happy with that and wrote a letter for him to take with him. She still talks about him, and often says she hopes he is happy.
Emily, mum to a girl, ten

My daughter was thirteen when her father and I separated. Her dad went to live with someone else and his children, and she was devastated – to her it was total abandonment and rejection. Her half-brother and sister – children from my ex's first marriage – also decided to cut contact with her, and a year later my dad died. She became very withdrawn, and hardly came out of her room. She was rude, obnoxious and horrible to live with, if I'm honest. I loved her but I didn't like her very much. I was struggling too because I had my own emotions to deal with, as well as trying to protect my children. At first I tried to get her to talk, but she totally withdrew. I decided to change tactics, and let her come to me. I don't know if it was the best way to deal with it, but leaving her alone seemed to be the best solution. That doesn't mean I let her do as she liked: I've always had rules, and she kept to them. Every now and then, she'd come to me for a silent hug. Gradually, as she got older and her hormones were kinder, her temper improved. Eventually she did talk a bit about what had happened. I'll never know how she really felt but I do know that she didn't blame me, which was a relief. She seemed to accept the situation and she started to join in with us as a family again.

Ali, mum to a girl, eighteen, and a boy, eleven

My brother-in-law died without warning last May when his sons were thirteen and twelve, and my stepson was twelve. The three boys are very close, and each dealt with it a bit differently, though they all wanted to stick together. The eldest wanted to be involved and chat about it, just like all the adults were doing, and whilst we tried keeping the tears for when he wasn't around, he saw us crying and each of us dealing with it in a different way, which I think was good for him. The middle one, my stepson, seemed to put his grief aside to help his cousins and the rest of us. The youngest seemed at a loose end and mooched around a lot. There have been many very sad times and I'm sure they hurt a lot, but very quickly it was business as usual for them in their day-to-day lives. Even at the funeral, they were running around on the steps outside. Children seem so resilient. As long as they get outlets to vent when they need it, and loads of support, they seem to cope so well.

Hannah, mum to three boys aged seventeen, fifteen and twelve

After a difficult separation from my ex-partner, who flew into a rage when I asked him to leave and smashed our home up, my daughter was left distraught. I sought professional help from Women's Aid, and they provided a children's counsellor who came to her school once a week and spent time talking and making things with her. She never really told me what she and the counsellor talked about, but I was fine with that – as long as she was speaking to someone. It was a difficult time for us all, but the help we got really enabled her to deal with it.

Elaine, mum to two girls aged twelve and six

Last year my nephew – my daughter's cousin – died suddenly at the age of twelve. It was and still is a traumatic time for all of us. She had to cope with seeing a lot of raw adult grief. We have dealt with this by allowing her to talk about her feelings with the family and with support from the pastoral manager at her school. She read in church at his funeral and devised and performed a dance at a celebration of his life that his mum – my sister – organised on the date he would have become a teenager. Some people believe that children shouldn't be allowed to attend funerals as it would be too upsetting. But I think that allowing her to be fully involved has helped her to come to terms with the death of someone she loves and misses dearly.

Jane, mum to a girl, thirteen

My partner of seven years died of a rare form of cancer after an eighteen-month illness. My twins were very close to him and it was devastating to us all. Initially, there were lots of tears, lots of questions and lots of insecurities. After a couple of months the tears have gone, in the main, and questions have been answered, but the insecurities still raise their heads. There's a lot of comforting and reassuring still to be done, but they're getting there. They have had counselling and we have a good support network. I've always felt that it's important for them to be able to talk to me, so I will always listen and perhaps gently probe to find out more, should I feel there is more to 'let out'. If I can't help or cope myself, I will ask for help. Talking and listening, as well as watching, is *so* important.

Julie, mum to a girl and a boy, both thirteen

Getting help

Some ups and downs are totally normal in life, but if serious emotional problems persist for your tween or seem to be significantly impacting on her life, get some professional help: chatting to a sympathetic GP would be the best place to start, or you could try tapping into her school's pastoral system and enlisting the help of a school counsellor, pastoral officer or nurse. It may be that you are referred to your local CAMHS (Child and Adolescent Mental Health Service). Some kind of talking therapy is the most likely form of help you'll be offered, although in a small number of cases, medication may be prescribed.

There's more advice and lots of useful contact numbers as well as information about what help is available in your area on the website of Young Minds. Details for this, and other helpful organisations, are included in the back of the book.

8 Independence and responsibility

Your tween is growing up. He's going to want – and need – increasing amounts of independence. This may mean walking to school alone, or with friends, or it may mean opting to stay at home by himself rather than accompany you to the supermarket. He may want to play in the park, without you watching from a bench nearby, or be dropped off at the local leisure centre to meet his mates for five-a-side. Whether these bits of independence are granted to him early or late on the tween-age spectrum, he's very likely to embrace them keenly: after all, independence equals freedom, and that's something most tweens crave.

With increased independence comes increased responsibility. Your tween has a responsibility to keep himself safe as best he can, and to adhere to whatever rules you deem sensible for his safety's sake. He must also show he can cope with other sorts of independence: getting himself organised for school, for example, keeping his room tidy, and putting the kettle on, should you ask him!

Of course, it's early days. Your tween is merely starting to dip his toes in the choppy waters of real life, testing them out, practising for the future. When all's said and done, a tween is still a child. As parents, we may sometimes have to remind them of that!

Keeping him safe (but letting him go)

So, how much independence should you give your tween, and when? It's a tough one. Our instincts to protect our kids remain as fierce as ever during these years – in fact for most, they escalate, as we watch our children become gradually exposed to all the harsh realities and risks of life. Yet all sensible parents know that at some point, children must start striking out alone – a process which will usually start between the ages of nine and thirteen. They *have* to spend time on their own, and with their friends, if they're going to be able to gain the confidence, experience, assertiveness and risk-assessment skills that they'll need to negotiate first the teens, and then adulthood, and we must give them the trust they need to do this. (In fact, a lot of experts are concerned that modern parents are failing their children on this front; that we're raising a generation of 'cotton-wool kids' who are cocooned and stifled in a way that could affect their development.) Besides, your tween is very likely to start pushing for more freedom from you now – perhaps more than you are ready to give him. The key is trying to find a good balance between providing safety and security, and allowing them the freedom they need and want.

It's a difficult area to navigate: there are no legal guidelines to adhere to, and no hard and fast answers to the various dilemmas this issue throws up. No one – expert or otherwise – can tell you when the time is right to start letting your tween free: it will depend on your own values and feelings, your tween's character, and practical factors like where you live.

Whilst only you and your co-parent can make the ultimate decision on when and how it should be done, this is an area where other people's opinions will almost certainly be useful, and where you'll probably want to get your heads together with other parents in your community. Finding out what other people's kids are doing makes sense – it doesn't mean you have to let yours do the same thing, but if you ask a range of different people their opinion, it will give you something to go on when forming your own. Bear in mind, though, that there's wide variation in how people feel on this subject – and little about it that can definitely be said to be either right or wrong.

One thing everyone's agreed on, though, is that when it comes to granting independence, the best advice is to drip-feed your tween his freedom rather than bestowing it on him in one big leap. Start by allowing him to spend five or ten minutes at home without you, or getting him to walk the last leg of the school run alone, and make sure he's confident and capable with those steps before moving on to anything bigger.

You'll need some ground rules, and a basic safety code in place when your tween is starting to be independent, which you need to instil thoroughly without simultaneously scaring him rigid. It's another tricky balance to achieve. Set the rules that you think make most sense, and make sure he knows he must stick with them or face the consequences – more than likely, that will be a temporary loss of those new-found freedoms.

Home alone

There are no legally-set guidelines for parents who are trying to work out when it's OK to leave a tween on his own at home – although it's an offence to do so if it places him at risk and, in theory, you could be prosecuted for neglect if you leave your child unsupervised in a manner likely to cause 'unnecessary suffering or injury to health'. However, the reality is that many parents need to know if and when it *is* OK to leave their tween, often because work commitments mean they can't be around 100 per cent of the time, but are unable to find or afford childcare to bridge a very short gap. School holidays can be particularly difficult to cover for older tweens, especially if you're a lone parent – not helped by the fact that many play-schemes or holiday clubs have an age limit of eleven or twelve.

A few relevant organisations have offered up recommendations: for instance, the NSPCC says that it's just not a good idea to leave a child under the age of 'about twelve', other than for 'very short periods of time', whilst the Children's Legal Centre advises that thirteen is a sensible minimum age to be home alone. However, according to both organisations, the main consideration when weighing up this issue is the individual characteristics of your tween, since maturity and understanding differs so much from child to child. In other words, it's up to you to judge for yourself when your child is able to cope without you by asking yourself some relevant questions. For instance, is he self-confident and mature in general? Is he likely to cope well with a problem or even an emergency rather than panic? Is he open when it comes to talking with you so that you can be sure he'll let you know if something goes wrong or he has concerns? Does he know the basics of home and personal safety? And could you trust him to stick to any ground rules you lay down?

However, the bottom line is that, where a tween of thirteen or under is concerned, it's probably not a good idea to leave him home alone for more than an hour or two – however mature he is.

Think very carefully, too, before asking a tween of any age to watch one or more younger siblings in your absence. Although there are no legal restrictions to the age at which a child can be asked to babysit, organisations like the NSPCC, The Royal Society for the Prevention of Accidents (RoSPA), and The Children's Legal Centre, all advise that sixteen is the minimum age to ask this favour of a child – and again, you could in theory be prosecuted if any harm is caused as a result of you leaving a younger child in the care of an older one. Quite apart from which, your tween may resent having to take on the responsibility.

Laying down the ground rules

Before you let your tween stay home alone, for any period of time, be sure to educate him on basic safety matters, preferably without scaring him. He needs to know how to get hold of you, and what to do in the event of any emergency (however unlikely it may be). For most parents, a rule that he never answers the door is a no-brainer, unless he's very certain he knows who it is and that they're trusted. And there needs to be at least one other person he can easily contact or call if he can't get hold of you and, ideally, a close neighbour who'd be happy to be approached should he need help from an adult.

Talk him through the basics of accident prevention. If he's using the microwave, cooker or kettle now, perhaps you'd prefer him to steer clear of these things while you're not around, and stick with snacks and drinks he can just grab straight from the cupboard or fridge. There's lots more good general advice on safety in the home on the websites of RoSPA and the Child Accident Prevention Trust.

If leaving him alone is to be a regular thing, perhaps in the hours after school, that's all the more reason to prepare for the situation thoroughly. What will he eat and drink if he's hungry or thirsty? How's he going to pass the time without you? Where's he going to keep his door key – and who can keep a spare for you if he loses his?

Perhaps most important of all is making sure that your tween himself is happy with the situation, and confident about being left for any length of time without you. As ever, keep open the lines of communication between the two of you when you're setting out to negotiate this particular area. If he's in any way worried about something thrown up as a result of his developing independence, you need to know that he's going to come and tell you about it.

Out on his own

As with being home alone, there are no actual laws prohibiting kids from being out and about on their own, so you will have to decide for yourself at what point you will let your tween out beyond the home without you by his side, and more specifically where and when. But there's no doubt this is an important piece of freedom that's bound to come up during the tween years. Being out and about on his own and with friends, even if for short periods and even if it's never very far away from you, is fundamental to his emotional and social development – and vital if your tween's going to get streetwise.

It's very variable when parents decide to let their kids out alone. Walking to school, short runs to the shops, or periods in the park with their mates but without adult supervision are the most common examples. A recent Netmums poll revealed that fifteen per cent of members first allowed their tween to walk to school alone at age nine, twenty-eight per cent of members allowed it at age ten, and twenty per cent allowed it at age eleven, with a cautious fourteen per cent refusing to let a child of over eleven out on the streets at all, and a confident twenty-two per cent allowing a child of eight or younger to make that particular journey alone on foot.

Factors like the community you live in, the sort of roads in your area, your own confidence on the matter and, as ever, your tween's maturity and character, will all add up when it comes to the decision you make. Chances are you'll take into account the views of at least one other parent here and, more than likely, you'll take the view that there's safety in numbers – so you might not be happy for your unaccompanied tween to walk to school, take a bus into town of a Saturday morning, or hang around the local adventure playground, but feel it's a different story with one or more (sensible!) friends by his side.

Staying safe outside

It's our job to educate our tweens to the potential risks out there in the real world, and arm them with strategies for coping should they need to, without alarming them so much they'd frankly rather stay at home. For many parents, the fear of a tween being scared, harmed or even abducted by a stranger will be the main reason for struggling to let them loose – even though we know that, in reality, the risks of anything seriously bad happening at the hands of a stranger are tiny. Bullying and mugging are probably more realistic worries, so it's certainly a good idea to chat – without being alarmist – about how he'd cope with either of those. In particular, mobile phones can make tweens easy prey, so it's a good idea to talk through security strategies if your tween has one: advise him to keep his safe and out of sight, and only to stop to respond to calls or texts when he's in a busy, well-lit area.

No doubt you've already talked to your tween about the basic laws of personal safety, and he'll also have had useful lessons at school. But if you're letting him out and about for the first time, it's a good point at which to offer some revision on the subject. Reiterate the obvious: that he should never accept gifts, sweets, or a lift, or be tempted to go anywhere, with a stranger; and that if he *is* approached, he should 'Yell, Run, and Tell' – in other words, he should get quickly away from any source of potential danger, and make plenty of noise while he's at it. The Safer Strangers, Safer Buildings campaign also has some useful ideas about where a child can go and who they can ask for help. You can get more information on the Child's Eye Media website, details for which are in the back of this book.

Do sit down with your tween and calmly talk all these issues through. Test his knowledge, by putting some likely scenarios to him and asking him how he'd cope. And go through your golden rules on the matter together, so he's in no doubt what your demands are – there's a suggested list of likely guidelines in the box below, although of course your own may be different. You might even like to draw up a written contract so you both know exactly what you're aiming for.

On the road

Traffic is definitely the biggest threat to your tween's safety in the big wide world: 2,800 children under sixteen were killed or seriously injured in 2008, and road accidents are the biggest cause of accidental death among this age group. So, whatever you do, make sure your tween is wised up to road safety issues before you let him loose on the streets without you. Hopefully this is a lesson you've been passing on for many years before-hand, anyway, but now's the time when knowing his Green Cross Code off by heart really matters. Make sure he knows any route he's taking, and all its features, back to front, and caution him over dangerous distractions such as mobile phones, MP3 players and chatting to friends. If he cycles, make sure he's undergone appropriate cycle training, that he wears a helmet, that he's visible, and that his bike is roadworthy.

There's loads of good road safety advice, including fun, tween-appropriate interactive resources at the websites of RoSPA and at The Department of Transport's Think! Campaign. Details are in the back of the book.

> ### Going it alone: Some likely golden guidelines for tween independence
>
> - He must let you know exactly where he is at any given time. He should always make sure it's OK with you before going anywhere without you, and tell you where he's going and when he'll be back. He must always let you know if his plans change.

- He must call or text you every time he reaches a particular destination, just so that you know he's there. He should call or text you when he leaves, so you know what time you can reasonably expect him home.
- He'll always keep his mobile switched on, if he has one, and will always answer your calls and respond to your texts as soon as possible (bearing in mind he should be in a safe place before bringing out his phone).
- He will always let you know who he's with, and it will always be with someone you know. In the case of new friends, you'll need to meet them, and preferably their parents, too, before he spends any time with them.
- He must always stick to whatever curfew you set him, particularly if it's in the evening.
- He can convince you that he knows what to do in the event of a problem or emergency, and where to go for help in your absence, if necessary.
- He won't go out with anything that might attract muggers, for instance, expensive trainers or a top-of-the-range mobile. He won't, in the event of being approached by a mugger, attempt to fight back.
- He must be open and honest, and let you know immediately if there's been a problem or he's in any way concerned.

Other ways of being independent

Of course, gaining independence for your child isn't just about freedom to spend time on his own. There'll be many more things he'll want to do for himself now – or things that he really should start doing for himself, even if he doesn't want to – and giving him the opportunities to do so is all-important. For instance, you could allow him to make his own choices in the fashion or music he likes; the activities and hobbies he takes up (or drops); how he decorates or maintains order in his bedroom (or not, as the case may be!). You could also give him as much responsibility as is practical in appropriate tasks – for instance, in getting himself ready for school, caring for pets, helping you out around the house and garden, and choosing and preparing his own snacks. By the time your tween hits his teens, he should be able to make himself – at the very least – a cup of tea and a sandwich.

Do whatever you can to consent to all these small examples of independence, and give plenty of praise when he does manage to do something on his own, big or small.

Help in the home

Now's definitely the time – if you haven't done this already – to start asking for some help round the house. If you've tended to let him get away with not doing basics such as replacing the toothpaste top, putting dirty clothes in the laundry basket, and returning toys to the toy box at the end of the day, tackle it now, before it's too late. Most parents of tweens also feel it's reasonable to start setting chores over and above these basics: ease your tween into the concept of helping round the house by suggesting small, enjoyable tasks for starters (there are some ideas in the box below), and make sure he has plenty of instruction so he knows what he's doing. If you're perfectionist about these things but your tween's standards are not quite up to scratch, you may have to grit your teeth and let him get on with it (or return to do a better job, later): at this stage, it's probably the thought that counts!

Whether or not you reward this help with cash or other incentives, or expect it as a matter of course, is down to you. There's more on rewards and earning power further on in the chapter.

Whistle while you work: Simple tasks to ease your tween into domestic duties

- Keeping his room tidy
- Clearing the table after dinner and stacking dishes by the sink
- Putting clean laundry away in the right place
- Dusting, polishing and vacuuming
- Cleaning out the animals or walking the dog

- Sweeping the patio
- Weeding
- Emptying waste paper baskets
- Filing bills and other paperwork
- Assisting in more skilled jobs such as DIY or preparing a meal

Moving away from you

Although it's important to allow your child more independence as he gets older, be aware of your own emotional response to it. You may feel that your tween's increasing independence means he's moving further away from you. Although it may feel a little hurtful, it's a natural process. Try to make sure there's still plenty of family time on offer to your tween. Push it, a little, if you have to: chances are he'll protest but in fact, will still very much enjoy your company.

What the experts say

Crissy says: Your tween needs you more than ever. Although it may feel like he values his mates above you as his sights become firmly set upon greater independence and autonomy, he still needs to know you're there, providing a secure base from which he can launch himself out into the exciting new world that lies before him. Don't make the mistake of withdrawing from your child. This is a time to wait patiently in the wings. Don't worry. He'll return in time if you maintain that connection and keep the lines of communication wide open.

As parental influence is usurped by peer pressure and the need to belong to a whole new tribe, feelings of powerlessness can lead some parents to become overly strict or punitive. But the closer you try to pull your child to you during this period of development, the further you risk pushing him away. Make sure your boundaries are firm, but also fair-minded and reasonable. Be prepared to reconsider and adapt house rules as he gets older, and when he pushes against non-negotiable limits, try to be empathetic rather than dismissive.

If you're really not sure which freedoms are and are not age-appropriate, it's fine to ask around. Chances are you'll find, contrary to your tween's complaints, that you're not the only parent stumbling around in the dark here. It's a big old scary world out there, not just for tweens but for parents too, and it's natural to worry. But tweens need to grow emotionally as well as physically, and they need the challenges that greater autonomy brings. Keeping your tween safe is top of the list of parenting requirements, but he does also need to practise risk-taking. If you make sure you're around to dust him off if he falls, he can learn as much or more from his mistakes as he can from his triumphs.

Elaine says: When to give a tween his freedom is an individual matter that will be based on his personality and level of maturity. Overall though, I think parents tend to err on the side of being too cautious and overprotect their children. There are many ways of letting children develop independence in small steps, starting within the home, so encourage them to demonstrate simple new achievements so they know that we believe them to be capable and will grow in confidence as a result. When it comes to going it alone, small steps remains the best policy – so they might first of all walk to the post box on the corner a few times, before then heading for the shop in the next street, and so on. What's really useful in preparing our children for successful independent forays into the world is chatting through the issues and the likely scenarios with them in advance. That means asking questions to establish that they know what they are doing when you're not around, and that they could handle any situations that might arise. It's important to allow your tween to take the lead in these chats: it should be about him exploring his own knowledge of the subject, rather than you lecturing. Practise any skills he's sure to need – double-locking the front door, for example, or making himself a hot drink – together, well in advance of when he will need them.

What the netmums say

When's the right time to let go?

Kris and Molly have to walk a mile and a half to school, and have done so for over a year. We started by letting them walk to primary school while in Year Six, then slowly letting them go further and further. Now, they're out and about a lot more – I've had to get used to them being all over town, because that's where their friends are. But they always have a phone with them, and have to let me know where they are. If it's a new friend, I like to have an address. My ten-year-old stays local: he can play with his friends around the corner, and walk to school ahead of me.
Jennie, mum to a girl, twelve, and two boys, twelve and ten

I've only just allowed my daughter to walk to school by herself as she's just started secondary – even then, I expect her to text me when she gets there. She's been into town once with her friends, but as she wandered off without telling me where she was, I've said that she can't do it again for a while. I certainly wouldn't let her go out on an evening on her own just yet. I do think we have to keep our tweens safe, but although it's important to encourage independence, I think my daughter's age is still too young for a lot of things.
Emma, mum to a girl, eleven, and a boy, nine

We moved recently from a big city to a small town, and here my kids have far more freedom. They walk to school, which is a mile away, play outside with local children in a nearby field, and walk to friends' houses. Everyone here allows their children a huge amount of freedom. I believe it's important to learn independence, gain confidence and manage risk. It was one of the incentives for leaving the city. But it does depend upon where you live. In the city our children couldn't roam around, as there was too much traffic and bad influence.
Louise, mum to a boy, eleven, and a girl, ten

Zoe has been walking to and from school by herself since she was eight. We're very close to it, and I have no concerns. I let her go to her friends' houses in the evening or to the play-park, which is fully staffed. She's expected to be home at 8 p.m. and is not allowed to just wander the streets. I won't let her go into town at this point. We live in Glasgow and it's such a huge city. I'm not confident she would be able to find her way about and get on the right bus home!

Naomi, mum to two girls aged twelve and five

My son has quite a lot of independence. From a young age, he was taught about road and personal safety, but it's only since he started at senior school that he's had a lot more freedom outside home. He walks or bikes to school every day, either alone or with friends, and in summer he often stays out until 9 p.m. with his friends – winter's more limited. On three days a week he comes home to an empty house for about an hour. He has his own key, which he's very proud of, and when I'm not there he texts me as soon as he's home to let me know he's safe and sound. He has a mobile phone so that we can contact each other at any time, and we frequently do. I believe that independence should be encouraged. He's a lot more confident and happier for it. He likes to be treated like an adult and he knows that I trust him. He also knows that if he does anything to jeopardise that trust, his freedom will be reduced and he desperately doesn't want that. I do worry about him when he's out, but I have to hold back those protective feelings for his sake. If he ever feels threatened or worried, he calls and I tell him to come home, which he does. I wish more parents were like me and would let their children play out. It would be less worrying, as there's safety in numbers.

Ali, mum to a girl, eighteen, and a boy, eleven

All my boys were allowed to walk to school on their own from the summer term of Year Three, but we were lucky in that school then was just around the corner, with no main roads to cross.

They were allowed to go out and about to local parks with friends from around age ten, but they had (and still have) strict instructions about what time to be home and they have to keep in contact with me by phone so I know where they are. I expect them home exactly when agreed and if not, they're in a lot of trouble! I've explained that I'm happy for them to be out and I trust them, but for safety I always need to know where they are. From secondary school age I have been happy for them to bus into town, and they have to do this for school anyway. I would leave the boys alone for a short period of time at home from around ten if I was walking up to the shops, for instance. My eldest I left a little younger as he's very responsible; with the middle one it was a bit later, as he has less common sense. There's no set age that a child is 'ready' to be left alone, you need to judge them individually. I think it is important to encourage independence as it increases their self-confidence and self-esteem if they feel that they are capable of this sort of responsibility and that they are trusted. But I do think it's important to give them this independence gradually so they can learn to deal with it in manageable chunks! It's hard as a parent. On the one hand there's a huge sense of pride that your child is capable and that you have helped facilitate this, but on the other you start to feel worried that your child may just be able to cope without you one day!

Jo, mum to three boys aged seventeen, fourteen and eleven

As a working single mum, I'm grateful, to be honest, that my son is now old enough to look after himself for a couple of hours after school, as it saves on after-school childcare fees. He's bright and mature, and I trust him completely – I wouldn't leave him if I didn't. The summer holidays are difficult, though, as I don't feel I could leave him for a whole day and obviously my own holiday just doesn't cover it. I still rely on a mixture of holiday clubs and goodwill from other parents, friends and relatives. Maybe in another year or so I won't have to worry about that, either.

Maria, mum to a boy, twelve

Coming from South Africa where there was no way I'd let Kevin walk to school or even ride his bike on the road, I found it really hard to let him out of my sight for a long time. Now he goes to the park and down the road to the football fields and into the woods with his friends. It's too far to walk to school so I drive him there, although I'd let him take the bus if he wasn't too lazy to do so! We started leaving him home by himself recently. He has a phone and the landline, and we lock the door and leave him keys. We've also taught him how to cook his own lunch (or at least, to make a sandwich). I have to say, I worry every time he leaves the house but I know I can't keep him inside forever. He's sensible and has our phone numbers if he feels unsure.

Kirsty, mum to two boys aged thirteen and nine months

Earning his money

A bit of cash in the pocket – whilst by no means an absolute right – is a positive privilege that the majority of tweens enjoy. Giving a small, regular allowance has advantages for parents, too. Not only can it help you keep pester power in check – because you can reasonably suggest that he buys, or at least saves to buy, his own things – but it's a great way to pass on lessons about the value of money, making sensible consumer choices, the benefits of saving, and the importance of keeping cash in a safe place (perhaps even in a bank account). It's also another of those areas where you can help nudge him towards general independence without losing control over anything really important.

Exactly how much you give – and what if anything you expect in return – is down to you. There are different schools of thought on 'earning' rights for tweens: lots of parents feel it works well to offer pocket money as reward for good behaviour and/or for doing chores round the house – and sometimes with a corresponding 'docking' system when expectations are not met. Others, however, feel that helping out and/or good behaviour shouldn't be conditional on financial reward and that making it so can lead to problems.

There's no right or wrong in this matter, just different views, so you should do what seems to work best for you and your tween. Maybe you'll look at a compromise: perhaps you'll offer a small, unconditional amount of pocket money every week, and have a reward system on top that allows your tween to bump up his earnings with good behaviour and helping out round the house beyond the basic chores that you can reasonably expect to be carried out for free.

If you have an agreement to pay an allotted amount regularly, try to stick with it and be consistent – especially if you *are* linking it to good or bad behaviour. Your tween needs to know it can be relied upon and that it's definitely worth keeping his nose clean that week!

Encourage saving by all means – some tweens can be surprisingly parsimonious and get a great deal of satisfaction in seeing their cash stacking up – but don't force it. Once his allowance, or savings, becomes significant, opening a bank account for him is a good move: it's the ultimate in safe places for him to keep his dosh. Most banks and building societies allow kids of eleven or more to have a cash card, which means he can make his own withdrawals and make regular checks on his balance.

Give him as much autonomy on spending as you can bear, but set out any rules on items you *don't* want him investing in – even if he *could* afford to – in advance. Think hard about where you'll stand if he's flush enough to buy what his heart desires, but what his heart desires is not, as far as you're concerned, suitable – inappropriate videogames, sweets by the bucketload, or pricey branded trainers that might as well have 'mug me' stitched on the side, for example.

What the experts say

Crissy says: There's something hugely empowering for your tween in having a bit of money in his pocket. As well as going some way towards teaching him the value of money, an allowance also has the more symbolic value of making your tween feel trusted to make his own choices – and inevitably his own mistakes. However, my personal feeling is that offering pocket money as part of a reward system, withdrawing it for bad behaviour or using it as a bargaining tool, can leave you high and dry once your tween decides that getting his own way is worth more to him than his allowance. On the whole, pocket money, if you can afford to provide it, should be freely given on a regular basis without prompting from your tween. Setting up the expectation that it's conditional on good behaviour, or that it's a payment for certain duties, is likely to engender a power struggle and ultimately could cause more trouble than it's worth. Your tween is now old enough to understand that he has a team role to play within the family and so it's not unreasonable to expect him to perform certain household duties or tasks without payment.

Elaine says: Parents have mixed thoughts on pocket money. My view is that from the age of eight, nine or ten, children could be earning it, by doing small household chores such as bringing down dirty laundry; emptying the dishwasher; polishing shoes; or doing a bit of vacuuming in order to pay for treats such as sweets, magazines, or small toys. As your tween gets older the amount can increase, and so can the level of responsibility. And as his earning power increases, he could also be encouraged to occasionally buy things for others, such as an ice cream for a sibling when on an outing. Handling money gives children an awareness of the value of things and is great practice for adding and subtracting in practical situations – both really useful life skills. They can learn to save up for things and will appreciate them all the more when they eventually buy a coveted object with their own money. I'll always remember the first item of clothing I bought with my own money at thirteen!

Every family will have very different values when it comes to the amount of pocket money to give. My own daughter, age twelve, earns 50p per day for completing her homework and emptying the laundry basket and that adds up to £14 a month. I call this 'pocket money' rather than an allowance, as it's not significant enough to pay for stuff like cinema outings or clothes. Once your tween becomes a teen, you'll probably need to start rethinking your system and replace the pocket money with an allowance, which will mean setting clear guidelines on what you expect the money is to be used for. Until then, giving a little money and, with it, some responsibility for spending it, will be good practice!

What the netmums say

Pocket money, allowances and rewards

James and Jake get £20 a month pocket money each, for doing chores around the house like washing the pots and helping with the laundry. If they want a new book or magazine, they tend to buy it from their own money, or if they want a new computer game they'll save up, or club together to buy it. If they get a good report or an award from school they get an additional bonus to their pocket money as a reward. If they're naughty at home or school, they lose £1 each time, and if they damage something on purpose, I make them pay all or some of the cost of replacing it.
Claire, mum to five boys aged eleven, nine, six, five and one, and a girl, three

After continually handing out money for the cinema, accessories, notebooks and iPod downloads, we started giving our thirteen-year-old a set amount of money, about £20, to last the month. She's realised quite quickly that when it's gone, it's gone! So she now takes a drink with her to the cinema and buys sweets in the supermarket before she goes. She gets a bit extra every now and again, especially if she's done well at something or been thoughtful towards someone else. You just have to ensure that you stick by it and never advance money on next month's tab.
Laura, mum to two girls aged fifteen and thirteen

My children don't get pocket money. They don't have to do chores with the exception of keeping their own rooms tidy. But if I ask them to help out with sorting the washing and they 'choose' to help they will get rewarded. If they 'choose' not to

then they don't get berated, but they don't get rewarded either
. . . they just get nothing.
Peta, mum to two boys aged nine and seven

We pay £15 a month into a bank account for Kester. He has a
cash card that he can withdraw money with, but he can't make
payments with it. Out of this, I expect him to pay for small Christmas and birthday presents for his two brothers, and his dad and
I. (I'll sub him if he wants to buy someone something in particular that's more than a few pounds.) The rest is for saving or
spending as he pleases and it seems to last him well – as he gets
older I'll up his money as he needs it. My kids' pocket money is
paid to them, regardless of behaviour. Neither do they get paid
to do jobs around the house – as they are part of the family, I
expect them to help out for nothing.
Jo, mum to three boys aged seventeen, fourteen and eleven

I don't agree with rewarding kids financially for helping around
the house! Kids should help out and not expect to get paid for
it. George has to make his bed, tidy his room, and feed the cats
twice a day. Once a fortnight I'll ask him to empty the dishwasher.
I think childhood should be just that, a time of fun and relaxation
in equal measures, but kids should have some responsibility, and
help when asked.
Natalie, mum to a boy, ten, and a girl, two

My boys get £10 per fortnight each if they've done their chores
and behaved well at home and school. It decreases if they
happen to be lazy on a particular week or don't behave or are
rude and answer back! I think it's important for my boys to help
around the home, otherwise they'll assume that it's just a
woman's job!
Caroline, mum to two boys aged twelve and eleven

For their £1.50 a week pocket money, my kids have to do small
household chores such as setting the table, polishing shoes and

cleaning out the guinea pigs. If at the end of the week they've not done their chores, or they complained too much when they did them, they get money deducted. With their money, they're expected to buy any toys or sweets they want through the year. It means they think very carefully about spending, and even manage to save. I want them to learn the value of money, and that you don't get something for nothing in life!

Louise, mum to a boy, eleven, and a girl, ten

My son gets £2 per week, my daughter a pound. To receive it, they have to make sure their bedrooms are kept tidy and their beds made every day. They both have the option of 'earning' more money throughout the week and when we started it, we all agreed a payment for different jobs – for example, emptying the dishwasher is 25p, setting the table 10p, clearing it 10p. It doesn't sound much, but you'd be amazed at how much it costs me when either of them is saving up for something! I know not everyone agrees that kids should be paid for helping, but I think it's a great system. I'm helping my children understand that you don't get anything for nothing in this life, hence they can 'earn' extra pocket money. They do also help out around the home without being asked to (or paid) because they understand that we all live here and need to look after our home.

Lesley, mum to a boy, twelve, and a girl, eight

We pay £20 per month into Kevin's bank account, which we set up so he can learn how to handle his money. He then gets extra money for doing jobs or good behaviour. I run my own business and I often pay him for helping me, and sometimes during the holidays he also helps his dad, which he gets rewarded for. (I'm not sure if it's given him much of a taste for working, though, as he's recently declared he would like to be a full-time student!)

Kirsty, mum to two boys aged thirteen and nine months

I don't give my son pocket money. If he needs some to go swimming or to the cinema, I give it to him. If he asks for some sweet money and he hasn't had any that day, I'll give him some, if I can afford it. Sometimes he'll ask to do chores to earn some money, which I always allow him to do. He negotiates a price, and we usually meet in the middle somewhere. Actually, I wish now that I'd given both of my kids pocket money to give them more of a sense of the value of money. I've never used any kind of reward system for good behaviour, however. I expect them to respect me and do as they're told without bribery, which fortunately has always worked for me.

Ali, mum to a girl, eighteen, and a boy, eleven

Dealing with pester power

Tweens these days are ruthlessly targeted by marketing men, who've realised that theirs is the age when consumer durables become desirable, and peer pressure really begins to bite. And they're keen to exploit it – in fact, the marketing industry has tweens marked out as a group of consumers in their own right. Thanks to the growth of the mass media and our tweens' constant exposure to advertising, there's no doubt as to what exactly these wonderful products are, and where they can get hold of them. The result is that almost all parents of tweens must fend off repeated requests for new possessions – or find the money to indulge them.

No one wants their child to miss out, or to be targeted as odd by unkind peers. Furthermore, it's natural to want to give in, in the face of nagging, for an easy life. But if your tween makes demands that are simply undesirable, unreasonable or unaffordable, stand firm in saying 'no', regardless of how unpopular it makes you. He'll survive without whatever it is he wants, and he'll eventually forgive you for not providing it. Take any claims that 'everyone has one' with a pinch of salt – you'll almost certainly find, if you look into it, that everyone *doesn't* have one. And remember that saying 'no' sometimes will help teach your tween the importance of being a 'discriminate consumer'. In other words, it will help him understand that, in life, financial necessity usually dictates that we can't have everything we want, so we need to work out which things we *most* want. Besides, no doubt some of the things your tween asks for will be off limits because they simply aren't appropriate for his age group. So, even if you're rich enough to afford to say 'yes' every time, you shouldn't. Explain to your tween why he can't have it, or why he can't have it *yet*, rather than just saying 'because I said so'. If you're on a budget – as most of us are – make sure he understands that. And once you've said a definite no to a particular thing, do stick with it. If your tween comes to suss out that, given enough whingeing and whining, he will eventually get what he wants, he will never let up!

Meanwhile, look for simple strategies for beating pester power. The most obvious is not to take your tween shopping with you.

Being reasonable

Don't always say no, though! Try to be flexible when dealing with pestering, and look for compromises wherever possible. Listen to your tween carefully before dismissing demands, and always consider whether there's a genuine need for something – if it turns out that everyone really *does* have one, perhaps it's only fair that he does now, too.

Telling him 'not now, but later' may be a sensible compromise, rather than rushing out to buy it straight away. And if you can't afford to foot the bill on your own, perhaps he can pay for it himself, or save up sufficient funds to do so. Or maybe you can come to an agreement where you both chip in.

Give love, not money

If pester power gets you down, try to bear in mind that material goods can never be better than your time, love and attention – and even in his greediest moods your tween will almost certainly accept this. If you can't or won't buy him what he wants, fill the deficit by offering him some of your time instead. Equally, if it sometimes feels that you're buying him stuff because you don't have much of in the way of time or attention to give him, maybe you should look for ways to redress the balance.

Don't forget to set a good example! If you're the sort of person who dashes out to blow money on the latest flat-screen TV and doesn't hesitate to splurge on your own desires, as opposed to needs, don't be too surprised if it turns out your tween wants it all, too.

What the experts say

Crissy says: The advertising industry spends billions each year targeting our tweens. And it works! Whether through necessity or choice, many women are delaying having children until later in life, often mid- or post-career. With shrinking family size and the growth of dual-income families, parents often have more to spend – and they are choosing to spend it on their kids. Today's tweens are no longer seen and not heard. They have a voice and they're using it to get what they want, not just by nagging their parents into a corner but also by sending us the message that they 'need' the latest brand trainers or pop-star paraphernalia. And as parents we are buying into this pestering, big style.

Marketing is a sophisticated business with the industry employing an army of experts to determine precisely how best to hook our tweens. Bombarded by subliminal messages from sources as diverse as the high street, the media, the internet and even schools, it is no wonder that today's youngsters often end up equating products with popularity and success. So the next time pester power is grinding you down, spare a thought for your tween. Chances are he really does believe that this game, outfit or gadget will change his life for the better.

That doesn't mean we should automatically flash the cash. We all want our kids to be happy and standing firm in the face of pester power can be a tough challenge. Hectic lifestyles and work schedules can leave parents wishing they had more time to spend with their tweens and there's nothing like a quick retail fix to assuage those horrid feelings of guilt. But it's always worth bearing in mind that these trends quickly pass, and today's must-have accessory will be next month's 'wouldn't be seen dead in' item. So yes, it is OK to say 'no', but in making your decision, always take a moment to consider why. Having a certain brand of backpack for school may seem pointless to you but if it lends your child a little extra self-confidence, perhaps it's a wise investment after all? If he's really desperate – or you're really skint – why not suggest he saves up for it himself? You can always contribute to the pot, but it will still be a great opportunity for him to learn the true value of money.

Elaine says: We live in a consumerist society, in which we're encouraged to buy and to value ourselves by our possessions. Tweens are particularly susceptible to specifically targeted marketing, at a time when they're working out their own identity and values. They're bombarded with advertising in many forms and need help to develop some discernment and judgement about what they see. We need to educate our kids so they can see through the hype and the hard sell, hopefully to the extent that they can pride themselves on not being duped, and on being wise to commercial pressurisation. We need to be firm about saying no – even when money is not the issue – to help children who are fast approaching adolescence learn about the value of money, budgeting, saving, delayed gratification, and to appreciate what they've already got. It's not easy to resist a child who whines and moans and complains that all his friends have one and how left out he'll be if he doesn't get one, particularly if you know your child is struggling to make friends. Even if it's true that everyone else has those particular trainers or the latest mobile phone, you need to be clear about the values you want for your child and stick to your plan. You need to know what's important to you. If you intend to say no or to have parameters for what can be spent, decide on this in advance before going shopping with him. Tell your child what you've decided and ask him how he needs to behave. Praise anything sensible in his answer. Empathise that he may be tempted by the things on display (of course he is – a lot of thought has been put into how to tempt him) and don't make him feel it's wrong to want things. It's normal, it doesn't mean he's greedy.

Adopting a relaxed, non-judgemental attitude in the face of pestering will allow you to stand firm while staying calm. If he asks for something that's beyond your budget, respond with sympathy. You might say: 'I understand you really want those jeans. They're really cool but they cost more than I said you could spend today. So what can we do?' If you get sensible answer, praise any aspect of it. If a tantrum ensues, you might say: 'You're obviously really upset and cross with me for not saying yes. It can be hard to have to wait for something you really want.'

Clearly, if we can show our children that we too are able to wait and save up for something we want, we'll be more successful in passing that value on.

What the netmums say

Can I have one, Mum?

I try to encourage Emma to buy the things she wants from her own funds. She was desperate for a pair of Ugg boots and waited over a year for them: she finally got them for a Christmas present. She had asked for an iPhone too, but I told her that she's too young, and it's out of the question. She doesn't bother too much about named trainers and although there are some fashion labels she's keen on right now, most are impractical so I haven't given in yet. She has just got a new BlackBerry phone and I pay for her contract, which is £15 a month.
Nicola, mum to a girl, eleven, and a boy, four

There's no doubt that tweens are under pressure to have the latest fashions and gadgets – especially once they start at secondary school. Alysha was never that interested until then, and suddenly she wanted this coat, and that bag. She understands that she won't get what she wants when she asks for it, she will have to wait for it, mainly because I'm a single parent

who's not working at the moment. Sometimes it makes me feel bad that I can't buy her what her friends have.
Kerrie, mum to two girls aged twelve and one

I don't take *ever* take my kids out shopping with me. They might still see things on television adverts, or come to me after school because someone they know has something they rather fancy, but I find the worst pressure of all comes whilst actually out at the shops. So I just leave them at home with their dad. They're still pretty young, mind you. I'm sure the lure of the shopping centre will become greater with time and I will start needing really good excuses for not taking them with me – or I'll just have to sneak out.
Julia, mum to two girls aged nine and six

At this age they're definitely affected by advertising, and experience envy for what their peers have. Children's TV channels are flooded with adverts for the latest music, toys, fashion, shows and DVDs, and it annoys me that they have such a huge influence. It seems that if our children don't have the latest videogame, gadget or designer outfit they think we're neglecting them! I'm afraid I don't buy into this at all. My son has what I can afford, not what the advertising world wants me to buy him. Both of my children have only had treats like this for birthdays or Christmas: I will not be pressured into buying things just for the sake of it. They complain, but it doesn't wash with me. My response is, when they have jobs and earn their own money, they can have what they like, until then it's a big no. If they get birthday or Christmas money, then yes of course they can choose what to spend it on.
Ali, mum to a girl, eighteen, and a boy, eleven

My tweens do tend to get what they ask for, but not straight away. They usually ask for computer games, football gear or trading cards. Many people think them to be spoilt, but they don't realise that they earn what they get, by doing chores for me. Sometimes I'll suggest they use their pocket money for it.

They've learnt that asking for it over and over means that they will end up not getting it at all. But the stream of adverts that are on between children's programmes really annoys me.

Claire, mum to five boys aged eleven, nine, six, five and one, and a girl, three

Consumerism – don't you just love it? Gemima does ask for things, but I've always tried to explain that bills and food must be paid for first, and we'll see what's left once those things are sorted. I admit I probably do spoil her by getting little bits here and there without her asking, like a magazine when I do the weekly shop, or something from the 99p store if I'm passing and have a spare pound. She gets pocket money from me and from her grandparents, and at the moment she's saving to buy a new DS. She's doing so well, I've told her that if she saves £80, I'll make up the rest.

Emily, mum to a girl, ten

Zoe wanted a BlackBerry for Christmas, but I said no. It's too much money and she doesn't need a phone for anything other than texting me or her friends. She's settled for a cheaper model, but still insists she needs internet access. Again, I've put my foot down and said no. She doesn't need it, she just wants it! She also has a laptop and a DSi, but she doesn't own any other high-end stuff. I did buy her a £65 Paul's Boutique bag for school, but then again, she needs a good-quality one – the previous two we bought broke under the weight of all her books. I don't think giving them everything they want immediately is good for them: they need to have something to save up for or something to look forward to. Giving them everything on a plate is setting them up for a lifetime of disappointment, as life is just not like that. I want my children to appreciate what they do have and not think that all they have to do is say 'I want', and they'll get it.

Naomi, mum to two girls aged twelve and five

My son always has a list of things he wants but rarely pesters. He's a typical ten-year-old, who wants all the latest console games and clothes. He makes a list for his birthday and Christmas, and then family and friends get him most of it – he has to save his £2-a-week pocket money for the rest. (He also earns extra money for good school reports, and gets lots of money here and there from my parents, who are divorced and desperate to be the favourite so try to buy his affection – he learned from a young age how to play them!) He sells all his console games once he has completed them and then buys the next one he wants second-hand, as he sees no point buying new. I'm strict on him saving for the things he wants as I was raised to accept that 'if you can't afford it, you can't have it'.

Natalie, mum to a boy, ten, and a girl, two

Too much, too young?

So they're growing up, and becoming independent. Hormones are stirring, and bodies are changing – or likely to be soon. And they're arguably more knowledgeable, and more streetwise, than tweens of previous generations. But your tween is still in his childhood. And lots of people these days are worried about the way the latter years of childhood are being eroded. Technology takes the burden of the blame: huge changes in the way we all communicate and the way we're entertained mean that our tweens are exposed to so much more than they would have been once – much of it far more 'adult' than they can get their heads round. Consumerism, too, is widely considered to be at fault: market forces, bolstered by peer pressure, have more influence than ever, putting inappropriate clothing, shoes, accessories, hairstyles, games and high-end gadgets on even young tweens' wish-lists. Some fear the modern education system, with its culture of tests, inspections and rigid curriculum demands, applies pressure that young children could well do without (sadly, a pressure that's sometimes compounded by the demands of 'pushy' parents). And then there are big changes in the structure of the family, with high divorce rates and blended families common, which mean that many tweens have to get to grips with the complexities of adult love lives – and all their consequences – whilst still very young. Finally, some people say that all of us – adults and kids alike – are just too busy pursuing work and formal activities to relax and enjoy the simpler pleasures of family life and old-fashioned, 'free-range' play.

It does all sound a bit scary on paper. But before you rush to drop out of society and enrol your family in a hippy commune, consider the possibility that it's not as alarming as you might fear. Discovering and exploring inappropriate influences is, to one extent or another, pretty much inevitable for kids, and always has been. And let's face it: none of us can turn the cultural tide. We can only make sure our kids are strong swimmers.

Keeping it appropriate

You can't protect your tween entirely from external influences that threaten to taint what's left of his childhood – and you'd be foolish to try. Even if you don't allow your tween exposure to anything unsuitable at home, he'll soon be introduced to it elsewhere. And if you do discover he's been playing '18'-certificate videogames, downloading worrying stuff from the internet, or listening to rap songs with offensive lyrics, your best bet is to stay calm and avoid showing a strong reaction – if your boundary-pushing tween realises something riles you, he may be tempted to try it again soon. Furthermore, he needs to know he can always come and talk about something he's seen or done that he's not comfortable with, without you freaking out about it.

You *can*, however, have firm boundaries at home, in line with whatever your particular values are. What your tween is watching, wearing, reading, listening to and playing with under your roof really is down to you.

Don't make a major song and dance about censoring anything – nothing's more likely to boost something's appeal. And bear in mind that 'because I said so' is not a good phrase with which to satisfy a rebellious tween. Instead, always involve him when you lay down the law and talk to him about why you've done so. Avoid being hysterical or alarmist about it, though – don't tell your tween daughter that wearing make-up will attract sexual predators, or your tween son that if he plays violent videogames he's likely to end up a serial killer. Always listen carefully when he seeks permission for something, consider it reasonably and look for possible compromises wherever possible, before rushing to say 'no'. So maybe your daughter can't wear a full face of make-up to a party, but you're OK with a bit of lip gloss and a touch of mascara. Perhaps your son may not play *Assassin's Creed* on his Xbox as it carries a 15 certificate – but you've checked out *Super Street Fighter* and that's an acceptable alternative.

In the end, our job as parents is not so much about prohibiting and censoring every little thing that worries us, but about bolstering all the characteristics that will help our tweens take these things in their stride – namely confidence, self-esteem and openness.

Child's play: How you can help preserve your child's childhood

- Keep careful tabs on those screen habits. Turn back to Chapter 5 if you need reminding how.
- Encourage your tween to play in 'old-fashioned' ways – building a den, making mud-pies, or playing a game of hide and seek. Play with him, sometimes, but give him time to play alone, too, and lots of time to play with friends.
- Don't buy your tween consumer products that just don't seem right for his age – put your foot down if necessary, however much pressure you're under.
- Take a look at your lifestyle and, if it seems as though family and fun time seems lacking, try to find ways you can change that.
- Lay down firm boundaries and rules, on everything that you have values on. Look for ways you can fit routines into your tween's life. He needs and will thrive on these (in spite of what he says!).
- Give your tween loads of love, reassurance and attention: these things will help him have the strength to reject what he's not truly ready for.

What the experts say

Crissy says: For generations, parents have bemoaned their offspring's eager desire to be seen as older than their years, but it seems this drive to leave childhood behind is coming so much earlier these days. Go back a decade or two and you'll find no mention of the tween phenomena – we dreamed sweetly of The Bay City Rollers, whilst our tweens are locking and popping to hip hop. Our tweens are living in a brave new world with a whole new range of pressures coming from the media, peers and the education system, which would previously have been soaked up by parents but now is all coming to bear firmly on their narrow shoulders.

As parents we have to accept that we can't hold back the sands of time. The onset of puberty has been creeping ever forward and society continues to change. To a certain extent it's becoming increasingly inevitable that our tweens will grow up too fast for our own comfort. In their desire to fit in they will often tune us out, but we mustn't be taken in by their outwardly mature and self-assured appearance. Underneath, they're just kids trying to find out who they are in the world, so aim to guide rather than propel your tween down the path that works best for you both. A willingness to negotiate and to share the personal value system that lies behind your decisions is helpful, but be prepared to set firm limits and stand your ground if needs be. A good rule of thumb when you're feeling backed into a corner is to ask yourself whether you're overreacting, or whether it really is that bad? If the answer's no, maybe it's better to turn a blind eye on this occasion.

Elaine says: Values in this area will vary hugely and are likely to depend on our own upbringing and culture. But whatever our values, it's important to communicate these to our children by our own example and by the rules we set. It's vital to stand firm, but this doesn't mean we can't empathise when they want it to be otherwise. It's hard if your values are different from their friends' parents. TV or computer game usage is a classic example, as parents have very different views on what is suitable. Personally, I would always follow the age guidelines on games and films. It eliminates many arguments if you're very consistent about this – your tween will know that he simply can't watch a film that's a '15' certificate if that's your value on that. It won't work, though, if you *sometimes* allow them to watch films or play games above their age level. Encouraging innocent enjoyment of childhood is not just about what we protect them from, but what we put in front of them as appropriate and enjoyable. So, don't put your nine-year-old daughter in knickers with saucy messages, but do encourage lots of imaginative play! It also helps if you reduce the level of electronic media your child has access to, as this will restrict the amount of external and sometimes inappropriate input, and will encourage him to use his imagination more, be more creative, and more active. What you pay attention to and take pleasure in will influence his interests. So if you spend time riding bikes, cooking or making crafty things as a family, then he is likely to enjoy those things.

What the netmums say

Growing up too soon

Although Gemima has make-up that she experiments with at home, she doesn't wear it out, other than a bit of light-coloured lip gloss sometimes. But I know others in her year at school are allowed to wear it, and sometimes quite a lot. I can't see the point of encouraging it at such an early age.
Emily, mum to a girl, ten

I don't think my son is growing up too fast, but I see a lot of kids that are. It infuriates me – kids nowadays grow up too quick, and some have too much independence. He wants a mobile phone, which is ridiculous. Who would he phone? Me, in the next room? I think the only way to halt the rush towards adult-hood is to take responsibility for your child and not let them rule the house. The only thing I let him have that he's technically too young for are certain console games. I always review them before he buys them, though.

Natalie, mum to a boy, ten, and a girl, two

Since she started high school, I've noticed Emma is growing up a lot quicker. She wants to wear make-up daily now, which I won't allow. I know I will have to give in one day, but at nearly age twelve, she will have to wait a bit longer!

Nicola, mum to a girl, eleven, and a boy, four

My daughter wants to do everything *now*, because 'her friends do'. I've always said that no, her friends probably *don't* do all these things, but I was shocked to the core by their primary school leavers' party: eleven-year-old girls in skin-tight short dresses, tons of make-up, spray tans – some of them could have got into nightclubs! I'm not totally against leavers' parties for this age group, but the pressure on parents to cough up for limou-sines and special dresses for these kind of events is unbelievable – everyone feels guilt about not being able or wanting to give them so much at this stage in their lives. In fact, I'm under constant pressure as she endlessly tells me she gets teased because I won't let her wear short skirts and over-the-knee socks to school. It's a case of 'over my dead body', though. She's only twelve!

Naomi, mum to two girls aged twelve and five

Being tall, my daughter looks older than her age anyway, and she wears make-up, which I don't mind. I think it's just harmless fun. It's a funny age because one minute she's trying to be a grown-up, the next she's playing with her Bratz dolls, or mucking around with her baby sister's toys. Children are encouraged to grow up so quick now. Some of the bras available for girls of Alysha's age are padded and lacy. What's that all about?

Kerrie, mum to two girls aged twelve and one

Some video games are clearly unsuitable for my son, but what can you do if you don't know what they're watching or playing when they aren't with you? He plays *Call of Duty* when he visits his father, which is completely inappropriate as far as I'm concerned. And when he's at friends' houses, I have no idea what they're playing, or what the parents' rules are. All I can do is tell him how I feel and why I don't want him to play these games. He's aware of age limits, but he pushes it if he can.
Ali, mum to a girl, eighteen, and a boy, eleven

I will not rush 'adulthood' on to either of my children. If my daughter wants to still play with dolls at eleven (which she does, regularly), then I will not stop her. I won't dress her up, or get her clothes that are too grown-up for her age. Perhaps I'm too strict sometimes, but I'd just rather they act their age.
Emma, mum to a girl, eleven, and a boy, nine

Appendix: Sources of information and help

General advice

Family Lives
Web: www.familylives.org.uk (Helpline: 0808 800 2222)

The Parent Practice
Web: www.theparentpractice.com

Education

School Home Support
Web: www.schoolhomesupport.org.uk

Young Minds
Web: www.youngminds.org.uk (Parents' helpline: 0808 802 5544)

Advisory Centre for Education
Web: www.ace-ed.org.uk (General advice line: 0808 800 5793)

Home Education UK
Web: www.home-education.org.uk

Education Otherwise
Web: www.education-otherwise.org (Helpline: 0845 478 6345)

Bullying

Kidscape
Web: www.kidscape.org.uk (Parents' helpline: 0845 120 5204)

Beatbullying
Web: www.beatbullying.org

Bullying UK
Web: www.bullying.co.uk

Anti-Bullying Network
Web: www.antibullying.net

Red Balloon Learner Centres
Web: redballoonlearner.co.uk

Puberty and sex

Brook
Web: www.brook.org.uk (Helpline: 0808 802 1234)

FPA
Web: www.fpa.org.uk (Helpline: 0845 122 8690)

Like It Is
Web: www.likeitis.org.uk

Modern media

Microsoft online code-of-conduct contract
Web: www.microsoft.com/uk/protect/family/guidelines/contract.mspx

Childnet International
Web: www.childnet-int.org

Chat Danger
Web: www.chatdanger.com

Safe Kids
Web: www.safekids.com

GetNetWise
Web: www.getnetwise.org

Wise Kids
Web: www.wisekids.org.uk

Cyber Mentors
Web: www.cybermentors.org.uk

Think U Know
Web: www.thinkuknow.co.uk

Music Matters
Web: www.whymusicmatters.org

The Industry Trust
Web: www.copyrightaware.co.uk

Get Game Smart
Web: www.getgamesmart.com

Health

Vegetarian Society
Web: www.vegsoc.org

NHS healthy weight calculator
Web: www.nhs.uk/tools/pages/healthyweightcalculator.aspx

Change4Life
Web: www.nhs.uk/change4life

Drinkaware
Web: www.drinkaware.co.uk

Frank
Web: www.talktofrank.com (Helpline: 0800 77 66 00)

BEAT (Beating Eating Disorders)
Web: www.b-eat.co.uk (Helpline: 0845 634 1414)

Winston's Wish
Web: www.winstonswish.org.uk (Helpline: 08452 03 04 05)

Child Bereavement Charity
Web: www.childbereavement.org.uk (Support and information line: 01494
    568 900)

Grief Encounter Project
Web: www.griefencounter.org.uk

Independence

NSPCC
Web: www.nspcc.org.uk

Children's Legal Centre
Web: www.childrenslegalcentre.com

Royal Society for the Prevention of Accidents (RoSPA)
Web: www.rospa.com

Child Accident Prevention Trust
Web: www.capt.org.uk

Think! Road Safety
Web: www.dft.gov.uk/think

Child's Eye Media
Web: www.childseyemedia.com

Index

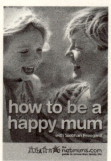